THE GENESIS
OF ETHICS

The Genesis of Ethics

Burton L. Visotzky

Three Rivers Press
New York

Published by Three Rivers Press, a division of Crown Publishers, Inc., 201 East 50th Street, New York, New York 10022. Member of the Crown Publishing Group.

Originally published in hardcover by Crown Publishers, Inc., in 1996.

Random House, Inc. New York, Toronto, London, Sydney, Auckland
http://www.randomhouse.com/

THREE RIVERS PRESS and colophon are trademarks of Crown Publishers, Inc.

Printed in the United States of America

Design by Karen Minster

Library of Congress Cataloging-in-Publication Data
Visotzky, Burton L.
The genesis of ethics / by Burton L. Visotzky.—1st paperback ed.
Originally published: New York: Crown Publishers, © 1996.
1. Bible—O.T. Genesis—Criticism, interpretation, etc.
2. Ethics in the Bible. 3. Ethical problems. I. Title.
[BS1235.6.E8V57   1997]
222′.1106—dc21   97–18258

ISBN 0-609-80167-8

10 9 8 7 6 5 4 3 2 1

First Paperback Edition

FOR SANDY,
GEN. 2:23

CONTENTS

THE GENESIS
OF ETHICS

1

THE DILEMMA
OF GENESIS

THE CBS FILM CREW is unobtrusively taping—which is to say that the three extra men in the room are trying not to knock anything over with their cables or blind anyone with their lights. It's rare that they film in such close quarters as a boardroom, rarer still that the gathering around this particular table should allow their conversations to be on record. We're ensconced in the inner sanctum of a public-relations guru on the nineteenth floor of a Madison Avenue office building. The power brokers of America sit here, quietly yet vigorously discussing the texts scattered before them. Remnants of a meal sit on the sideboards. CEOs of some of America's largest corporations are here: a chemical giant, a clothing retailer, a soap company, a business machine manufacturer. On occasion, there's been a steel mill owner, a publishing mogul, a real-estate baron—even a managing editor of the *Wall Street Journal* has been present for these particular negotiations. Of course, there are the bankers and lawyers, each from Wall Street's most prestigious firms. These latter gentlemen are the deal makers, Masters of the Universe, the so-called barbarians at the gate. The room reeks of wealth, privilege, and a sense of strength.

That CBS might wish to film this conversation is of some interest. The discussion does not concern a leveraged buyout, not even a friendly takeover. Nor is this a board meeting or a public-relations brainstorming session. I know, because I sit at the table, facilitating the session. We're debating the biblical book of Genesis. We meet once a month for a light supper and then we study. The film crew taping us this evening will use the footage on *CBS Sunday Morning with Charles Kuralt* for a show on "Religion in America."

Why do America's business leaders, perhaps even a shark or two among them, why in God's name do they gather monthly in a boardroom to study the Bible?

While we're at it, why does Charles Kuralt think this is newsworthy? Rather than offer an immediate answer, allow me to digress a moment to tell you a story told to me by Rabbi Josef Solomon.

Once upon a time there was a wealthy businessman who was a generous donor to his local synagogue. One day he went to visit his rabbi and said, "Rabbi, you know I've given generously to the synagogue for many years now. Truth to tell, business isn't so great anymore. I've had some serious setbacks. But I felt I owed you an explanation about why my contribution is going to be so small this year."

The rabbi replied, "Is there anything I can do to help you? You've always been a good friend to this synagogue. If you need help now, it's our obligation to you. It's what I'd do for any congregant."

The businessman thought for a moment and then said, "Rabbi, I'm very touched that you would think to offer help. I can't begin to tell you how much your support means to me, especially after I told you I'd be giving a lot less than in the past. But you know nothing about my business. What possible help could you offer?"

The rabbi responded, "Well, our sages of blessed memory knew a great deal about business. Entire tractates of the Talmud are given over to business discussions."

"Even so," countered the businessman, "my particular business is too esoteric and, frankly, my losses simply too severe."

"Well," said the rabbi, "when our sages were troubled, sometimes they looked to heaven for advice."

"Whaddya mean?"

"When our blessed rabbis no longer knew what to do, they would take their Bible and let it fall open at random. Whatever the first words they read, they took these words to have the power of God's voice and acted accordingly. Perhaps you should try this method of seeking the good Lord's favor."

"To tell you the truth, Rabbi," the businessman said, "it sounds a bit meshuga to me. But hey, nothing else seems to work. When I get back to my office, I'll give it a try. Thanks."

With that the man left and many months passed without the rabbi hearing from him. Then one day, after the rabbi had all but forgotten the conversation, a limousine pulled up at the synagogue. The businessman got out and marched proudly to the rabbi's office. He was tanned, relaxed; he looked confident and sure of himself. No sooner did the rabbi greet him than the man pulled out a check and handed it to the rabbi. The amount of his gift to the synagogue was ten times larger than any previous gift he had given, even in his best years.

"Rabbi," he began, "I owe this all to you and that conversation we had some months ago. I took your advice, and look at me now!"

The rabbi was quite astonished, particularly since he was not at all used to his congregants actually heeding his advice. "Just what did you do?" he asked.

"I went to my office, pulled out a Bible, let it fall open on my desk, and read the first words that came to my attention. I'll be damned if they weren't just the advice I needed," the businessman said. "So I followed the advice and here I am today, stronger and more successful than ever."

Amazed, the rabbi asked, "Tell me, just out of curiosity, what were the words of sacred Scripture that caught your eye?"

"Oh, those?" The businessman reported, "The first words I read when I opened my Bible were 'Chapter Eleven.' "

Usually, reading the Bible doesn't produce such direct yields as the punch line of a joke. But yields there are, and my business leaders, very, very busy men and women each of them, felt the profit strongly enough to come back month after month to continue studying together. Among them were people who flew in from Columbus, Ohio, and from Pittsburgh, who arranged their flight schedules back from deal-making in Japan or hopped the Concorde from Paris just so they could sit in that room to read Genesis together. These were not necessarily what you would call "religious" people, although some of them came from religious backgrounds. There were Southern Baptists who could recall their stern preachers and some Orthodox Jews who remembered their yeshiva days. But there were also wholly secular Jews and Gentiles, Christians who hadn't seen the inside of a church in decades and Jews whose idea of kosher meant consultations with their attorneys. Like any group, there were also a few churchgoers and synagogue attendees. But they weren't on Madison Avenue to study doctrine.

Some years earlier I had founded and directed another study group, the Genesis Seminar. This one was made up of writers: fiction writers, essayists, critics, screenwriters. There were also editors and film directors, journalists and poets. This group, too, drew media attention: The Canadian Broadcasting Company filmed us for television and taped us for radio. We were featured on a show on NBC and written up twice in *The New York Times*. There, our Bible study group was described as "the best conversations in New York City." As with my CEOs, the writers' group had a varied population. There were observant Jews and secular Jews, Protestants and Catholics both lapsed and active. The group was also spiced with writer Bharati Mukherjee, born a Bengali Brahmin. We also had visits from Bapsi Sidhwa, a Pakistani novelist who was raised in the Zoroastrian tradition. In other words, the Genesis Seminar was very much a nondenominational study group. Those writers who had no religious ties to Genesis nevertheless saw it as a monument of Western literature.

What is it about Bible study that can exert such a hold on people outside of a church or synagogue context? I suppose one might contend that the writers were happy to gather and discuss a book that none of them had authored, so their tongues had free reign. Besides, writers are a lonely lot; they sit and write all day and long for someone to talk with—especially if it's only once a month and there's a free meal involved, too. And as for businesspeople, well, networking is what it's all about. Deals were cut as we read of covenants being cut. Bargains were struck as Abraham bargained with God over the fate of Sodom and his nephew Lot.

Of course, this may have some grain of truth to it, but is far from the answer to the "why" question. Writers need not study Genesis to talk with one another about literature, nor do business moguls need to gather over the Bible to network or cut a deal. There was a draw, a fascination, something that made them each return, month after month—something beyond the standard trappings of organized religion, something in the study itself, in the book and its stories. When, after five years of monthly study, the writers' group finished Genesis and I announced an end, they insisted on more and continue to study to this day. When the CEO group was brought to a close after its round of Genesis, members asked if we might not continue, and I agreed to reconstitute a somewhat different group in a boardroom on the Avenue of the Americas in midtown Manhattan.

Now, the lure of the Bible isn't news. Synagogues and churches have been engaged in this kind of study for literally two millennia. It's worth reviewing this veneration for a moment because it sets my "Why do they study?" question into even sharper focus. If anything, the fact that the book is canonical, is revered, is read with a very sacred intention makes my question all the more acute. Piety exacerbates the question of why the Bible is read, if you will, by the "unchurched."

Many years ago, when I first began as a rabbinical student at New York's Jewish Theological Seminary, I used to attend Sabbath services at a nearby synagogue. I liked it there because this *schul* (Yiddish for synagogue) seemed like the "genuine article." I am a Conservative rabbi, but this particular synagogue was Orthodox. The rabbi was Polish and had served in Poland before World War II. After a long and harrowing journey, he now resided in New York City, where he still preached in Yiddish. The *schul*'s women's gallery was way high up in nosebleed territory, like the five-dollar seats at the opera. (This particular feature eventually led to my abandoning the synagogue in favor of a place where men and women could participate equally.) The synagogue is located in what once was a flourishing Jewish neighborhood, on Old Broadway off 125th Street in Harlem, but even twenty years ago when I attended, that neighborhood was virtually entirely black.

One Sabbath, we had finished our usual prayers and repaired to an antechamber to offer repeated toasts to the Sabbath and to all present. We were very pious about early-Sabbath-afternoon kiddush, a chance to drink some schnapps and say L'Chaim! For reasons that elude me now, the drink of choice at that *schul* was Southern Comfort (perhaps the aged rabbi was a secret Janis Joplin fan). In any case, as we rolled out of the synagogue into the bright light of a Harlem Saturday afternoon, there on the stoop of the *schul* were two little black girls. One of them fluffed her skirt and looked up at me and asked, "Hey, mister, is that the place where they kiss the books?"

Even as I gently answered yes, I realized that this young child was an astute observer. She had obviously peeked through the door and seen praying Jews kissing the Torah as it was marched through the congregation and read in public. And, all things being equal, her characterization of a synagogue was sweet and to the point. I chose not to elaborate beyond my "yes," satisfied that if a black child of Harlem had to characterize the synagogue, calling it "the place where they kiss the books" was about as good as anyone could ask for.

And she was right, we do kiss the books. In fact, Jewish veneration for books borders on the extreme. One ninth-century critic of rabbinic Judaism said it was practically idolatry. We take the Pentateuchal scrolls, we dress them up in velvet, we adorn them with silver crowns and bells, we parade with them (and everybody loves a parade) through the synagogue so everyone can rise and kiss them, and then everyone who is called up to the public reading of the Torah kisses it before and after!

The church also reveres the Old Testament. While it means something different to Christians than it does to Jews, and while the church doesn't exactly kiss and hug the scroll, there is a long history of Christian veneration of the Bible. Art historians can show you countless illuminated Bible manuscripts gessoed in gold, bound in silver, and bedecked in precious gems. From high on their lecterns priests and pastors read the Old Testament selection every Sunday to somnolent parishioners. The text is valuable to the church as a testimony to the Good News, its prophecies esteemed as authoritative proof of the coming of Christ.

It's precisely this canonical valuation of the Bible that gnaws at me when I ask my "Why do they study?" question. For in both church and synagogue the sacred status of Scripture affects the very ways in which the Bible is read. By forming communities around the Book, church and synagogue, perforce, learn ways of reading that preserve the sacral quality of the Bible and so reinforce the presumed holiness of the community. In the church this reading strategy is determined by the magisterium and it serves to find church doctrine within the verses of the Testaments, Old and New. Even in Protestant denominations there is a penchant for reading the reflection of the church into the mirror of the Biblical text, Luther's understanding of Paul as though Paul were a Reformation Protestant being a prime example.

In the synagogue this method of preserving the text, of reading the rabbinic agenda therein, is called midrash. I don't wish to devalue this type of reading, far from it—I earn my living as a scholar of midrash, and as a rabbi I engage it daily. But midrash and magisterium can serve to obscure the biblical text as much as they elucidate it—something that the fathers of the church and the rabbis of old reluctantly admitted.

Each community confessed that there was a tension between the contextual narrative and the communal understanding. In the Jewish community this separation between text and interpretation became formalized in rabbinic vocabulary. The Hebrew term *peshat* was coined for the narrative in context. Literally translated, it means the "simple" reading, what we sometimes (erroneously) call the literal reading. The more communal, ideological reading was called the *derash*—that is to say, the text and its midrash. Here the text is read in light of the current situation of the community. Verses are often rent from their context, for the lesson of the homily becomes paramount. There is, after close to two thousand years of rabbinic exegesis or reading of the Torah, sometimes a gap between the *peshat* and the *derash* on any given verse or story.

One simple example should suffice to demonstrate the difference between *peshat* and *derash*. In his commentary on Genesis 1:4 ("God saw that the light was good, and God separated the light from the darkness"), the medieval French commentator Rashi writes:

To explain this we need a *derash*. God saw that it was not appropriate for evil-doers to make use of the [primordial light by means of which they could see from one end of the universe to the other], so God separated the light for the righteous to use in the messianic future. But according to the *peshat,* God saw that light was good and that it was not seemly for light and darkness to be mixed up together, so God set the day as a border for the light and the night as a border for darkness.

It is clear that his first explanation, the *derash* about evil-doers making use of primordial light, is a flight of Rashi's rabbinic imagination, offered to explain the special nature of the light created before the sun was made. The second explanation Rashi offers, his *peshat,* is more in keeping with the context of the narrative.

The church of the fourth and fifth centuries recognized this dichotomy as well. They contrasted the "simple" reading, which they called *historia,* with more complex and doctrinally motivated readings, *allegoria.* The very distinction granted to the two phenomena bears witness to the possibility that Jewish or Christian religious readers may be reading a far different text than secular readers, even when the words are the same. Religious readers are faced with a problem that secular readers need not suffer. For all that the Bible is canonized, called sacred by community after community, it—particularly the early narratives of Genesis—remains a difficult book, a set of stories St. Jerome once described as "rude and repellent."

That a saint of the church bears testimony to the problem brings my earlier "Why do they study?" question back into focus. Religious readers generally read their community's midrash. They read the text through the lenses of church and synagogue, and this is as it should be—those lenses define the membership in those religious bodies. But there remains a disparity between the received communal traditions about the texts and the actual words of the narrative. There is cognitive dissonance, if you will, in mediating the chasm between *peshat* and *derash.* This dissonance is particularly acute in the family narratives of the very first book of the Bible, Genesis.

So, if religious readers may experience some difficulties studying Genesis, what is it about the book that brought writers and business leaders to study groups, month after month, to doggedly make their way through the text? Why did they read it? What did the study of Genesis give them? In business parlance, what was the bottom line? I will not contend that it was the high ethics of the book that drew them. Most people are, frankly, not all that drawn by high ethics. Furthermore, Genesis presents its own acute problem—the dissonance referred to above—if we wish to think of it in any conventional Western sense as an ethical book.

Read simply, in fact, Genesis is an ugly little soap opera about a dysfunctional family. Four generations of that family dynasty are charted, their foibles exposed and all the dirty laundry, as it were, hung out in public for millions to see. It is a story about rape, incest, murder, deception, brute force, sex, and blood lust. The plotlines and characterizations of Genesis are so crude as to call into serious question how this book became and remained a sacred, canonical text for two thousand years and more. Later we will delve with more detail into the foibles and peccadilloes of the patriarchal clan, but for now it suffices to recognize that like soap opera itself, it is the unattractive component of Genesis that causes us to have such a strong identification with it in the first place. When we read of the dysfunctional family with strong lust and murderous intentions, we recognize that it is our family—although we may be reluctant to admit this revelation out loud.

This is the common ground between the religious and nonreligious reader alike. I want to dwell on this a bit as a prelude to stating my thesis. It is not the niceness of Genesis that makes it attractive to generation after generation of readers. Quite the contrary, it's the gut-wrenching quiddity of the narrative that draws us in year after year. Genesis is all those dirty little secrets we know about one another strung into a "family" narrative. This family is so "nuclear" it's fissile. Genesis is R, it's NC-17. Genesis is what spouses hide from the neighbors, hide from the children, hide from each other. The narratives of Genesis are roiling in repressions we refuse to tell our therapists. It's not pretty, it's not nice, it's not for polite company—and it's canonical Scripture for hundreds of millions of Jews and Christians, the background for a revelation to hundreds of millions more Muslims, and the inspiration to zillions more secular folks who just happen to enjoy reading Western literature. What could they all have been thinking when they made this doozy of a book their Bible, and just what did they think they were reading?

The stunning dissonance between what the text says and how it has been received remains a subject largely undiscussed. The vast chasm between what Jews call *peshat* and *derash*, between the actual narrative and the way generations of communities have interpreted it, is an object of wonderment and dismay. Genesis is a text full of stories about a brutal and dysfunctional family whose morality bears little resemblance to the mores we hold dear in Western society. Yet both church and synagogue read this book as though it were the very model of propriety, as though the families of Genesis were just like those we viewed on television throughout the 1950s. There is a stark contrast between the *peshat*, the story in its context, as it is nakedly told, and the *derash*, the way in which the religious communities who hold the Bible sacred have chosen to make it "nice."

It is the thesis of this book that the very dissonance between *peshat* and *derash* is what makes genesis so attractive.

The narratives of Genesis, with all their brutal power, teach us about ethics utterly independently of our normative notions of "nice." The stories are, for better or worse, a rich mirror of readers' lives. Yet there is often a disparity between these stories and the subsequent Judeo-Christian ethic that has been derived from them throughout the centuries.

This book focuses on the unmediated narratives of Genesis. Throughout the following pages, by uncovering the troubling tales of the characters of Genesis, we will gain access to texts that allow us to ponder modern ethical issues that beset us in daily life—at home, in the community, and in the workplace. By holding up the characters of Scripture with all their flaws to the light of critical inquiry, we will learn something about ourselves and the construction of our own behavior. One need not make the Bible "nice" in order to learn from it. On the contrary, we will see that the brutality of the tales of Genesis can serve to teach us about our sense of self and community and about our construction of ethics.

Each of us shares the same dissonance we observe in Genesis. The narrative of our lives is not always nice. It is often messy, sometimes brutal. There are parts of each of us that we carefully hide from our neighbors, our children, our spouses, our therapists, even from ourselves. Like Genesis, there is a disparity between who we really are and who we wish to be, the face we present to everyone else. The gap between those parts of each of us, between, if you will, the profane and the sacred, is what draws readers so powerfully to Genesis. It is not sufficient that it be read as prurient soap opera. God knows, there is enough daytime drama already in the world without finding it in sacred Scripture. But let us not deny that Scripture becomes sacred only when, by communal will, we learn not to read the nastiness of Genesis but to find it, instead, an ennobling text. We redeem the narrative from its slough and elevate it, redeem it by making it a sacred narrative about our sainted ancestors of old.

Of course, it's just this that we yearn to do with our own lives—become something beyond the sum of mundane moments in the daily round. To the extent that Genesis mirrors our lives and our desires, it surely mirrors this, too. We wish to make our own narrative as well respected, as universally acclaimed, as canonized as Genesis. It is this possibility of mediating the dissonance that is the powerful appeal of Genesis. When we observe the disparity between the stories in Genesis and their sacred reception, we yearn to accomplish the same for ourselves. Our very community is formed upon this myth of redemption, of reaching beyond ourselves, of being better, holy, sainted—even if we, too, began as wandering Arameans, slimy shepherds, or NC-17.

In short, then, it is not the narrative of Genesis that makes the work sacred. Rather, it is in the process of *studying* Genesis that the transformation takes place. It was for that, for study together, that CEOs and writers came month after month. The communities they formed in study taught them, transformed them, gave them enough to have them come back again and again. There was something in the interaction, in the dialectic, in the conversation that was a rich gift. The benefaction they received in the exchange of ideas was the moral development they experienced. *In the study of the family narratives of Genesis moral education occurs.*

It is apposite at this juncture to talk a bit about moral development, moral reasoning, and moral education. It's a topic that has attracted attention, on and off, since World War II. The waves of popularity for the subject of moral education seem to come in direct proportion to the amount of corruption, graft, crime, and oppression of the poor and needy our society revels in at any given moment. The worse things are, the more we wring our hands and speak of the need for moral education. Sometimes, as an educator, I fear that we feel we've actually accomplished something by promoting moral education when moral action is what's called for to cure any of the ills just lamented. Real moral education must lead to moral behavior.

But this is easier said than done. Teaching values is a tricky business, since as my teacher, the late Professor Lawrence Kohlberg was fond of pointing out, one man's "bag of virtues" may not be the values the next guy cherishes. Kohlberg tried, instead, to educate his students in the ways of moral reasoning. Since Kohlberg focused on teaching reasoning, he ran the frustration that one might equally well reason one's way to a morally repugnant answer as to a virtuous one. In a way, Kohlberg taught something that seemed the opposite of religion, for religious communities each hand down specific content, while Kohlberg attempted to teach students how to develop reasoning structures. Without specific content there was no way to predict what conclusion the study of a dilemma might produce. Yet there was, in the end, reason. This is a form of pessimism inextricably wedded to optimism. On the one hand, we cannot predict or guarantee the "right" behavior in the end. On the other hand, reason, that great Grail of the Enlightenment, prevails.

Kohlberg demonstrated his passion for reason in his Harvard classroom. Although he was the type of absentminded professor who could pull out of a parking lot and blithely drive the wrong way down a one-way street, when discussion of his theory of moral education was the agenda, Socratic dialogue was the means. I have never been more intellectually challenged or more entertained than when Professor Carol Gilligan entered Kohlberg's lecture hall to debate him on the fundamentals of his theory. She was passionate in her insistence that the very essence of his theory was unfair to women. He was passionate in his insistence that discussion was the only way to test the theory, and rational dialogue was the vehicle of choice. In that vehicle, moral reasoning was always a two-way street. Only by engagement with oncoming traffic could one make any progress.

Kohlberg's theory of moral education reflected the privilege he gave to reason. If one could learn to reason in a more sophisticated manner, that was progress. Kohlberg posited six stages of moral reasoning, from the least sophisticated to the most. Stages one through three, the less sophisticated levels, were most commonly found among toddlers and preadolescents. By stage four, people could reason their way to a law-and-order stance, understanding the necessity for law to govern the community. Stage five thinkers reasoned that there were moral issues that required the individual to stand outside of the community for what is right—civil disobedience was a case in point. Stage six was limited to the select few. Kohlberg generally would list three examples of stage six thinkers—Mahatma Gandhi, Martin Luther King, Jr., and, well, Larry Kohlberg.

Kohlberg was a good social scientist as well as an educational philosopher. His theory of moral reasoning was philosophically grounded in the work of his Harvard colleague Professor John Rawls. Kohlberg made us read and understand Rawls' *Theory of Justice* as background for moral development theory. While we're at it, I should mention that Kohlberg also had us learn Jean Piaget's developmental theories since they lay behind the stages of moral development that Kohlberg proposed. Yet it was not enough for Kohlberg to have a good theoretical underpinning to his work. Larry wanted to prove that his theory was valid, and cross-culturally valid, at that. So he field-tested his stage theory by traveling worldwide to differing cultures and testing subjects. His tests were meant to show that his stages of moral development could be found anywhere one looked.

It is his method of testing that is the focus of my attention here, and explaining it is the real reason for this long excursus into educational philosophy. Kohlberg tested his theories by questioning his subjects about short narratives they had read. By persistently asking them "why," he uncovered the structures of reasoning that indicated the stage of their moral development. The narratives Kohlberg exposed his subjects to were called moral dilemmas. His favorite example of such a dilemma was called "Should Heinz Steal the Drug?"

In this moral dilemma the tester would read a narrative which indicated that Heinz was basically a nice guy and good citizen in a small town. Poor Heinz's wife was dying of a horrible disease, one that was curable, but with a drug that was very expensive. The local pharmacist refused to lower the price of the drug, and Heinz went through every means of procuring it legally and attempting to persuade the druggist to lower the price. The druggist could not be moved, Heinz could not pay for the drug, Mrs. Heinz was dying.

"Should Heinz steal the drug?" asks the tester. The yes or no answer is of less significance than the follow-up, "Why do you think that? Can you explain your reasoning?" The answers having been given, the tester could assess the stage of moral reasoning the subject offered.

Sometimes these moral dilemmas were the subject of discussions. Classes would have the opportunity to talk amongst themselves about Heinz and his drug problem. As might be expected, in any given room of discussants, there were participants at a variety of differing stages of moral development. One of Kohlberg's graduate students, testing Kohlberg's moral dilemmas in the afternoon Hebrew school where he taught, noticed a curious phenomenon. It seems that his students did not have the developmental tools that would enable them to grasp arguments offered at two stages or more above their own. This was not all that surprising, as Jean Piaget had demonstrated similar limitations in the development of scientific modes of thought. Students who were exposed to a stage of development one above their own, however, generally "got it."

More surprising was the finding that students who were exposed to moral reasoning a stage above their own developed more rapidly than students who were not exposed to more sophisticated moral reasoning. In short, talking about why one might behave in a certain way and exposing the ethical structures behind those behaviors accelerated moral development. This was a new finding, and one that took Kohlberg's theory of moral development out of a theoretical framework and into the practical educational world. People could learn to reason morally in a more developed fashion through continued exposure to more developed reason. Stated this way, it seems obvious, but the implications are rich. Talk actually does accomplish something!

What (among so many other things) Professor Kohlberg had to teach us was this: In communities that study together, their very conversation is a tool of moral development. My CEOs or my writers or my other groups of students have benefited profoundly from studying Genesis in a group. Not only have they gotten the intellectual pleasure of wrestling with a text or the frisson that comes from reading about a dysfunctional family; not only have they learned the rules of civilized discourse and the pleasures of actually hearing another person's point of view; not only have they learned to articulate their own viewpoint coherently; not only have they learned to answer why their opinions are what they seem to be; but the very process of doing so in a study setting, with a group, helps them develop more sophisticated tools and structures for moral reasoning. *Genesis is rich in moral dilemmas, the study of which promotes moral development.*

Story after story in Genesis serves as a moral dilemma worthy of careful consideration. Generations of readers in religious communities have been forced to confront these dilemmas as they face the dilemma of the Genesis text—how does one make this particular text into the sacred document of a community? Jewish and Christian congregations throughout the ages have struggled to mediate the cognitive dissonance between the dilemma and the moral discussion it evokes, on the one hand, and the desired outcome on the other: a Bible text that could serve as the source of ethical inspiration for millennia. The very discussion that ensues provides the means for bridging the gap between dilemma and desired outcome: midrash. Each generation's record of the discussion of the moral dilemmas of Genesis has offered the means for moral development. The record of midrash, preserved in rabbinic literature and, if you will, by the magisterium in the writings of the church fathers, is precisely the discussion that itself elevates readers through the study of sacred text.

Without communal study, Genesis would be just another soap opera. With a community formed around it, Genesis helps religious and nonreligious readers to confront the moral dilemmas of our time.

Since Scripture is such a rich mirror of the daily dilemmas that confront us—a pastiche of tabloid headlines (Daughters Each Bed Drunken Father! Wife Turns into Pillar of Salt!)—it serves eloquently as the sourcebook for moral education. The very nastiness of Genesis not only draws us to read it, but teaches us something as we ponder its meaning. In mediating the dissonance between *peshat* and *derash,* readers can find a way to moral reasoning.

Over the past decade I have been teaching these biblical texts, these moral dilemmas, in a variety of public settings. I have taught the CEOs and writers, mentioned above. I have also studied these texts with women's groups, teachers, synagogue and church groups, and in a variety of interfaith settings. This brand of study, using the disturbing narratives of Genesis as the texts of dilemmas for moral development, is but one of many ways of studying Scripture. I am not, here, advocating that it replace denominational study. I believe each religious tradition has a useful and vested interest in transmitting the teachings that have helped form spiritual communities over the centuries. The rabbis of the Talmud, some fifteen hundred years ago, spoke of seventy facets of the Torah. For religious communities, let this be but one of the seventy.

Here, in *The Genesis of Ethics,* I am offering a window to a type of discussion that seems to work cross-denominationally. Moral education is something everyone can benefit from—Jew, Christian, Muslim, Hindu, agnostic. The conversations that follow are universal conversations. Beyond the melting pot, they allow us a way to speak with one another and learn from one another. Differing traditions will be brought to each text. Different voices will be heard. Differing stages of moral reasoning will be offered for the interpretations we suggest. I hope to translate to the page these different voices, spoken in different rooms across the last decade. What binds them all is a common text—an ancient text that serves as an all-too-accurate mirror for today.

In the pages that follow we will study passages from Genesis together. I have made a decision, a difficult one, not to study all of Genesis. As a rabbi, I am obligated to see every passage of the Bible as worthy of study, but here, I'm more concerned about accessibility. I am all too aware that most moderns do not know the biblical text. This is true of many religious people as well as secular folks. One can no longer assume, as one did in the days of Shakespeare or Milton, that readers know their Scripture, so I am choosing passages that I think work best in our discussion of ethics. I focus on family narratives for the simple expedient that most of us grew up in some kind of family. The narratives are immediately familiar, even clothed, as they are, in the garb of the ancient Near East. Yet my interests run beyond the confines of family to a more global moral development.

I do, however, follow the biblical narrative in the order it occurs in Genesis. Rather than isolate themes, I prefer narratives, for they more closely mirror life. Which is to say, like life, they are messy. More than one idea will crop up in a narrative, more than one moral value must be weighed in a narrative. Often, conflicting values must be mediated. Further, decisions taken in one narrative may have consequences for other, later stories. Along the way, we'll be forced to stop and isolate factors, identify dilemmas, and then regroup and see how the parts affect the big picture.

It of course hasn't escaped me that following the order of Genesis makes this book more useful for study groups. It's possible to follow along in your own version of Genesis, whether it's in a church or synagogue study group or in the Plumbers' Union Local discussion group. I recommend a regular study group with set hours. It can be once a week or once a month. Less than that gives little if any continuity. More than that might simply demand too much from busy people facing the demands of work and family. But if I may again quote my friends the rabbis, "Don't say 'I'll study when leisure arises.' You might not find the time."

Finally, I will point out now that I translate the Genesis narratives into English for each chapter. I do so for the convenience of my readers and the convenience of my argument. But *caveat lector*, I implore you not to trust me. It would please me enormously to know that you asked: Does the Bible really say that? It would please me even more to know that you pulled a family Bible down off the shelf to check and contrast my readings. Bible translation is a difficult business—in fact, all translation is. Vladimir Nabokov used to tell his undergraduates,

"Oh, those ignoble, treacherous, and philistine translators!" In the seventeenth century, author James Howell wrote, "Some hold translations not unlike to be/The wrong side of a Turkish tapestry."

Bible translation is even trickier. I remember a story my Israeli colleague Gershon Shaked told me about an Israeli writer who had gone on a tour of Europe and was privileged to meet the then prime minister of Sweden, Olaf Palme. Palme was giving this writer a hard time about being an Israeli citizen.

"Why," the prime minister accused, "even though your own Bible says, 'Thou shalt not kill,' you Israelis fight in wars and take on terrorists, let alone bombing civilians!"

The Israeli novelist countered, "Actually, sir, the Bible says, 'Thou shall not murder.' In Hebrew it's *Lo Tirtzah.*' But that means we may kill in self-defense." Palme demurred, sure he was correct. When the Israeli invited him to look it up, Palme called his aide and asked for his Swedish Bible. Turning to Exodus 20, he triumphantly read aloud in his native language and then said, "See, 'Thou shalt not kill!'"

The Israeli was unmoved and insisted, "The Hebrew text says, '*Lo Tirtzah,*' thou shalt not murder.'"

"Very well," responded Palme, "but are you sure you are using a good translation?"

The problem of finding a good translation from the Hebrew original is an old one. Even St. Jerome gave up on the Greek and Old Latin and reverted to the Hebrew text for his Vulgate translation. But not all of you read Hebrew, Greek, or Latin (to say the least), and not everyone will agree on the correct translation into English of a millennia-old text. So don't rely only on me. Get out those translations. I personally prefer Everett Fox's *Schocken Bible* translation, precisely because it captures the flavor of the Hebrew original. Other times, I use the Jewish Publication Society's Bible. But there are those of you who would use the Revised Standard Version; still others, the New Revised Standard Version. Some of you will use yet other denominational texts. There are even some who still delight in the cadences of the King James Version. All well and good. What is the correct Bible translation to use? Answer: All of the above. So grab a Bible, turn the page, and let's study together.

I invite readers to join this discussion, whether alone, as consenting adults in the privacy of your own homes, or in study groups formed from your religious community, your offices, your bowling league. The study of these texts is a transformative experience. If you study with a group, you will soon find you are part of a vibrant community. Everyone, each member, has something to offer, some experience, that lends expertise to his or her opinion about the text. Each member must be heard and validated by the others with whom you study. As the rabbis of the second century point out in a text called *The Lessons of the Fathers*, "Who is wise? One who learns from every person."

Study and discussion of these texts help us hear a nagging and in-sistent voice. It is the voice of moral authority. We have to work to hear this voice. It takes some study. Yet the dissonance we experience when we study these texts of Genesis forces us to listen really care-fully. When we do so, we realize that the nagging voice of moral au-thority we are hearing is *our own voice*. Its echoes stay with us wherever we go.

2

ABRAHAM AND SARAH—
ON THE ROAD

JEWS DO NOT BELIEVE in astrology, or so my colleague and teacher Joe Lukinsky reminds me. This is not to say that there aren't plenty of Jews who read their horoscopes daily. What Rabbi Lukinsky is thinking of is a Talmudic adage that says "There is no *mazal* for the Jews." Now, while some folks might translate from the Yiddish and think this means that Jews just don't have any luck, in fifth-century Babylonia it meant something different. In a land ruled by Magi and under the influence of the stars, as it were, the rabbis insisted: Jews don't have *mazal*, they have no constellation, no sign.

Now, lest we all fret over vanished opening lines for the singles' scene, Lukinsky is quick to point out that while rabbinic Jews do not have astrology, they do have the weekly Torah reading cycle. This is particularly true of all the Jews who have been Bar or Bat Mitzvah. At the tender age of twelve or thirteen, kids are called upon to read in public from an unpunctuated, unvoweled Hebrew scroll, written on parchment with a quill. It's quite a rite of passage, and those who have done it, even those who have done it and never again stepped foot in a synagogue, are likely to remember their *parashah,* the Torah reading for their Bar or Bat Mitzvah week. Years later they can still say, My *parashah* was *Vaera* or *Pinhas,* or any of the other fifty-four weekly Torah readings in the annual cycle. I imagine them at cocktail parties, at bars in Soho, at the local Barnes and Noble, sidling up to an attractive single and asking, "Hey, cutie, what's your *parashah?*"

I am acutely aware of this, not only because I am single, but because I have been singularly shaped by my *parashah*. Of course, I had no idea as a kid of thirteen that the choice of my Bar Mitzvah reading would shape my life in the way it did—to be honest, I don't know whether it's karma or coincidence that has led me to a career based on my Torah reading. My Bar Mitzvah *parashah* is (not "was," but "is," as it remains so in a very active sense) *Lekh Lekha,* that section beginning at Genesis 12:1, the so-called Call of Abraham and the subsequent events that unfold. It is here that I begin discussion of the "moral dilemmas" in Genesis.

I've used this portion of Genesis over the past decade in at least seven previous study groups. It works well, it's a good jumping-off point. No complex creation stories or messy floods to muddy the waters of our discussion, just good old family conflict, the kind all of us are experts in. And what a family conflict this narrative begins with; it's the stuff of *Geraldo* and *Oprah,* or maybe a good soap opera. I know, we could call it *Dynasty:* a rich family, four generations, interactions with world leaders, beautiful women. Instead of Alexis and Krystle, we'll have Sarah and Hagar. . . .

Before my fantasies grow too baroque (although I quite like the soap opera idea, Genesis having a much longer run than most—in fact, it's in its zillionth rerun), maybe we should turn to the text of my *parashah* and follow the basic plot. Some text "facts" to inform our discussion, if you please. To be completely honest, the Scripture I will quote starts a few verses earlier, back in Genesis 11 (the Torah reading there is named after Noah). That way, we'll have a running start to Abraham's journey, and the introductions and background necessary to follow the characters through the plot.

When I read these words at age thirteen, I thought I knew what the story was all about. Thirty years later, the words are the same, but the story seems radically different. It's no surprise that I've changed in thirty years—Kohlberg's developmental theory assures us that that should happen. High school, college, graduate school, marriage, two kids, a divorce, and sixty pounds later, the narrative isn't as innocent as it was when I was a Bar Mitzvah boy. Not Abraham, nor Sarah, nor I seem to be saints anymore. To be honest, it's hard to listen to the Torah reading in the synagogue these days, it just cuts too close to the bone. I suppose that's why Jews read it every year, year in, year out. Same words, different story. Here we go.

This is the history of Terah: Terah fathered Abraham, Nahor, and Haran, and Haran fathered Lot. Haran died before his father, Terah, in his birthplace, Ur Khasdim. Abraham and Nahor took wives. Abraham's wife was Sarah . . . Sarah was barren, she had no child. Terah took his son, Abraham, his grandson, Lot, and his daughter-in-law, Sarah, and went with them from Ur Khasdim to go to the land of Canaan. But when they got to Kharan, they settled there. Terah lived two hundred and five years and he died in Kharan.

God said to Abraham, "Go from your land, your birthplace, your father's house, to the land I will show you. I will make you a great nation. I will bless you and make you famous. You will be a blessing. Those who bless you, I will bless. Those who curse you, I will curse. Through you all of the families of the earth will be blessed." So Abraham went, as God had told him to, and Lot went with him. Abraham was seventy-five when he left Kharan.

Abraham took his wife, Sarah, and his nephew, Lot, and all they had amassed, and the people they had acquired in Kharan, and they left for Canaan. When they arrived in the land of Canaan, God appeared to Abraham and said, I give this land to your offspring. So Abraham built an altar to God, who had appeared to him . . .

There was a famine in the land, so Abraham descended to Egypt, to stay there a while, for the famine was bad. When they were nearing Egypt, he said to his wife, Sarah, "Now, I know you are a beautiful woman. When the Egyptians see you and ask whose wife you are, they will kill me and keep you alive. Tell them you're my sister, so I'll turn a profit on it and they will keep me alive on your behalf."

So it happened when Abraham arrived in Egypt that the Egyptians noticed how beautiful the woman was. Pharaoh's courtiers noticed her and praised her to Pharaoh, so the woman was acquired for Pharaoh's household. Abraham profited from her: He got sheep, oxen, and donkeys, slaves and maidservants, mules and camels.

God plagued Pharaoh, mighty plagues on him and his household, because of Abraham's wife, Sarah. Pharaoh summoned Abraham and said, "What have you done to me?! Why didn't you tell me she was your wife? Why did you say she was your sister so that I took her as my wife? Now, here's your wife, take her and go!" Pharaoh set a guard upon him and exiled him and his wife and all that was his. So Abraham ascended to the Negev from Egypt—he, his wife, and all he had, and Lot with him. Abraham was now very wealthy in livestock, silver, and gold.

What a happy little tale. As a kid I marveled at the music of the Torah reading of the last two lines, full of trills and flourishes. A triumph for Abraham, now rich, rewarded by God, marching with an honor guard, victorious, back to the promised land. Having survived the rigors of famine and the harrowing of Pharaoh, Abraham inherits his just deserts—the Negev and parts north. Gold and silver are his, sheep, oxen, and donkeys, slaves and maidservants, mules and camels. He began as a poor shepherd, but now father Abraham is a very wealthy man. God sure provides for His chosen.

How differently I read this text today. There's so much going on in this narrative, it's hard to know where to begin unpacking it. In not very many lines of sacred text, the Bible has drawn an extraordinary moral dilemma. How shall we characterize it? "What price success?" Or shall we opt for the Geraldo/Oprah title "Husbands Who Pimp Their Wives!"? But I'm getting ahead of myself, rushing to conclusions about the narrative that may not be there, one possible reading of many, and one not generally preferred by traditional interpreters of this passage.

So let's go back a bit and comment point by point. We'll do some exegesis, assuming for the moment that a line-by-line reading might help us get a handle on the action here. Before we do that, though, let me explain the word I used in the last sentence: *exegesis*. The roots of the word are Greek and it means "coming or going out." Exegesis is the art of drawing meaning out of a verse or text. Exegesis implies that the interpretation or reading we offer is somehow implicit inside of the text—we merely draw it out. Presumably we have some tools of reading and those tools help us first supply the context, then read between the lines, understanding first the *peshat* and then the *derash*.

All of this comes under the rubric of exegesis. But like *peshat* and *derash*, not everything I see in the text will be perceived there by the next reader. Therefore, sometimes what I assume is in the text, you may assume is a forced reading, an overreading, nonsense. I suppose it all depends on whether or not you agree with my understanding of the text. If you do, then you'll tend to say I'm doing exegesis—that is, correctly reading out what the text means. If, however, you disagree with my reading, then you won't credit me with being an exegete, just a fool. Actually, I would hope for better, especially since I will offer a wide variety of readings for every passage in this book. I'd like to think we'll learn to listen to a broad array of exegeses and recognize that each of them may have some validity as a reading of the text. If we can do that, we not only will broaden our understanding of the text, we will develop our moral reasoning faculties as well. While we're at it, we will also develop our listening skills—a good attribute for the building of community.

Let us begin exegesis of the story. It will be clear that our bias going into the narrative will profoundly affect what we draw from it. If we presume, along with much of Judeo-Christian tradition, that Abraham is a "saint," then we shall require a different set of lenses through which to interpret the action. If, on the other hand, we allow for the possibility that father Abraham was a scoundrel, our interpretation will differ yet again. These poles of interpretation, antinomies on the continuum of exegesis, have informed almost every discussion I have participated in regarding this passage of Scripture.

Traditional readers, rabbis of old, and their contemporaries, the church fathers—along with most moralists of our own era—all start with the assumption that father Abraham is in a pickle. Faced with the option of sure death at the hands of the Egyptians, he takes a risk that allows him to remain alive and perhaps rescue his wife from her role as "sister." When I read this story with my writers' group, we spent a full session agonizing over Abraham's moral dilemma. How can Abraham stay alive? Must he put Sarah at risk? Will their faith in God bring them rescue? Will their faith in each other allow their marriage to continue after such an episode?

There's more than a little of modern terrorism and hostage taking in this reading of the story. In essence, from the minute they enter Egypt, due to the life-and-death choice they have made, Sarah is taken hostage and runs the risk of abuse at the hands of the Egyptians. By faith, Abraham survives the ordeal, and with the help of God rescues her and is rewarded—not unlike the Israeli rescue of hostages at Entebbe during the July 4, 1976, weekend, two decades ago. One assumes, given this view of Abraham and Sarah, that their marriage is stronger than ever after their ordeal and that thanks to their faith, the once-childless couple will soon bear a son and live happily ever after.

When I read this passage some years later with my study group of CEOs, I was on guard lest too pious a reading might preclude the less trained readers from seeing subtleties in Abraham's dilemma. I gently raised the moral issue that might be considered when one focused on Abraham's short speech to Sarah as they entered Egypt. Had he said, "When the Egyptians see you and ask whose wife you are, they will kill me and keep you alive. Tell them you're my sister and they will keep me alive on your behalf," I would have had complete sympathy. But Abraham unfortunately added a clause, right there in the Bible. What he said to Sarah was, "Tell them you're my sister, so I'll turn a profit on it," which certainly adds an unsightly nuance to the narrative.

"Whoa, whoa, whoa!" one of the attorneys in the group jumps in. The speaker is, in fact, one of the most successful criminal attorneys on Wall Street. His reputation is that he never plea-bargains and also never loses. This makes his services highly desirable in the white-collar crime sector. He once said, I think in jest, but I confess I'm not at all sure, "There's no such thing as a guilty client."

"Let's look at this chapter," the lawyer instructs us, his jury. "At the beginning of the chapter, God takes a poor shepherd, a nothing, and tells him to become the head of a great and mighty nation. Now, that's quite a challenge. Yet look," our counselor points out, "*morality aside*—" (It was when I heard these two words that I knew I would be hearing something memorable, a novel interpretation of Genesis 12. I also realized that I wanted this man's phone number in my wallet just in case I was ever in the situation of having only one phone call to make.) "Morality aside," he repeats, "by the end of the chapter he's talking one-on-one with a head of state. And let's face it," he adds triumphantly, "he's earned start-up costs."

When we finished laughing, I filed "morality aside . . . start-up costs" in my memory, although I abashedly admit that I filed it with my repertoire of lawyer jokes. As the weeks passed between one study group meeting and the next, his words began to gnaw at me. What if he was correct? What did it mean if this seemingly cynical attorney had a *peshat*? What if the whole point of Genesis 12 was precisely that, "Morality aside . . . he earned start-up costs"? If that was the lesson, if we were meant to learn about survival at any cost, advancement without thought for morality, that it was okay to pimp your wife if the profit was sufficient, if, if, if . . . then I had to rethink the lessons of Genesis entirely.

I was reminded of the story about George Bernard Shaw and the duchess whom he propositioned, asking whether she might consider consenting to have sexual relations with him for five million pounds. When she replied that for that much money she surely would give the matter consideration, Shaw asked whether she would have sex for a few farthings. The duchess haughtily demanded of Mr. Shaw whether he thought her a prostitute! Shaw replied, "We've already established that, madam. We're now haggling over the price." What price did morality cost? Was life a matter of simply avoiding situations where the currency of morality was tested too severely? Were there hard-and-fast rules, or did situations change the ethics we held dear?

Growing up in Illinois, I had heard another story that reinforced my doubts. Again, it was an attorney at the center of the story, but this one even more famous than my study partner. They say that a criminal came to Abraham Lincoln in the days before he was president but already a lawyer of some repute.

"I'd like you to represent me, Mr. Lincoln," the fellow asked.

Lincoln, who had some inkling of the man and his activities, asked, "Are you guilty, sir?"

"Of course I'm guilty," the criminal replied. "That's why I want to hire you to get me off."

"If you admit your guilt to me," Lincoln explained, "then I cannot represent you."

"But you don't understand," the man replied. "I'm offering one thousand dollars for your services."

Even though one thousand dollars was a lot of money back then, Lincoln declined.

The man said, "Mr. Lincoln, I'll offer you two thousand dollars to represent me."

Again, Lincoln demurred.

"Mr. Lincoln, I came up to your office to hire your services, for it is said you are the best attorney in Illinois. I will give you four thousand dollars as a retainer."

At that, Lincoln unfolded himself from his chair, grabbed the criminal by his jacket, marched him to the door, and threw him out of the office. As the man rose and brushed himself off, he asked Lincoln, "Sir, why did you throw me out when I said four thousand dollars? Why not one thousand, or two thousand, or why not when I first came into your office and admitted my guilt?"

Lincoln replied, "You were getting close to my price."

Does everyone have a price? Is it acceptable to sell Sarah to save a life? Is it less acceptable if a profit is turned on the transaction even as a life is saved? If such barter is tenable, might we actually imagine that Abraham is to be admired for his wiles? That as a trickster he is to be praised and not condemned? That his ability to turn a profit in a rough situation makes him worthy of fathering a nation and being God's chosen?

Could we imagine that this is a scam? That Abraham knows only too well the horror Pharaoh and the Egyptians have of taking another man's wife, and that they would pay a high price for an attractive woman, but an even larger sum of hush money to quiet the scandal of adultery? That Pharaoh's pretensions to divinity forced him to hew to a high moral standard and that, once entrapped, he would quickly pony up to prevent any breath of scandal?

Imagine the cleverness of Abraham pimping his wife. A quick profit is turned, and then a second windfall as God enters the scene as enforcer. In fact, is Abraham emboldened to this scheme precisely because he knows that God will provide the muscle to preclude Pharaoh from keeping his wife and killing him?

Before you protest that the notion of "scam" is too radical a reading, remember that once successful at this type of extortion, Abraham pulls it off again in Genesis 20 with a local king named Avimelekh. He, too, pays off big, "sheep and oxen, slaves and maidservants," when he returns Sarah to Abraham. But Avimelekh goes even further. He says to Abraham, "Behold, my land is before you. Dwell where you see fit." And then, in case the fact of the scam were not clear, he says to Sarah, "I have given one thousand pieces of silver to 'your brother.' It is meant to serve as a covering of the eyes for all who are with you."

From this second scam it is all too clear that the cash is for the cover-up; everyone is bribed to look the other way. The scam is eminently successful. In fact, it's so successful that six chapters later in Genesis, Abraham and Sarah's son, Isaac, imitates the lessons he has learned from Mom and Dad and repeats the scam with his wife, Rebecca. Now, Isaac only knows about the previous episodes through hearsay—he wasn't alive when Sarah and Abraham took this particular show on the road—but Isaac's cousin, Lot, was with Abraham and Sarah in Egypt. We'll see in Chapter 6 what lessons he learned about sex bait from his saintly uncle.

While we're brooding about this ugly little episode, it's worth taking a breather, a step back to see where we are in our reading. I've suggested that Abraham is a fellow who, given the right opportunity, might sell his wife. Of course, this reading goes against the grain of everything we've ever been taught about reading the Bible. I know this interpretation of Genesis is upsetting and draws immediate resistance from readers. I know because I am so resistant to the iconoclasm myself. I hate the idea of smashing the idol I have in Saint Abraham.

Alas, it is Abraham's role, his lot in tradition, to be associated with iconoclasm. One of the most beloved stories of rabbinic, extrabiblical tradition shows us young Abe, in his father's idol factory, smashing the statues to bits. It should serve as a warning that when we read the story of Abraham there might be some sweeping up to do at the end. The questions Abraham asks his father in that legend ("Don't your ears hear what your mouth speaks?") may be appropriate at this juncture. The anger Abraham's father, Terah, feels when his idols are smashed may be an anger that longtime Bible readers are feeling at the reading I've just offered. What have we gained in raising the possibility that father Abraham is a scoundrel, a trickster, an amoral profiteer? Why must we be forced to rethink our accepted Judeo-Christian morality?

Why, indeed. Accepted morality may be nice, but it need not be our own until we rethink it. By now you should have pulled your Bible from the shelf to reread your version of the story. If these questions were provocative enough, you may have engaged a spouse, a friend, a parent, or a pastor about the implications of this reading of Genesis 12. The study and discussion of the moral dilemma *is* the process that we are after here. Do not reject the possibility of this interpretation out of hand. For a moment consider it, weigh its implications, follow the logic of the morality (or lack of morality) implied in this version of Genesis 12. Test whether this radical pole of interpretation can be sustained in the words of the text, and examine what hermeneutics, what biases, what assumptions you have brought to the opening story of Abraham and Sarah.

In one study group I taught, a literary agent, Jewish only in name, with very little formal Jewish education, passionately defended Abraham and Sarah against this cruel portrayal of them as scam artists. Since he was a professional reader, I insisted on pressing him: Wasn't this reading at least a possible interpretation of the text? He reluctantly admitted that yes, it certainly was. Maybe it was even an appropriately fair reading of the words. Why, then, I asked, had he so passionately defended the traditional Saint Abraham reading, especially if he had no apparent vested interest in it? His answer, which came a full month later, at the next scheduled study group, was no surprise: He defended Abraham because that was his notion of Judaism. He still held precious a naive view of religion and was not quick to abandon it. His simple reading of a nice Abraham offered him solace in what he knew to be an otherwise cruel world.

Is there benefit to a more nuanced reading? Can we profit from consideration that Abraham is deeply flawed yet nevertheless chosen? Can we learn something from a failure of morality against which we set our own? Is there solace to be gained from the fact that Abraham, despite his flaws and dubious decisions, remains on a pedestal in Western consciousness three thousand years after his death? Why do we need saints and heroes so badly that we choose a very human Abraham as our model? Or is his flawed humanity precisely the point?

While we achingly ponder this series of questions, let's return to the story with yet another point of view. In the world of the rabbis, where the method of multiple readings is highly valued, there is a term for this technique: *dvar aher,* "another interpretation."

Up till now we've focused primarily on Abraham and left Sarah in silent acquiescence. Might we give her some voice? She is utterly silent in this chapter, even though it is she who is put at risk. Later on in Genesis Sarah has a lucid, articulate, even ferocious voice. What could she have been thinking during the events depicted above? Can we offer a variety of thoughts that flit through her mind, across her lips, and into the conversation—even if between the lines—of Genesis 12? This, too, is a classical rabbinic method of interpretation. The rabbis were not in the least bit shy about putting words into the mouths of biblical characters. It was their way of drawing out the implications of Scripture, of earning the fullest profit of God's revelation. The rabbis surely knew that when they offered dialogue on behalf of silent characters in the Bible, they were offering readings from their own century, anachronising their thoughts into the mouth of a biblical character.

We, too, know only too well that the readings we offer here are late-twentieth-century readings. We do not pretend to biblical scholarship, rather midrash. That is to say, I am not primarily interested in understanding the contextual meaning of the narrative. Quite the contrary, I am interested in the biblical narrative helping us understand ourselves. So, with that in mind, what *was* Sarah thinking?

Let's begin with piety. Sarah is identified, the very first time we meet her, as a barren woman, she has no child. As if this weren't bad enough—and here I mean not only the barrenness, but the totality of identification with that state, as though children were the only thing by which a human being's life could be judged a success or failure—it is in her barren state that God promises Abraham offspring as plentiful as the stars, as numerous as the sands on the shore of the sea. How dismal for Sarah. Poor Sarah becomes practically obsessive about offspring, even as she is unsure whether it is she or Abraham, in reality, who is the problem. We will explore her doubts about her husband's potency further in the next chapter, but for now it is sufficient to note that Sarah will not shoulder all the blame herself. As she laughingly tells the angels who announce her imminent pregnancy in Genesis 18:12, "My husband's just too old."

How, then, might she react when that old husband, at the border to a strange and fearsome land, proposes to her, "Tell them you are my sister"? The famine in the land might well be sated by entrance into Egypt. Perhaps someone would get her with child, and this at Abraham's suggestion! Her sacrifice would save her husband's life and bring the child of promise, the offspring to fulfill God's covenant with Abraham and her.

Another interpretation: Sarah didn't give a fig for children, but she loved and cherished Abraham. Faced with a Sophie's Choice, she did what she had to. Like many women during the holocaust (and virtually every other war), she submitted, resigned to saving as much of her family as she could. If sleeping with the enemy would save Abraham and get them through the famine, so be it. Sarah, full of faith in herself, in her husband's judgment, in God Almighty, goes modestly into Pharaoh's house, prepared to endure whatever indignities are laid upon her, if only Abraham might live.

Another interpretation: Sarah is very tired of taking the heat for Abraham's impotence. She is ready and willing to call his bluff. It is bad enough that the old man can't get an erection any longer, has no more interest in her, and then blames her for being barren, to boot. It is bad enough that he makes her wander from place to place, brings her to a promised land wracked with famine, and then proposes that they enter Egypt as "brother and sister." It is bad enough that he smarmily tells her, "Now I know that you are a beautiful woman," as though it made a shred of difference to him, covered in sheep dung at the end of a day of shepherding. Married to a nomad, an uncivilized boor who talked to voices in the night, Sarah was not going to pass up a chance to enjoy the urbane pleasures of Egypt. Indeed, she was beautiful. Properly washed and oiled, she had a crack at Pharaoh's bed. Who wouldn't jump at the opportunity? He was so cultured (and bore an uncanny resemblance to Yul Brynner). Why *not* sleep with Pharaoh, and if she got pregnant, well, it served Abraham right. Sister, indeed!

I wish that I could tell you that these last few readings were the stuff of ancient midrash. Unfortunately, the rabbis of blessed memory were too constrained to imagine that their women might have such shocking thoughts. They preferred their women demure, at home, submissive. In *Genesis Rabbah,* a sixth-century Palestinian commentary on this passage, the rabbis suggest that Abraham's solution was to put Sarah in a box and nail it shut, lest the Egyptians lay eyes on her. The readings I offer above came from a women's class that I taught for a number of years, and here I had thought these club ladies would be as demure as their tailored suits and blue-tint hair led one to imagine (although I once stupidly gave voice to the opinion that given their average age somewhere in the sixties, they were middle-aged—a big mistake, which should have tipped me off to the radical readings they would offer).

This women's class ventured all of the above and more. "Why shouldn't Sarah be interested in a bit of adventure? After all," they asked, "hasn't she put up with all the crap of his career long enough?" "Don't you think it's time she has a chance?" "Wouldn't you jump at the opportunity of sleeping with a Pharaoh?" "How could Sarah resist such an adventure, especially once Abraham gave her that wife-sister line?" I confess, happy feminist that I think myself, I was taken aback by the radical nature of the readings and the vehemence with which they were offered. Once the door to this possibility was open, it seemed a wonder that Sarah might ever return to Abraham when the ordeal was over. In fact, as these women reminded me when we got there, Sarah never quite forgets the position Abraham has placed her in. The marriage is effectively destroyed, if intimacy may be any measure of marriage.

Now I hesitated, wisely on two counts, to ask whether there wasn't a certain amount of projection of their own suburban lives onto Sarah's. On the one hand, it wouldn't do to undermine such a strong and authentic feminist reading of the episode. On the other hand, if they were projecting their own fantasies, frustrations, and sexual realities onto Sarah, I wasn't at all sure I wanted to hear about it in detail. I have had enough experience watching my friend Peter Pitzele use biblical narratives as the texts for psychodrama to know that given the thin patina of Genesis narrative, everyone's neuroses just come pouring out. While the study of the Bible may be revelatory and even therapeutic, it is wise for me to remember that I am a rabbi and not a therapist. I am concerned with moral development, but I must also know the limits of my competence.

So we will leave Sarah to her still-unvoiced thoughts, satisfied that we have opened the door to possibilities of her motivation. In doing so we have not only offered women an entrée to the text, but have exposed a method of interpretation which gives rise to a great deal of dialogue for development. It is clear that Genesis, like any other narrative, has a point of view. I suppose that, even with its implicit critique, the point of view of Genesis is Abraham's, or at least one that is ultimately sympathetic to him and his offspring. And, if I may take a term from feminist film criticism, the "gaze" is decidedly male. When we ask a woman's questions, when we take a point of view other than that of the protagonist, we gain new perspectives into the narrative. It helps to see other people's outlooks when reading a dilemma. Arguing someone else's position helps us appreciate it and rethink our own.

This leads us to wonder about poor Pharaoh. It's hard to be sympathetic to a biblical character with the name Pharaoh, but there are certain few pharaohs who have done okay by the Jews—Joseph's patron or Solomon's father-in-law, to name two. In any case, our Pharaoh is the victim of circumstance, and a circumstance of Abraham's making. Pharaoh protests, "What have you done to me?! Why didn't you tell me she was your wife? Why did you say she was your sister so that I took her as my wife?" He is clearly upset, affronted. He cannot imagine the type of person who might put another man at risk of committing adultery, to say the least of someone pimping his own wife. Pharaoh is outraged, upset, he doesn't know what to do first, he's so befuddled. He certainly pays Abraham off, loads of silver and gold as hush money. But unlike the triumphal march I imagined as a child, Pharaoh sets armed guards on Abraham, declares him persona non grata, and boots him out of the country: " 'Now, here's your wife. Take her and go!' Pharaoh set a guard upon him and exiled him and his wife and all that was his."

It will be curious to note as we get to our next chapter that Pharaoh, here, is in much the same position as Abraham in Genesis 16. He listened to what was told to him, took what was apparently offered, and then found himself damned if he did and damned if he didn't. To make matters worse, God enters this already difficult scene and plagues Pharaoh and all his household. It is difficult to imagine what manner of plague God brings upon Pharaoh, and again it is difficult to think of Pharaoh and plagues without thinking of the story of Exodus. In any case, it is enough, more than enough, for Pharaoh, especially when added to the moral outrage. I can't resist adding, though, that when the rabbis of old imagine Pharaoh's plague at this critical juncture, they imagine a sexual disease that causes impotence. Sarah's virtue thus protected, the rabbis can rest at ease, perhaps unaware that they have imaginatively afflicted Pharaoh with the same disease that Abraham may suffer. Alas, poor Sarah.

This reading presumes that Abraham has been egregious in his mistreatment of Pharaoh. Either Abraham has been the deceiver suggested above, or, minimally, Abraham has imputed a baseness to Pharaoh that Pharaoh does not have. Is Abraham, then, projecting his own worst side? In the face of fear and uncertainty, does Abraham presume that Pharaoh must, of necessity, be as unsavory as possible? Is this, then, the only way to enter a foreign land? Are we fated to always treat the other as morally inferior, even if they are not? Must we reduce them to "the Other"? And what does that reduction of our fellow human beings say about our own moral development? Is not Pharaoh justified at his moral outrage?

But is it necessary to think of Pharaoh as more ethical than Abraham? Might one not equally well make the case that all of Pharaoh's bluster comes after the abduction of Sarah? Only when God has plagued him does Pharaoh suddenly become righteous. Is he saving face? Is Abraham not correct that the niceties of adultery were observed by the expedient of killing the husband and then magnanimously marrying the widow (just like King David and BathSheba)?

It is disturbing that given the bias of the account (the Jewish Bible) there is any room whatsoever to give Pharaoh the benefit of the doubt. Traditional interpretations, from rabbis and church fathers, presume Abraham to be righteous and Pharaoh a liar. But we are conditioned by our communities of reading, our biases, our knowledge of other Pharaohs. The words of the narrative leave us with a morally ambiguous situation. Consideration of all the sides of the story gives us pause, causes us to reflect, rethink our moral positions, and justify our responses.

Abraham and Sarah are father and mother of faith. How, then, in the very chapter where they are "called" to faith do they come to behave in such a morally ambiguous way? What is the nature of this call, this so-called chosenness? What moral responsibilities does it place on Abraham, Sarah, and their descendants? Or, we may ask, does the very fact that they have been chosen release them from the obligation of moral behavior? Will God always protect him, so long as Abraham is loyal to God? What cost does this loyalty carry? When there is a "teleological suspension of the ethical," as philosopher Søren Kierkegaard called it, can God demand anything as a test of loyalty, and must Abraham pay it? Is that, then, the price of a suspension of morality?

What is the nature of this faith and loyalty that Abraham and Sarah show to God? (To say the least of faith in and to each other.) It is true that when God bade them, they left their homeland and moved to the promised land without demurral, but once they got there, then what? Famine moved them into hostile territory quickly. The rabbis count the famine as a test of Abraham. Perhaps he was meant to stay firm. Had he said, "Here God wants me. I have faith God will provide, even in the famine," well, Genesis would have been a very different book. Had Sarah made stone soup, perhaps she would have been rewarded with a child, or at least with a husband who made love to her. Instead they embark on a journey that ends in a disgraceful deception, the only faith displayed, perhaps, that God will play the heavy and act as enforcer for their schemes.

In the end, they grow rich. We do not know, nor does the Bible give us any clue, whether Pharaoh had his way with Sarah before the plague. We do not know, although we will see many clues, what effect this misadventure has on Abraham and Sarah's marriage. We do not know yet, although we will be shown with stunning brutality, what nephew Lot might have learned by observing this bizarre behavior. And since the Bible delights in a fearful symmetry, we will see how this episode echoes through subsequent chapters of Genesis, all the way to Exodus and beyond.

As we read of Sarah and Abraham's interaction with another Egyptian, Hagar, we must recall that action breeds consequences that cannot be measured at the moment. When God delivers a son to Sarah after her own abortive attempts to become pregnant, we will see that this miracle, too, carries a fearsome price.

The rabbis count the famine as a trial by which God tested Abraham. In fact, by the rabbis' count, there are three trials in this narrative. First, there is the uprooting from home and hearth to a promised but nonetheless distant and alien land. Second, there is the famine, which leads to the third trial, the abduction of Sarah by Pharaoh. We have discussed how Abraham and Sarah endure these trials, for better or for worse. Perhaps it is apposite to inquire at this juncture who is this God who tests them so severely. As the rabbis put it, "Abraham was tried by ten trials to make known how great was the love of father Abraham." The rabbis do not explain whether these trials show Abraham's love for God, or God's love for Abraham.

Once, my old Talmud teacher Professor Saul Lieberman regaled us with a story of a quiz he had given one of the Bible professors at my seminary. He had asked the professor, "Who is the most tragic character in the Bible?"

After some thought, Professor Muffs replied, "Jeremiah."

"No, Muffs, not Jeremiah," Lieberman cackled. "Try again."

So Professor Muffs thought some more and then replied, "Ezekiel."

"Wrong again, Muffs," said Lieberman, "so I'll tell you. The most tragic character in the Bible is God!"

This story bears remembering as we read on through the Genesis narratives. God *is* a tragic character. Although I did not open our study with the story of creation, it is good to recall here that in that *parashah,* when the Bible opens, God creates a universe in seven days. Indeed, God sees what has been made and pronounces, "Behold, it is very good." For all of that optimism, though, it is worth remembering that in the rabbinic division of the Torah into weekly readings, by the time that *parashah* has ended, God regrets that humanity has been created and has decided to flood the world in order to destroy the very creatures that were made in God's image and likeness.

As we turn to the next chapters, we may ask what role God plays in these narratives. I remember one January, upon returning from a series of synagogue lectures on Florida's east coast, I found a student waiting to ask me an urgent question. "Professor," she earnestly began, "is it true that from a synagogue pulpit last Shabbat you called God a son of a bitch?" Apparently her colleagues in Florida had been on the phone.

"No," I replied reassuringly, "what I actually said is that God is a *mean* son of a bitch."

I then carefully explained to her that I was distinguishing for my Florida audience between biblical theology and rabbinic theology. In the latter, with its Hellenistic worldview, God was depicted as Nice or Good. The Bible had no such pretense. In Genesis 12, for example, God puts Abraham and Sarah to severe tests of loyalty and then beats Pharaoh as God acts the role of enforcer in Abraham's wife-sister scandal. It was the point of my synagogue lecture that an adequate theology for the twentieth century required a mixture of biblical and rabbinic views of God. But it is important to recognize that God is a difficult character, one whom we cannot afford to overlook if we are to understand the dynamics of the narratives we confront.

In studying the moral dilemmas of Abraham and Sarah, we may already begin to recognize issues that beset us in our own lives. We ask ourselves, Does this story from three thousand years ago teach us anything about ourselves or about the world in which we live? Or are famines and Pharaohs simply too remote to make the jump to our own, more comfortable existences? Although I believe that the Bible does speak directly to our own day, it is not the answers to the questions but rather the process of study that is essential. Whatever the answer to the specifics of the narrative, we are learning to analyze an issue, listen to other points of view, consider that there is more than one reading of every story, and articulate the reasoning behind our own opinions. The very act of study, the engagement it demands, teaches us to be part of a community that values moral reasoning. If Professor Kohlberg is correct, it is just this kind of study that leads, in fact, to moral development.

Let's turn now to the next episode in Sarah and Abraham's marriage. Sarah despairs of ever having children, and in desperation takes matters into her own hands. That appears to be the surface narrative of another challenge to Abraham and Sarah's marriage. Again, the outsider who completes the triangle is an Egyptian, only this time, the moral dilemma is made even more complex by the arrival of offspring for Abraham and his wife.

3

THE
OTHER WOMAN

DURING MY DIVORCE I learned an important lesson about other people's marriages: No one ever really knows what's going on. I learned this, of course, when friend after friend, confronted with my news, responded with shock. "But I had no idea. You seemed so happy." And how could they have had an idea? People can only see what they are shown. To make it worse, once they are shown, they only see what they wish to see. This is particularly true with the breakup of a marriage; if it seems too familiar, then it's already too threatening to look at very carefully. It's much easier to assume, with a nod to Tolstoy, that all unhappy marriages are the same.

Of course, Tolstoy's point was that each marriage is different, whether in literature or in reality. Whether it was Anna Karenina or me, the forms unhappiness takes are unique to each couple and the situation they have created for themselves. Sometimes otherwise happily married couples founder on the shoals of another love interest. Sometimes couples fall apart over arguments about their children. Sometimes couples cannot have children and rather than seek solace in each other, turn to subtle forms of torture to act out their anguish. The list of permutations here is endless, as many unhappy endings as there are marriages.

This is not to say that there are no happy marriages, for surely there are. Further, there are couples who have negotiated pitfalls like those above and grown stronger and more loving. These rare couplings are a blessing from God and should be celebrated. Often as not, in fact, couples stay together as break apart. Sadly, of those who stay together, many are unhappy, limping along unable to heal a wound struck early in the marriage. Such a disabling wound often compounds as the marriage progresses. Long memory is no friend in this type of marriage—scores are settled decades later, much to the detriment of all involved.

This unhappy background may be the necessary introduction to Abraham and Sarah in Genesis 16, the chapter of the Other Woman. It is, I confess, also possible to read this story and assume that Sarah and Abraham have found a *modus vivendi*. They are happy, content, and flourishing as each other's partners. Or, perhaps, unhappy and discontent, but flourishing as partners nonetheless. In any case, we contend here with an other woman, a surrogate mother, an adoption plan that goes awry, the physical abuse that results, and the marital stress and discord that accompanies this kind of family history. We have to try and read between the lines, and as with all undertakings of that sort, there's more than one way to read.

Sarah, Abraham's wife, had not borne him a child. She had an Egyptian maidservant named Hagar. Sarah said to Abraham, "Note, please, God has kept me from bearing. Go, now, into my maidservant. Perhaps I can be built up through her." So Abraham listened to Sarah's voice.

After ten years of Abraham's dwelling in Canaan, Sarah, Abraham's wife, took the Egyptian Hagar, her maidservant, and gave her to her husband, Abraham, for a wife.

He came into Hagar and she got pregnant, but when she saw she was pregnant, her mistress seemed less weighty in her eyes. Sarah said to Abraham, "I am furious at you! I put my maidservant in your arms. Now that she sees she is pregnant, am I to be less weighty in her eyes? Let God judge between you and me!" Abraham responded to Sarah, "Your maidservant is in your hands. Do to her as you see fit."

So Sarah abused her and she ran away. A messenger of God found her at a spring of water in the wilderness, the spring on the road to Shur. He said, "Hagar, maidservant to Sarah, where are you coming from and where are you going?"

She replied, "I am running away from Sarah, my mistress."
The messenger of God said to her, "Return to your mistress. Be abused by her."

The messenger of God said to her, "I will make your offspring very plentiful, uncountable in number."

The messenger of God said to her, "You are pregnant and will give birth to a son. Call him Ishmael, for God has heard your affliction. He will be a wild ass of a man, his hand against everyone and everyone's hand against him. Yet he will dwell in the presence of all his brethren.". . .

Hagar bore a son to Abraham, and Abraham called his son, whom Hagar had borne him, Ishmael. Abraham was eighty-six years old when Hagar bore Ishmael to Abraham.

Oh, Sarah, how you despair! When a woman is so bound up with having children, so defined by her childless state, how low she may sink into depression and despair. For how low must a woman feel to offer another to her husband of ten years? How desperate, how frantic for a child must someone be to conceive a plan such as Sarah's? Can you imagine, in any flight of fantasy, a suburban matron turning to her husband and saying, "Well, dear, you know we have no children after all these years. Why don't you sleep with the cleaning girl? Maybe she'll get pregnant and give us the baby as our own."

Of course, put like that, there are cases, all too regularly. Stories of surrogacy abound, and particularly the stories of failed surrogacy that fill the tabloid headlines. Usually, the conception is accomplished artificially, but even today there are cases where the methods are cruder, yet more sure—making babies the old-fashioned way. No wonder that the surrogate mother may change her mind. But it need not be only for love of the father. Women have self-respect. Women, lo and behold, learn to love the baby they deliver after carrying it for nine months as part of their own body. Come to think of it, it's a wonder that any surrogacy arrangement ever works out.

Even adoption is difficult. It's hard to watch all those white, middle-class parents, hungry for children, lining up to plead with the caseworkers, paying off the agencies, flying to South America to buy a brown baby on the black market. It's hard to watch them. Harder still to see the mothers give up their infants; whether it's due to over-population or poverty or shame is almost incidental. All too often it's about class and race. The mysteries of baby-hunger, the famine that forces desperate women to take desperate measures on either side of the birthing line, the mystery is powerful, something in God's hands.

That's just how Sarah sees it. Faced with the possibility of her bar-renness, with the increasing odds that it is she who is to blame, that her body has failed her, and failed her in a society where offspring are the measure of a woman, faced with an empty nest and an empty marriage, Sarah blames God: "Note, please, God has kept me from bearing." What else can she do? Blame herself? Blame Abraham? It's safer, somehow, to blame God. God is remote; blaming God is less likely to destroy the vestiges of a fragile marriage, or so Sarah hopes.

In blaming God, Sarah is freed to take matters into her own hands. God has put her in an untenable position. Now, ten years in the so-called promised land and still no offspring. God promised Abraham land, yes, but also children to work it, possess it. Where are the seed as plentiful as the stars in the sky, the sand on the shores of the sea? When God is not forthcoming, Sarah seeks to act. She acts to keep her husband, her marriage, the land, the promise, the commitments hinted at by God. Sarah offers Hagar, and in so doing, takes up God's cudgel, even as she acts for God. Oh, Sarah, how you despair! Of course, she does not have God's perspective, God's cosmic point of view. She has no clue how badly this will all turn out.

Sarah offers Hagar with the best of intentions, an act of faith in God and God's partnership with humanity. Yes, that's it! God has made a promise and it's up to barren Sarah to find a way to fulfill it. She will offer her maidservant, the Egyptian slave. It is about class and race. She knows she is taking a risk. She cannot even call Hagar by name when she offers her to Abraham, yet curiously, she offers her as "wife." Perhaps the wife status is required for the offspring to be legitimate, but it opens the door to disaster.

Or perhaps Sarah is unaware that she is reenacting the debacle with Pharaoh. The rabbis see the parallels to Abraham and Sarah in Egypt. In one neat connection they suggest that Hagar was part of the hush money, the payoff Pharaoh gave Abraham as he escorted him and Sarah to the border. The wages of sin, as it were. Could there be any other denouement but the one we read here? Couldn't Sarah see the parallels with Egypt past, if not with the Egypt of Exodus? Sarah couldn't have known enough to shudder at the thought of a Jew physically oppressing an Egyptian for her fecundity. Sarah couldn't have seen the irony, savored the foreshadowing.

But perhaps Sarah might have perceived that her good-faith offer of Hagar indicated a lack of faith in God, an inability, once again, to sit back and wait, to let God do things according to God's will, on God's own timetable. Sarah couldn't foresee Genesis 21:1, that "God remembered Sarah as God had said. God did for Sarah as God had promised." Sometimes a selfless gesture, when offered without thought of the consequences, turns to disaster of national proportions. How easy for us to judge, who have the gift of hindsight. How easy for God to judge, Who has the gift of foresight.

Let's shift gears now and consider another reading of this adventure. Let us assume that Sarah can see the parallels with her Egypt experience all too clearly. Sarah is cursed not only with barrenness, but with all too fertile a memory. It is almost incidental how she remembers her days in Pharaoh's harem, with fondness or with rancor. Does she smile when she thinks of the clean, smooth, white, Egyptian cotton sheets, cool beneath her—in stark contrast to the hot sand floor Abraham's tent offers? Can she recall the unguents and kohl, the careful makeup and costume that were part of the pageant of Pharaoh's boudoir? Or does she recollect the terror of the captive, the threat of rape, the fury at a husband who had sold her to this particular slavery? Either way, memory is malignant. It grows inside, it eats at her innards, consuming her body and soul.

So Sarah schemes, connives, concocts a plot patterned on her passion in the pharaonic court. She, barren, was given to an Egyptian by her husband, that he may live. Now, invoking the rabbinic principle of measure for measure, Sarah repays her husband his due. She, barren, will give to him an Egyptian, that she may live through adopted offspring: "Go, now, into my maidservant. Perhaps I can be built up through her." There is more than a measure of perversity here. Her own humiliations of the past are requited through humiliations of the present. Erase the shame of Egypt by yet more shame of Egypt. Deny the crude attempt to bear a child through Egypt by yet again attempting to bear a child through Egypt. Punish her husband for giving her to another man by giving him to another woman. Enough!

Another interpretation: "Sarah is barren; she has no child."

Who is to say that it is Sarah at fault? It is a truism that the Bible is a men's document, always written from the patriarchal perspective. So, obviously if there are no offspring, the woman must be to blame. But Sarah has her doubts. Let us not forget, Abraham is not a young man. In fact, he is eighty-five when this chapter unfolds. Nor should we forget Sarah's incredulity later, in Genesis 18:11–12, when the angels come to tell her she will bear a child: "Abraham and Sarah were old, getting on in years, Sarah had ceased menstruating. So Sarah laughed to herself, saying, 'After I've been worn out, shall I gush with pleasure? Besides, my husband's too old.' "

It's that last observation, a throwaway line, that opens the door to speculation. That it is damaging is confirmed in the very next verse of Scripture, when God repeats Sarah's doubts to Abraham but discreetly does not mention her jibe at Abraham. The rabbis point out that this is biblical evidence that sometimes glossing over the truth is justifiable, especially if it promotes household harmony. But what God covers up is Abraham's inability to perform adequately with Sarah. She cannot think of pregnancy when the old man simply cannot get an erection. Somewhere in Sarah's equation, whether it is a function of reality or simply her own denial, Abraham bears some of the blame for this childless state.

To be sympathetic to Abraham, for a moment, all of this sex for offspring can be depressing, daunting, detumescing, especially at age eighty-five. So let's be sympathetic to the old man and forgiving of Sarah if she is not quick to wholly bear the blame for barrenness. And if Abraham is less than sympathetic to Sarah's plight, let's understand and attribute it to his own macho bluster. No man, no matter how old, likes to admit that he cannot do what he once could do with vigor. As George Burns once quipped over the ash of his smoking cigar, "Now that I'm in my eighties, it takes me all night to do what I used to do all night." For father Abraham, even this may be but a fond memory.

But what, then, happens when Abraham accuses Sarah once too often of being the source of the problem? When Abraham bitterly blames her for the unfulfilled promises of God? When Abraham whines about how he would have seed as plentiful as the sand on the shores, if only his woman were not barren? How he'd have an erection up to the sky if only she could bear him offspring like the multitude of the stars? Is it not then that Sarah calls his bluff? Tired of the harping of a withered old man, does not Sarah, with a malicious gleam in her eye, offer, "Go, now, into my maidservant. Perhaps I can be built up through her"? Her challenge is implicit: Let's see if you can be built up through her, buster. And Abraham rises to the bait. He does sleep with the young maidservant. And he succeeds. "He came into Hagar and she got pregnant." Imagine Abraham's glee, however much he tried to keep it from Sarah. And then imagine Hagar, sleeping with that old coot, coaxing him to get hard, laboring under his huffing and puffing body. Hagar was young but not stupid. She was Sarah's maidservant. She knew of the troubles they were having. She knew that she had succeeded where Sarah had failed. She knew she would now bear the child of God's promise. How could she suppress some slight smile of satisfaction, if not with Abraham's sexual prowess, then at least with the situation? How could she resist that toss of the hair off her face that revealed her teenage contempt for her old mistress?

Is it any wonder that Sarah goes slightly mad? Betrayed and then betrayed yet again. Her bluff called, Abraham gets an erection for the little Egyptian when he hasn't made love to his proper wife in years. And then, the final proof, that it was she who was to blame after all. No longer could Sarah wonder if perhaps Abraham's impotence were at fault. No, damn it, he was potent, a father, but neither-nor with her. Her rage overflows and Hagar is the target. She beats the girl up and then turns on Abraham. Goddamn you! How could you? "I am furious at you! . . . . Let God judge between you and me!"

Another interpretation: Slavery is a bitch. It simply is not pretty, even by the elevated standards of the Hebrew Bible. By any measure whatsoever, it was simply better to be free than to be a slave. It wasn't just that one was the property of another (although that was certainly bad enough), but then there were the expectations of performance that came with the role. Female slaves were not merely expected to do laundry and windows. It was a given that they would perform other household services as well, though ones less frequently spoken of in polite company. Services to the master, if you will. In short, female slaves were there for the taking. No questions asked, no authorities to complain to, no concept of harassment, no choice.

Is it possible that patriarch Abraham had known Hagar now for years? A young mistress, as it were, to complement his older, barren wife? If so, what of Sarah? Does she countenance it? Has she a choice? Can she control it? If the husband is having an "affair" (although this admittedly is not an affair in any modern sense of the term), how does the faithful wife endure?

Does Sarah suffer this in silence, as she did the episode with Pharaoh, or does she passive-aggressively try to take control? "Go, now, into my maidservant. Perhaps I can be built up through her." Unfortunately for Sarah, her ploy to control the situation brings into the open what had previously been a secret of the bedroom. To exacerbate matters, young Hagar, now a wife and no longer a mistress, gets pregnant. Hagar begins to understand the shift in power. No longer the "other woman," she now is *the* woman, the mother of the long-awaited child. Is it any wonder that Sarah "seemed less weighty in her eyes"?

It is one thing to suffer a mistress in silence, but another thing entirely to have the mistress flaunt her elevated status with a smirk or a flash of the eyes. If Abraham had not started up with Hagar all those years ago, Sarah may never have felt the need to sanction the relationship by the surrogacy offer. Had Sarah satisfied Abraham, rather than Hagar having done so, perhaps Sarah might have felt less vindictive toward her servant and not plotted to take away her baby. In the end, either way, from Sarah's perspective it is Abraham's fault. He just wouldn't be satisfied, would he? So, "Sarah said to Abraham, 'I am furious at you! I put my maidservant in your arms. Now that she sees she is pregnant, am I to be less weighty in her eyes? Let God judge between you and me!' " And as for Hagar, well, Sarah will deal with her. "Sarah abused her and she ran away."

I confess, I have some sympathy for Abraham in all of this, whatever view of Sarah's machinations we may take. Like Pharaoh, who had Sarah dangled before him (if he only knew . . .), Abraham is damned if he does, damned if he doesn't. Imagine the old fool as Sarah offers Hagar to him. "I say what? You want me to do what? With who?" To say the least of his own battle. "Never mind should I, but if I try, will I be able to?" And, then, poor fool, then he is just self-satisfied enough to allow a grin to cross his face the morning after. Oh Abraham, focused on your petty triumph, how could you forget your wife, Sarah? Can't you see her pain? Don't you know that she wanted the child? That she wanted you? Couldn't you have had the sense of the moment when Sarah said, "Go, now, into my maidservant. Perhaps I can be built up through her," to respond, "Sarah, wife of mine, what matters offspring to me? If God wishes us to have children, God will provide. My pleasure is in you, my dear. Think not that any woman could hold a place in my bed but you. Come now, lay with me."

Of course, this last scenario ignores entirely the humanity and the attractiveness of the slave, Hagar. What confounds Sarah's plan is a reality the Bible seems to recognize in its legal codes when it treats the problem of slavery, which is that although slaves may be chattel property, they remain human beings. One may wish to treat them like cattle, but each slave has a face created in God's image, a personality with some likeness of the Creator. In part it is spiritual, religious; in equal if not greater measure, it is physical. The slave girl was not merely a vessel, she was sexy, attractive, charming, able to transcend her role as surrogate and become a rival wife to Sarah, for Abraham.

When young Hagar submitted to her mistress's order to sleep with Abraham, she may have endured Abraham's penetration in demure silence, or she may have resentfully survived what she saw as rape, her eyes flashing hatred at her tormentors. Hagar may equally have charmed and seduced Abraham, whether out of love and respect or out of an opportunistic sense that here was a way out of her predicament, a return ticket home to Egypt. In any scenario the outcome is the same: In becoming a mother to Abraham's child, she becomes, as well, a wife to the patriarch. Hagar has what Sarah hasn't. Hagar is fertile, Sarah is not. Hagar has Abraham's sexual attention, Sarah does not. Hagar has Abraham's child in her belly, Sarah does not.

It goes yet further, for when Hagar is abused and flees, she also has God's attention, as Sarah yet does not. Indeed, Hagar is in communion with God almost on a par with Abraham. When it comes to matters of the spirit, Hagar is a true wife to Abraham, as mother Sarah yet is not. Like Abraham, Hagar gets the promise. Like Abraham, Hagar hears God's voice. Like Abraham, Hagar receives an annunciation. Like Abraham, Hagar calls to God. Like Abraham, Hagar gets a well, a source of living water, a sign of God's grace in the desert. In the sense that a prophet is one who speaks with God, Hagar is a prophet, mother of a great nation, matriarch of a clan that will produce twelve princes, of seed too many to count.

Is it any wonder, then, that Sarah seems less weighty in Hagar's eyes? To Sarah, Hagar is nothing, a slave to be beaten, a vessel, once used, that can be ignored. When Sarah's fury flares, she abuses Hagar physically, but her argument is with Abraham: "I am furious at you! . . . Let God judge between you and me!" Hagar is no longer on Sarah's screen; she's already forgotten, a poor solution to a vexing problem. But Abraham cannot ignore her, and neither does God. From the moment of conception, Hagar knows she is no longer a slave, she has become a person. And, as a person, she has personality, status, relationship not only to Abraham, but to God. Perhaps her slave status has better prepared her for relationship with the Creator of the universe, to Whom all creatures are slaves. Although Hagar is cowed by God's messenger, the rewards she reaps for her offspring are great.

God deserves some consideration here, for the message of the angel is disturbing. Hagar is told, "Return to your mistress. Be abused by her." What kind of counsel is this? Are we to infer that there is some virtue in submitting to abuse? Is a message of this chapter that wives and girlfriends are meant to be kept in their place? That physical abuse, at anyone's hand, is acceptable? How distressing, too, that it is matriarch Sarah who is the abuser. One woman oppressing another. May we learn that oppression takes all forms? That God might countenance such violation?

Whatever the fierce Semitic background of this story, I cannot believe that we would learn such lessons for our modern times. To my mind, there is no circumstance that justifies such physical abuse. Nor could I envisage God countenancing this. I might possibly find some small solace by reading this story as a message of hope. The angel shows Hagar that there is an alternative to suicide. Rather than run from her mistress Sarah and face certain death in the wilderness, she is better off returning home and enduring. Sometimes, when there are no viable alternatives, endurance, survival, even submission to abuse must suffice.

I confess that this explanation leaves a bad taste in my mouth. I do not think it wise to counsel submission to abuse. Too many women and children suffer physical abuse to happily embrace this message as the lesson of the Bible. Even though as readers we understand that Hagar's endurance earns her vast rewards, it is a reward that her progeny reaps, not Hagar herself. I am acutely uncomfortable consigning her to passivity in the face of Sarah's abuse. I am all the more uncomfortable knowing that in Genesis 21, Hagar and her son, Ishmael, are sent at Sarah's insistence into the wilderness to die. It seems that if Sarah learns a lesson from her abusive behavior, it is this: Abuse can be repeated. If tolerated once, it can be wreaked again. I am deeply troubled that the Mother of Faith, matriarch Sarah, can be so encouraged in outrageous behavior, by none less than God's messenger.

Perhaps God already knows that in Genesis 21 Hagar will be amply rewarded. Perhaps, given the corporal punishments meted out in the Bible, Hagar's beating is only disturbing to a late-twentieth-century liberal psyche. Perhaps, given Hagar's role as slave, beatings were all too common, so too much importance shouldn't be given to this one. Perhaps the fault lies with Hagar for fleeing. Perhaps it is Hagar who shows the lack of faith, and God shows generosity by sending a messenger to save the runaway, rather than letting her perish in the desert. Perhaps the rewards that are showered on Hagar in this chapter and later are examples of God's beneficence and charity.

But then, perhaps, too, it is the abuse that makes Hagar's son Ishmael into "a wild ass of a man, his hand against everyone and everyone's hand against him." Abusive patterns tend to repeat themselves.

Given the traumas his mother endured and he himself experienced, one worries for the fate of his offspring. But here is not the place to discuss Ishmael and his offspring, for in order to do so, we must read more of his background, the early family life that shapes him into the man and tribal leader he will become.

It is at this juncture that we do well to recognize that Genesis is a complex book; the family histories are played out on more than one plane. For as much as we may read this as a family narrative, it is also a national narrative. Abraham is the father of more than one nation. Abraham fathers a son with Hagar, but he eventually also fathers a son with Sarah, too. His eventual offspring, Ishmael and Isaac, become the progenitors of two peoples and more—brothers dwelling together, yet often in conflict. Let us now turn back to Sarah so that we may bring all the players onto the stage of this two-level drama of family and nation, for in equal measure with the moral dilemmas addressed in the family saga, the ethical implications of this national narrative echo in our headlines to this very day.

4

Sex in
the Nineties

My daughter was born a few months after my thirtieth birthday. Like any first-time parent, I doted on her. I have the good fortune to be an academic and count myself a feminist, so I spent many, many hours with her, sharing parenting responsibilities equally with her mother. Sometimes it seemed as though the bulk of the hours I did my fathering were between 10:00 p.m. and 6:00 a.m. Like any new parent who was also working (in my case, teaching and finishing my doctoral dissertation), I was stressed, tired, and deliriously pleased with my little girl.

My second child, a son, was born a few months before my thirty-sixth birthday. Again, I was a very active parent, proud of the fact that I spent as much time with my children as their mother did, prouder still that I spent far, far more time with my kids than the average American dad. Yet I was naively surprised that getting up in the middle of the night was not as easy with my son as it had been with my daughter. It's not that he was any harder to raise—far from it, both of my children are just lovely, sweet peaches. I, however, had changed. I was a little less tolerant, a lot more stressed, and far, far more tired. Although many factors could be weighed in why my life had changed, one single fact seemed to account for my startling increase in tiredness: I was five and a half years older when my son was born than I had been at the birth of my daughter.

I find it nothing less than stunning that Abraham, at the birth of his first child, was fifty years older than I was when my second was born.

Imagine getting up to change a diaper at eighty-six years old. Well, don't imagine too hard; Abraham probably left that task to Hagar, much as my own father left diapers to my mom. Nevertheless, the fact remains, "Abraham was eighty-six years old when Hagar bore Ishmael to Abraham." The very next verse jumps thirteen years, past the nights when Ishmael kept his parents awake fretting and teething, plunging the reader into his adolescence. Abraham, now ninety-nine, has another revelation. God renews the covenant with a change of name to Abraham: "No longer shall you be named Avram, but Abraham, for I have given you to be the father of many [*av hamon*] nations" (Gen. 17:5).

So far, good news, although Ishmael, if he could listen carefully, would hear in God's promise the possibility of an end to his status as an only child. It gets worse, for God now insists, "Circumcise your foreskin, as a sign of the covenant between Me and you" (Gen. 17:11). God demands that every male in the household be circumcised. It sounds as though this clause should certainly fit Ishmael, yet, curiously, the requirement is for circumcision on the eighth day after birth. This, too, might make Ishmael worried and confused. I cannot imagine a thirteen-year-old male, just beginning to grow into his sexuality, just sprouting pubic hair, I cannot imagine any such boy/man would happily hear the news of this particular impending surgery. What a *rite de passage* to endure! Yet here, too, the command is complicated by the eight-day rule. Yes, Ishmael will be circumcised, along with all other male members of the household, including father Abraham, yet the command seems designed for one who is yet to arrive on the scene.

Indeed, there is a hiatus in the biblical text between the command to circumcise and the carrying out of it, which is reported at the end of Genesis 17. Let us jump ahead, now, to the circumcision itself and then backtrack to the interruption, rather than leave poor Ishmael hanging even a moment longer. "Abraham was ninety-nine years old when he circumcised his foreskin. His son, Ishmael, was thirteen years old when he circumcised his foreskin. On the same day, Abraham and Ishmael were circumcised" (Gen. 17:24–26). Poor Ishmael. Whatever bonding might have occurred between father and son sharing this cruel ritual together must have been dissipated by the intervening verses. There, to his credit, Abraham's love for Ishmael is manifest. It is clear that for Abraham, Ishmael is son enough—all the offspring he may desire. And if not that, at least an offspring he is ready to protect.

Given the complexity of the Freudian moment, when a teenage son has his penis cut by his laconic, elderly, patriarchal father, Ishmael can surely use whatever reassurances Abraham has to offer. But the event is undermined even further by the promise God gives Abraham. Following the repetition of pledges to give Abraham land and a multitude of offspring, God also changes Sarah's name. "No longer will her name be Sarai, but Sarah. I will bless her and give you a son through her" (Gen. 17:15–16). Abraham responds to this astonishing news with a mixture of incredulity and compassion for his firstborn, Ishmael.

> Abraham fell on his face in laughter. He said to himself, "Shall I have a child at one hundred? Or shall ninety-year-old Sarah give birth?" Abraham said to the Lord, "Would that Ishmael might live before you."
>
> But the Lord said, "Nevertheless, your wife, Sarah, will bear you a son. You will name him Isaac [meaning laughter], for with him shall I establish My covenant as an eternal covenant for his offspring. As for Ishmael, I have heard you. Now I have blessed him. I will make him be fruitful and multiply many fold. Twelve princes shall he bear; I will make him a great nation. But My covenant I will establish with Isaac, whom Sarah will bear to you at this season a year hence." ...
>
> On that same day Abraham did as God had told him and took Ishmael, his son, and all in his household ... and circumcised their foreskins (Gen. 17:17–23).

On the very day that Ishmael enters the covenant through circumcision he is replaced by the promise of a son through Sarah. Many are the stories of couples who wish to adopt, going through incredible contortions to obtain a child, only to find that when the adopted child is finally settled in his new home—lo, the barren wife is pregnant! The story before us is more incredible, still. Abraham, father of a teenager by his second, trophy wife, now has a child by his first wife of many years. It's almost a comic reversal of the coupling patterns in certain socioeconomic circles in the nineties. Usually, the successful husband—you know the one: handmade shirts, thousand-dollar suits, tuxedo studs of gold and balls of brass—now divorced from his no-longer-useful first wife, remarries a second, blond, young, horsey woman, only to learn with dismay a short while afterward that somehow the birth control has failed and he once again will have a baby in the house. I actually know of a case where a successful political journalist is seeking a wife "of childbearing age" so he can prove his virility in a measure other than column inches.

Of course, the usual antidote to this syndrome is for the aging first wife to hold on to her man by bearing another child herself, late in life. Never mind the strain on her career, the genetic roulette, the possibility that one more child may effectively end the marriage and guarantee that he leaves, these little "accidents," or to more optimistic and/or pious families' "gifts from God," happen all the time. Babies in the house do wreak havoc on a husband's ability to carry on with a mistress. And they shift the balance of relationship between the parents and the older children in the household, too.

In order to understand what transpired between Abraham and Sarah, it helps to imagine what happened in their household during the thirteen-year hiatus between the birth of Ishmael and the promise of Isaac. Hagar, Sarah's maid and Abraham's mistress, had been abused by Sarah, fled, returned to the household, and borne Ishmael to them. It is difficult to chart smoothly the relationship structure in the household during these years. First, let us remember that Abraham's favorite nephew, Lot, son of Abraham's dead brother Haran, had been living with them and was there during the momentous sojourn in Egypt with Pharaoh. Whatever his special relationship was with Abraham (see Genesis 14), he was off on his own now, living in Sodom, with his own wife and children. While Sarah no longer felt threatened by his presence, she also no longer had a young man around the house. Until Hagar bore her foster child, Ishmael.

Ishmael was not exactly what Sarah had hoped for. During Hagar's pregnancy the surrogacy arrangement had soured to the breaking point, but for God's intervention. Are we to imagine, after the episodes discussed in our last chapter, that Hagar returned to Abraham's tent, content to give her baby up to Sarah? Or should we assume that Hagar, now with wife status, takes her place alongside or ahead of Sarah as the mother of Abraham's firstborn son? Or does Hagar presume wife status while Sarah assumes that it is she who is now Ishmael's adoptive mother? As long as Sarah remains Hagar's owner/mistress, this ambiguity exists, particularly if Abraham does not forcefully resolve it.

Of course, Abraham would be a fool to resolve it. Why alienate Sarah, who is a powerful and active mother to his son, and a woman from within his clan, unlike the slave, Hagar? On the other hand, Abraham will not wish to alienate Hagar, either, as she may yet avail him of sexual favors that he cannot or will not receive from Sarah. There is, of course, no precise parallel to Abraham's situation in our modern world. We frown on bigamy (perhaps this very story offering the reasons why). Divorce and remarriage is not quite the same as the Hagar/Sarah dilemma (at least not yet, but by Genesis 21 it will seem much closer). Nor is a husband with a wife and mistress quite the same. Nor, I suppose, an unmarried father with children by more than one woman (though we're getting warmer). I think that to appreciate the moral dilemmas of this situation we do not need to have precise congruence with our own lives. Rather, what is called for here is an active sympathy to each of the four parties affected—Abraham, Sarah, Hagar, and Ishmael.

Since we will soon push Ishmael out of the way, let's take a moment to consider his situation. He is Abraham's only begotten son, if you will. Born to the Egyptian slave Hagar, he is (or is not) mothered through adoption by the aged Sarah. Does Sarah cling to him, baby him, woo him for her own? Is she good to him? Or does she shun him as the cleaning girl's child, the mistake, Abraham's bastard son? The relationship between Sarah and Ishmael is prickly, hard to fathom.

For that matter, it is equally difficult to imagine how Ishmael gets along with his birth mother, Hagar. Is she honored or despised? Does Ishmael know of the abortive surrogacy arrangement? Does he imagine that his real mother tried to sell him? Has Sarah poisoned him against Hagar? Can he discern Hagar's lesser status in the household? Is he ashamed of Hagar? Does he yearn to be Sarah's son after all? Or is Ishmael protective of Hagar? Is it clear to him that he is Abraham's only son and through him, therefore, his mother is exalted? Has Hagar told him how she endured beatings at Sarah's hands so he could be born to Abraham? Has Hagar tutored him in his promise, in the words of the angel, in his potential?

Ishmael is a "wild ass of a man, his hand against everyone." How does Abraham treat his son? Is he the plaything of Abraham's old age? Does Abraham dote upon him, think Ishmael is a lovely, sweet peach? When he looks at Ishmael, does Abraham grin with recollection of his nights with Hagar, his great performance, his resurrection into a life of sexual pleasure? Or does Abraham remember the sorrow Ishmael caused in his household, the unfixable breach he caused between Abraham and Sarah? Is Ishmael simply too much for an old man to handle? Does part of his wildness come from Abraham's disinterest? Or Abraham's inability to discipline a child eighty-six years his junior? Or does Abraham love Ishmael so dearly that he simply cannot say no to his precious child?

Maybe Ishmael is simply a good son. Not too special, not too bad. No attention deficit disorder, no acting out. Just a good boy. Maybe Ishmael has learned to be very quiet, keep his worries to himself. Maybe Ishmael knows the price of being noticed in that household. Does Hagar hit him? Does Sarah slap him, as she did his mother? Does Abraham lift a hand to the boy? Or is this too much to impose on a preadolescent (though surely Ishmael would neither be the first nor the last to suffer any of these indignities)? Perhaps we might try to hear Ishmael speak for himself, although I suspect that as he turns thirteen and gets circumcised, as he grows to puberty and finds himself replaced by baby Isaac, his voice will surely change.

Let us turn now from Ishmael and his mother, Hagar. For now, let us focus on the covenantal family and the long-awaited announcement that they will have a future after all.

Abraham was sitting at the flap of his tent in the heat of the day when God appeared to him at the Oaks of Mamre. He looked up and saw three men approaching him. When he saw them, he hurried from the flap of his tent to greet them.

Bowing low, he said, "My lords, if it may please you, do not pass by your servant. Take a bit of water to wash your feet; relax beneath the tree. I'll bring you a loaf of bread, that you may eat to your heart's content before you move on. It is for this that you have passed by here."

They said, "We accept your invitation."

Abraham rushed to Sarah in the tent and said, "Hurry! Take three measures of white flour and knead three loaves of bread."

Then Abraham ran to the cattle and chose a nice, tender calf, which he gave to his servant, who hurried to prepare it.

He served them butter and curds and the veal he had prepared and waited on them beneath the tree where they ate.

They asked him, "Where is your wife, Sarah?"

He replied, "Here, in the tent."

He said, "When I return to you, she will be quickening. Your wife, Sarah, will have a son."

Now, Sarah was listening at the tent's flap, which was closed. Abraham and Sarah were old, getting on in years; Sarah had ceased menstruating. So Sarah laughed to herself, saying, "After I've been worn out, shall I gush with pleasure? Besides, my husband's too old!"

God said to Abraham, "Why did Sarah laugh asking, 'Will I indeed give birth when I have aged so?' Is anything too wondrous for God?! In time I will return to you, when she is quickening, and Sarah will have a son!"

Sarah denied it, saying, "I didn't laugh," for she was fearful. He said, "No. But you did laugh."

Notice Sarah, caught listening behind the tent flap. And where in this precious annunciation scene, I wonder, are Ishmael and Hagar? Their very absence from the action foreshadows things to come. This is good and well, for the story is complex enough without it. No longer a story about Hagar and the sexual competition she offers to Sarah, it is a story of an aging husband and wife and the problems they face in their marriage relationship. Sarah has endured menopause; she describes herself as "worn out," though it must be noted that some translations read "withered." An old lady who laughs aloud at the thought of finding herself moist with pleasure.

How poignant Sarah's words, and what a world of disappointments they betray. We have already reviewed the sorry sexual history Sarah and Abraham may have shared. Sarah's own despondence over her barrenness. The debacle with Pharaoh in Egypt. The desperation of her offer of Hagar to her husband. Her rage when Hagar flaunts her pregnancy. And, as alluded to in the last chapter, her sexual dysfunction with Abraham and the possibility of impotence, which her scoffing "My husband's too old" may well betray.

Let's begin with menopause and the terrors it holds. I write, of course, as a man, and a particularly sheltered one at that. In my home, growing up, things such as hot flashes simply were not spoken of before my virgin ears. I divorced too soon to have any exposure to a wife experiencing "the change." I'm not a physician or a therapist, not even a congregational rabbi with a sympathetic ear to aging female congregants. So, in order to sympathize with Sarah, I have to stretch, to imagine, to put myself in her shoes in a way that half the reading population (i.e., the men, and perhaps some women) does not.

To stretch our imaginations in this way is good. Moral development comes when one is able to imagine one's self sympathetically sharing another's predicament. In John Rawls's theory of justice, it is basic fairness to imagine a situation where you could be the other person. Once you can imagine sitting in the other person's seat, you might try and find your way to solving a problem so that the solution would seem fair no matter what seat you *were* sitting in. Of course, the risk involved in this exercise is the limits imposed by my imagination. I open myself to the possibility of being clobbered—by other men, by feminists, by gynecologists, by menopausal women, *ad infinitum*. Imagine though I might, I am not a woman; how much the more so, I am not a childless woman, postmenopause, contemplating a possibly impotent sex partner and a sterile (in the broadest sense) marriage.

Yet try I must. How might it feel to be Sarah in these circumstances? I am reminded here, again, of the important work my friend and teacher Peter Pitzele does. His biblical psychodrama, living midrash, requires participants to ask precisely these kinds of questions. This role playing helps them understand the feelings of various characters in the story. I use these pages to ask similar questions, with the further conviction that such an act of sympathy leads to moral development. But I digress, I confess, because this particular act of sympathy seems so distant from my own life. I, now single, having fathered two children already, debate vasectomy versus condoms as an effective form of birth control. I have fulfilled my obligation to be fruitful and multiply. As is clear from the opening of this chapter, the thought of waking to the cry of an infant in the middle of the night is best recollected for me, rather than relived in my mid- to late forties. My sympathies are with Abraham, not Sarah.

What might it feel like to be betrayed by your own body? In a society that values women as child bearers, above all, what might barrenness feel like? How deeply is that ache exacerbated when, after years of quiet hope and vocal despair, the menses stop, the blood flow ceases, and in a flash the future holds only death?

Here, I am assisted by a conversation I had at the hospital bedside of a friend who endured an emergency hysterectomy. This woman is thoughtful, articulate, already in her fifties, and the mother of three. She, who is one of the most intelligent and cerebral women I know, confessed to terror. It was not the terror of surgery; that had already successfully passed. It was a terror of mortality, a cessation of possibility, a confrontation with the surety that there would be no new life issuing from her body ever again. I learned from this brave and intelligent woman the power women carry in their bodies, the gift of life. Only once it was cut out could she not take her body for granted. Only then could she even recognize (at least before me) that she had, in fact, a body. I imagine that this might be what menopause does for many women. It's bad enough the hormones run wild. Menopause requires courage.

Could I, then, were I Sarah, summon the courage to laugh in the face of an absurd annunciation: "When I return to you she will be quickening"? Would I slip into a deep depression instead of laughing? Or would my fury flare, my anger boil over, as it had at Hagar, if a goddamned messenger provoked me so? Could I bear the thought of trying yet again with that despicable old man, who first berated me and then betrayed me? Would I remember once being in love with him? Of having pleasure way back when? What it felt like to grow moist at his touch? I despair of my ability to do this. My own imagination is too poor to enter Sarah's head, let alone her aging body.

Yet I do know, only too well, what it is to have an aging body. I do remember, with the terror shared by every man who has ever experienced it even once, what havoc the body's betrayal during sex wreaks on the psyche. If not the terrors of Sarah, I can resolutely understand why Abraham, too, laughs at hearing the annunciation. I suppose, were I to consider vasectomy seriously, I might face the terror of no-child-ever-again. A longtime friend, who never had a child of her own, confessed to me recently that she was missing her periods. I, alarmed, asked if she was pregnant. Her answer, almost scornful of my idiocy, was that it was not pregnancy she was fearful of, rather the lack of it forever. She, however, obstinately refused to connect this with her own mortality. I still don't know whether this was a wise denial of the "no-birth-equals-death" formula, or a fearful evasion of a terror she cannot yet confront for herself. No matter, I cannot do justice to Sarah, even with the help of women friends who love me enough to share their terrors. So I look again to Abraham.

He has just left the decade of his nineties. Sarah has just entered her nineties. Are these two truly meant to have sex again, and at the command of God, no less? I have alluded more than once to the real possibility that Abraham was impotent with Sarah. Now, it is established fact that even if this were the case, Abraham is able to have sex with Hagar. So I look not to a medical condition plaguing poor old Abraham, but to a marital problem. Abraham and Sarah just do not have sex any longer. They may have once, long ago, but too much time has passed, too many hurts, too much misadventure. No need to recount, yet again, the litany of lacerations their entanglements with Egyptians have caused over the decades. They are bled dry. So Abraham, too, laughs when he hears he is to father a child after all with Sarah. A different quantum weight of laughter, but enough to name his son. Isaac's is not necessarily a laughter filled with joy.

And as for Abraham, on the very day God tells him he must have sex with Sarah again, he cuts off part of his penis.

Another interpretation: Abraham is a dutiful and loving husband, sharing Sarah's frustrations at never having produced offspring to fulfill God's covenantal promise. Sarah is so beautiful, it is easy for Abraham, even now, to imagine the precious child they might have had. And so, despite his love for Ishmael, when God tells him he will yet father Sarah's child, he laughs with the sheer deliciousness of life. With alacrity he fulfills the command to circumcise, to enter the covenant, to enter into the blessings God has given him—especially this most blessed one of all, another chance with Sarah.

And Sarah, too, is mirthful, delighted, thrilled. Long after all hope has died, hope and Sarah experience resurrection. She, old woman, shall gush with pleasure, her belly grow with child, her breasts with milk. He, old husband, will grow and fill her, lovers again as they were once, who can remember when. Is it any wonder that they laugh? Truly Isaac is a blessed child, fulfillment of the covenant, bearer of the promise. Is there any sound more enchanting, more graceful, than the laughter of old lovers thanking God for their pleasure?

Well, who knows? But what a great mystery and discovery. The love and joy of God are truly abundant. Yes, they may be fearful, incredulous, but they must also laugh. Abraham and Sarah are to be father and mother, their abundant faith rewarded and restored. They are mother and father to Isaac; in laughter they are mother and father to us all.

5

Bargaining
for Justice

With Abraham's and Sarah's laughter still echoing uncertainly in our ears, it might be a good time to take a closer look at the three visitors who have set them laughing. They are described as three men, travelers with dirty feet, tired and hungry from their journey. They readily accept Abraham's offer of refreshment. Every descriptive marker indicates them to be but men. Yet they are angels, God's messengers, and Abraham is the purpose of their journey. The announcement they have is for him and his wife. They know without asking what Sarah's name is, they predict the future. The Bible tells us, first at the outset, again in the middle of the narration, and once more at the end: It is God who appears to speak with Abraham.

The personality of God is important to this chapter, if not for purposes of theology, at least for character. This is not because theology is uninteresting to me—far from it; I find God fascinating, in fact, compelling. But I am concerned with ethics here—and ethics takes place in communities of humans, in our relationships one to another. God is metaethical. This means that when God, as God rather than as character, intervenes in human affairs, there is Kierkegaard's teleological suspension of the ethical. For God is not bound, nor does God bind according to the ethical rules of human relationships or society. This problem of theology may be at work in our story, and it certainly will come under discussion in Chapter 8. But I prefer to treat God, here, as another character in the story. I follow the lead of the Bible itself, which while recognizing that God speaks, nevertheless presents God with a human face. It is with this face that Abraham dares to argue. It is from this still extremely powerful character that Abraham and we may learn about bargaining for justice.

So the men left there and headed for Sodom. Abraham went with them to send them on their way.

God said, "Shall I hide what I am about to do from Abraham? For Abraham is to be a great and mighty nation, through whom the peoples of the land will be blessed. I have known him in order to command his children and his house after him, that they may observe the way of God, doing righteousness and justice, so that God might bring to Abraham that which he was told about."

So God said, "Loud is the cry of Sodom and Gomorrah; their sin is very weighty. I am going down to see whether what was reported to me has ended, and if not, I will know."

So the men left there and headed toward Sodom, and Abraham still stood before God. Abraham drew near and asked, "Will you sweep away the righteous with the wicked? What if there are fifty righteous in the city? Will you sweep it away and not show favor to the place because of the fifty there? Far be it from you to do anything like that, to kill the righteous with the wicked. Far be it from you that righteous and wicked be equated. Shall the Justice of all the earth not do justice?"

God said, "If I find fifty righteous in the city of Sodom, I will show favor to the entire place on their behalf."

Abraham replied, he said, "I presume to speak with the Lord, I who am but dust and ashes. But perhaps the fifty righteous will be lacking five. Will you destroy the entire city for those five?"

God said, "If I find forty-five there, I will not destroy it."

He continued to speak to God and said, "What if forty are found there?"

God replied, "I won't do it then for the sake of the forty."

He said, "Please do not be angry, Lord, so I may speak yet more: Perhaps thirty will be found there."

God said, "I will not do it if thirty are found there."

He said, "I presume to speak with the Lord, but perhaps twenty will be found there."

God said, "I will not destroy for the sake of the twenty."

He said, "May my Lord not be angered if I speak once more, but perhaps ten will be found there."

God said, "I will not destroy for the sake of the ten."

When God finished speaking to Abraham, God left, while Abraham returned to his place.

We do have to talk some about theology, for in order to understand this dialogue, a lot depends on what God knew, and when. If God is the omniscient (all knowing), omnipresent (ever present), and omnipotent (all powerful) God that modern theologians generally presume God to be, then we might have a problem. If God is not omniscient, omnipotent, and omnipresent, then we have a different problem. Allow me to explain. If God is omniscient, then God knows perfectly well that Sodom is corrupt enough to destroy. If God is omnipresent, God also knows that in the future there will no more be ten righteous than there might be when God is bargaining with Abraham. If God is truly omnipotent, God can destroy them in any case, since ethics need not constrain an all-powerful God.

It's too fine a point to argue whether ethical constraints really impugn the omnipotence of God, whether by being limited by ethics God ceases to be all powerful. So I won't pursue the argument here. Let me dismiss the other side of the problem, too. If God is not omniscient, omnipotent, and omnipresent, well, God isn't really all that "godly" after all, although I certainly am ready to admit that this limited picture of God may, in fact, be the theology of this portion of Genesis. In other words, the Bible at this point in our narrative may not have a very sophisticated theology at all, but in order to consider God's role in this part of Genesis, I think we will have to return to this knotty problem if we are to do justice even to the character called God.

Before we consider theology, there is a question not only apposite to God's character in this story, but a question with some distinct applications to modern life. For this discussion we benefit by considering God to be all knowing (omniscient), all powerful (omnipotent), and ever present (omnipresent), if only for heuristic purposes. If God is the three O's, then God knows, in advance, that Sodom gets destroyed in the end, no matter what agreement is reached with Abraham. Well, not exactly no matter what, so long as Abraham stops arguing at ten righteous citizens of Sodom. With all of Abraham's power of argumentation, I wonder why Abraham didn't bargain God down to one righteous person and save the city.

Maybe Abraham got shy because his naked self-interest at saving his favorite nephew would be all too clear. When self-interest, rather than true justice, is the driving force in the bargaining, perhaps it is doomed to fail. Although it must be noted with irony that even as Sodom melts down, Abraham's seed gets saved through his clout. So God destroys the city and still saves Lot. But what lesson might Abraham take from this outcome, then? Avoid self-interest? Own up to it at the outset? Disclose that there is a conflict of interest? Might any of this have helped Abraham, or is this just a "justice" principle useful when a free and voracious press is likely to make inquiries that might affect your public image—like whether you paid Social Security taxes for Hagar?

But it is not merely Abraham's self-knowledge that his nephew's life was at stake in the bargaining that sullies the ethics of this wonderful passage. This whole God business is very problematic. God may not be bargaining in good faith here, for if God knows that in the end Sodom goes down the tubes, then why bother negotiating with Abraham? The whole 50, 45, 40, 30, 20, 10 is a charade. God slams them anyway.

The seeds of my grumble are embedded deep in the story line. Watch how Abraham approaches God. It is clear who holds all the cards. God is "Justice of all the earth," even as Abraham questions him. He knows he has temerity; repeatedly he begs, "Please do not be angry, so I may speak." It sounds an awful lot like an abused wife or child speaking to a drunken husband or father. Abraham abases himself even further. "I presume to speak. . ." he twice offers. Why should demanding justice be a presumption? Should that not be what God expects? Demands? Abraham does have a clear logic on his side.

"Far be it from you that righteous and wicked be equated." This is an argument to save God face. Here, too, Abraham offers a "Far be it from you" argument more than once. It sounds as if he is placating a particularly disagreeable godfather. Whatever the sins of Sodom, God is thinking of something much more sinister than a horse's head in bed.

Finally, there's Abraham's "I am but dust and ashes." This beautiful line of Scripture has given rise to many sermons, stories, even jokes over the years. In one rabbinic tale humans are accurately measured as creatures with their ups and downs. So, the good rabbinic sage suggests, every person should carry two slips of paper in his or her pocket and take them out and read them as the occasion calls for. On one it should be written, "I am but dust and ashes." On the other it should remind you, "For my sake the universe was created!"

Another interpretation: In a large, modern suburban synagogue on the eve of Yom Kippur, the holiest day of the year, the rabbi wraps his cashmere prayer shawl around his Armani suit. With the practiced timing of years in the pulpit, as the last congregant slips into her seat, the rabbi throws open the ark and falls prostrate before it. Flat on his face, he proclaims before the Lord, "Master of the Universe! Today it is Yom Kippur and we must beg your forgiveness. I am overwhelmed by the task! I am an unworthy vessel. I am but dust and ashes!"

The cantor, shrouded in a white silk robe covering his Calvin Klein summer-weight suit, takes his cue and falls before the ark. Flat on his face, he proclaims before the Lord, "Master of the Universe! Today it is Yom Kippur and we must beg your forgiveness. I am overwhelmed by the task! I am an unworthy vessel. I am but dust and ashes!"

Finally, the beadle of the synagogue, an old European Jew in baggy mismatched jacket and trousers, takes his turn before the ark. He, too, falls prostrate and sobs, "Master of the Universe! Today it is Yom Kippur and we must beg your forgiveness. I am overwhelmed by the task! I am an unworthy vessel. I am but dust and ashes!"

At this the cantor hisses to the rabbi, "Will you just look at that! What gall! Just who does he think he is to call himself but dust and ashes?"

Unfortunately for Abraham, when he says it he is dead serious.

Lives are at stake, perhaps even his own fate. His terror and self-effacement are very real. Abraham faces the recognition that God will destroy a city in which his nephew, Lot, abides. Abraham does not doubt for a second that God will sweep away the city, any more, I suppose, than he doubts that God has "known him in order to command his children and his house after him, that they may observe the way of God, doing righteousness and justice, so that God might bring to Abraham that which he was told about (Gen. 18:19)." If this God can abundantly reward, so God can abundantly punish. This is a God of power, power Abraham has witnessed unleashed on his own behalf in the house of Pharaoh. What Abraham cannot countenance is that God might use that power to sweep away righteous and wicked in equal measure. Is there no justice?

Oops, thinks Abraham. Why didn't I see that coming when I let God act out the role of my enforcer in Egypt? If God can protect the less than ethical, God can equally well destroy the righteous. We're back to Kierkegaard's suspension of the ethical "will he, nil he." Just who does Abraham think he is to call himself but dust and ashes?

Another interpretation: What kind of bargaining takes place when one side holds all the cards and all the other side can do is bluff and bluster? Worse, what lessons are learned when the very powerful position completely overwhelms the inferior one, when the powerful knowingly agrees to conditions that will never come to pass? I am deeply concerned about this last question because it may matter very dearly to Abraham. The lessons he learns from this exercise in bargaining with the Almighty may cloud his judgment in the future. I am thinking about his stunning silence in the face of God's command to slay his son, Isaac (Genesis 22). One could as readily look to his feeble protest and immediate acquiescence in Genesis 21 as well. It is ironic that Abraham may learn lessons about bargaining that affect his role as a parent.

For Abraham is a parent when this dialogue with God takes place. In fact, it occurs immediately after God has notified Abraham that he is about to be a father yet again. Can God serve as a model parent to Abraham in this story? Does God demonstrate to him how an all-knowing parent might teach an eager child to bargain for what is just? Is God proud when Abraham demands of his parent-in-heaven, "Shall the Justice of all the earth not do justice?" Has young Abraham learned his lesson well when God takes leave of him? If you think so, try to imagine what Abraham must think of his bargaining session with God when "Abraham rose early and went to that place where he had stood up to God's face. He looked off toward Sodom and Gomorrah, toward the entire plateau and behold, he saw a cloud rising from the earth, like dense smoke from an oven" (Gen. 19:27–28).

Let's not even think of the terrible meaning of that cloud mushrooming over the cities of the plain (although readers would do well to contemplate Celia Gilbert's stunning poem "Lot's Wife"). Let us only focus here on bargaining from a position of power. Parents and children often play out the same charade that God and Abraham just went through. It is, of course, difficult to know who is more frustrated in this kind of a "bargaining" session. Children often feel impotent, put upon, mistreated. It's not fair, they whine. Parents, for their part, feel logic failing them. In the end they resort to creative arguments like, Because I'm the dad, that's why! But sometimes bargaining is far more complex. The message given in the end may not be the outcome of the bargain.

This is, I suspect, what happens in the case of God and Abraham and often happens in the parent-child (or boss-employee, teacher-student, just about any uneven negotiation) dynamic. The superior conducts negotiations with, as it were, insider knowledge. The outcome is already a foregone conclusion. Yet while the superior gives the appearance of actually bargaining, in fact, there is no bargain. What does take place is an empty ritual that leads nowhere. The subordinate to the process thinks that there is justice, real negotiation, fairness. In the end, he or she learns that he or she has been manipulated, that the outcome was known from the start. The subordinate feels like a fool, gulled, duped. This is not a feeling conducive to good-faith bargaining in the future. If anything, this kind of bargaining teaches that it is silly to negotiate at all—only power or deception counts in the end.

As for the superior position, it is at best disingenuous. The one with insider knowledge is not only bargaining unfairly, but demeaning the lesser party in the transaction. Ivan Boesky, who knows quite a bit about bargaining with insider knowledge, once confessed to me that this was, in his words, "a sin." Since I was startled to hear him use this precise language, I asked him what he meant. He said, "The sin is using the other person as the means to the next transaction." He is right about that: it denies them their personhood. Instead, it treats the inferior position as a necessary, if annoying, step to the next transaction. God asks, "Shall I hide what I am about to do from Abraham?" But then, God reveals it to Abraham in a way that seems like it is an opportunity for real give-and-take. Instead, it is the means to the next transaction—the destruction of Sodom.

I fear what Abraham may have learned is that when one is powerless, one must either submit or deceive. These are Abraham's tactics. He is a master of submission to God and a master of deception with his fellow humans. It is a lesson he teaches his children. The story of Sodom and Gomorrah may be the source of the knowledge that either submission or deception is preferable to real negotiation. If so, it is a very costly bargaining session God holds. It is not only Sodom that is overturned. "Shall the Justice of all the earth not do justice?"

Another interpretation: Let us return briefly to the problem of theology. At the outset of the story God tells Abraham, "Loud is the cry of Sodom and Gomorrah; their sin is very weighty. I am going down to see if whether what was reported to me has ended, and if not, I will know." Now, Sodom and Gomorrah have already been described in Genesis (13:13) as full of people who are evil and sinners, so there should be no mistake about their wickedness. Nevertheless, God explicitly tells Abraham, "I am going down to see." This could be a valuable lesson in justice. God is teaching Abraham, Do not rely on secondhand knowledge or upon gossip. Go for yourself and investigate. When the stakes are this high, justice is only served if you know firsthand, for sure, to the best of your ability. Indeed, God seems to second this interpretation when God explains, "if whether . . . if not, I will know."

There is, yet, another way to read these last words. They are not rhetoric. They are not there for the didactic purpose of teaching Abraham about justice. God means it when God says, "I will know." In other words, God does not know and has to find out. It is for that reason that God goes down to Sodom to see "if whether . . . if not." God does not know, for God is not depicted here as omniscient or omnipresent. God neither knows nor is God there to know. God must go and find out. I stress this ignorance for it is important theologically. The God of this story in Genesis is limited, not the God of theologians who would insist that God be omniscient, omnipresent, omnipotent.

The limitations of God in this reading are telling. They offer us a vision of God as a character with real limitations. God gets frustrated with humans, especially sinners. God may have the power to destroy Sodom and Gomorrah, but there are powers God is lacking in this telling. If God truly does not know whether Sodom and Gomorrah's sin is sufficient for destruction, then God does not know the outcome of negotiating with Abraham. Being neither omniscient nor omnipresent means that God here bargains in good faith with Abraham. Since God may, indeed, find ten righteous in Sodom, Abraham and God are negotiating from positions of greater parity. This does not mean that God is not superior—far from it; Abraham is appropriately deferential to the awesome power that God can unleash. But at least God bargains in good faith. There is no insider information.

Ironically, a lower theology, in which God is more limited in knowledge, makes God a better partner for negotiations. The fairness comes from the equal blindness on each side. God, in fact, may be making a very reasonable bargain, even a generous one. Why wouldn't God expect to find ten righteous in Sodom? God's very faith in humanity is exhibited here, though it is, alas, disappointed when Abraham's ten righteous do not materialize. In this instance, God is more than just, God has, as it were, bent over backward to be fair. Abraham has learned many valuable lessons: It is worth arguing for justice, even if cities are not always saved. It is worth bargaining for justice, if for no other reason than to build faith in God's justice. It is worth negotiating with God, for in the end at least some lives are saved.

We also learn the paradox of our relationship with God. The more transcendent we presume God to be, the more wholly other God appears, the more difficult it is for there to be any form of justice in which humanity can participate. In a covenantal relationship there must be sufficient parity, even if uneven, so that partners can bargain in good faith. God must be open to the possibility of learning new things about Sodom, of having Abraham change God's mind about what might be fair to humans. So, too, parents, bosses, and others must learn that if they engage in dialogue with children, employees, and so forth, it must be genuine. A bit of ignorance, a willingness to learn the outcome as part of the process of negotiating, rather than as a hidden stipulation at the outset—these attributes allow for justice to develop in the course of negotiation. True negotiation is a process of discovery. What is discovered, what is the best bargain one may hope for, is an outcome in which every party benefits.

Another interpretation: In the study groups I lead, we always begin each session with the same introductory ritual. We go around the table, and each participant introduces him- or herself. I do it because there are often people who come and go, so not everyone always knows every other person's name. As a group leader, I also find that it gives the participants permission to speak. Having already said something at the table (their name), they feel freer to continue speaking when something comes to mind. It is always fascinating to hear how people's brief self-definitions change or stay the same from month to month.

Once, at one of my Madison Avenue CEO sessions, four people in a row were attorneys. The first introduced himself as a lawyer and mentioned a prominent firm where he was a partner. The second member identified herself as an attorney, a graduate of the Harvard law school, now on long-term maternity leave (her son was five years old at the time). The next group member identified himself also as an attorney, but explained that he had never practiced law, having opted for entrepreneurship instead. We all waited to hear what the next person would say. He was a famous law professor, a founding dean of a small but prestigious New York law school. He now serves as president of a foundation. We all laughed as he opened in the best AA tradition, "Hi, my name is Charlie and I'm a recovering attorney."

When some months later I read this biblical passage with my CEO group, we were treated to a rare display of lawyering as yet two other attorneys in the group, one a corporate type, the other a criminal lawyer, went at each other hammer and tongs. Since we were neither in a courtroom nor was I wont to play the judge, the two of them debated uninterrupted. Everyone leaned back and listened, fascinated. What intrigued me about their dispute was how abstract it was. Both of the lawyers were masters of the seemingly petty details and procedures that make or break cases, yet what this passage of Scripture elicited from them was an impassioned argument about whether bargaining ever achieves justice. If justice is an absolute, if it is black and white, if it is clear, then how, one asked, how can one ever bargain for justice? Bargaining by definition presumes compromise. Yet justice by definition admits of no compromise.

Not so, advanced the other. Compromise is exactly what justice is about, which is why bargaining is the best of tools for achieving it. Since I recognized that these two attitudes were, indeed, keys to understanding the passage, I finally interrupted and pointed it out. Abraham may have been a good attorney, then, I suggested. In the end, his client Lot, his nephew, avoids the death sentence God has passed on the inhabitants of Sodom and Gomorrah. His argument seems lost; he has not saved the city, for there are fewer than ten righteous there and God rains fire and brimstone down upon it. However, I continued, let us assume that he wanted to save his client, no more. If so, his tactics were perfect. Lot walks.

The attorneys ignored me. They went on to argue whether any lawyering achieves justice, indeed whether justice has anything to do with lawyering. If the job is defense of the client, then the client's welfare must be put above the dictates of pure justice. If being an attorney or judge meant proper application of the law, then regardless of whether a law is just or unjust, lawyering seeks to apply the law. There can be no search for justice if one is to be a faithful attorney. The rebuttal was simple: Why bother being an attorney if you do not believe you can achieve justice? Is that not, in the end, why we go to law school and slog through our careers? Is it not to achieve justice, law and the client be damned?

If Abraham is the lawyer who seeks only to acquit his client, he has
succeeded. Lot survived the sentence of execution. If Abraham is the
lawyer who seeks justice no matter what, perhaps he has also succeeded. In the end, the innocent (Lot and family) are saved while the
wicked are destroyed. Both ways, Abraham and God win, the client
wins, justice wins. And our particular study group won that night, for
we had seen two prominent attorneys, both decades out of law
school, engaged in a passionate argument about the very nature of
their calling. Why were they lawyers after all? What moral and ethical
reasons stood behind their daily round of detail and procedure? What
made them tick, pushed them to succeed? To my mind, it was a pris-
tine moment of the power of Bible study, for both a passage of Genesis and two careers were brilliantly illuminated.

6

SURVIVORS

EIGHTEEN HUNDRED YEARS AGO an anonymous rabbi suggested, "One who says, 'What's mine is mine and yours is yours'—this is the ethic of the average person. But there are those who say this is the ethic of Sodom." On the face of it, it seems as though the first rabbi may already be engaging in wishful thinking. Would that it were the case, we think at the end of our twentieth century, that people would be satisfied with their own and let the other guy worry about his or hers. The need for greed, cultivated so carefully in the eighties of this century, has taught an entirely different ethic: "What's mine is mine and what's yours is mine." For many of us, blue and white collar alike, this is the formula for success. Get ahead at all costs. But the same anonymous rabbi described this second principle as "the ethic of the wicked." If greed is wicked, then isn't a *laissez-faire* attitude at least average, if not desirable? After all, what's mine is mine and what's yours is yours. Seems reasonable, if not necessarily noble. So how, then, does that other voice, "There are those who say," how could they possibly liken this attitude to "the ethic of Sodom"?

To put it another way, what are the sins of Sodom?

That evening, the two messengers came to Sodom. Lot was sitting at the gates of Sodom and when he saw them he rose to greet them. They bowed to the earth in greeting.

He said to them, "If you please, my lords, won't you turn toward your servant's home, that you might wash your feet and lodge there tonight. Then may you rise and head on your journey."

But they replied, "No, we shall lodge tonight in the square."

But he constrained them until they turned his way and came to his house. He served them drinks, baked flat bread, and they ate. Before they bedded down for the night, the men of the city, the men of Sodom, from young to old, every single one of them, surrounded the house. They called out to Lot, "Where are the men who came to you tonight? Bring them out to us so we may be intimate with them!"

Lot went out on the porch, shutting the door behind him. He said, "My brothers, please, do not do harm. Please, I have two daughters who have not been intimate with men; I'll bring them out to you. Do with them as you see fit. Just don't do anything to these men, for they have come under the protection of my roof-beams."

They said, "Move over! This one came here as a stranger, and now he judges us? We will do you more harm than them."

They constrained that man, Lot, very much and they moved to break down the door.

The men inside reached out and pulled Lot back into the house with them, then shut the door. As for those men on the porch, the men inside blinded them in a flash, from small to big, so they couldn't find the door.

The two men asked Lot, "Who else is here with you? Sons-in-law, sons and daughters, everyone you have in the city—take from this place. We are going to destroy this place, for the out-cry against them before God is enormous and God has sent us to destroy it."

Lot went to speak with his sons-in-law, those who took his daughters. He told them, "Arise and flee this place, for God is going to destroy the city!" But his sons-in-law assumed he was kidding.

When day broke the angels pressed Lot: "Arise, take your wife and your two daughters who are here, lest you be swept away in the sin of this city."

He tarried, so the men took him and his wife and his two daughters by the hand and took him and set him outside of the city, for God's compassion was upon him. When they had removed them from the city, one said, "Run for your life! Do not look back, don't stop anywhere on the plain. Run to the mountains, lest you be swept away." . . .

God rained brimstone and fire down from heaven upon Sodom and Gomorrah. God overturned those cities and all the plain, and all the inhabitants of the cities, even the vegetation of the earth. His wife looked back and she became a pillar of salt . . .

Lot and his two daughters with him went up to the mountains from the town of Zoar, for they feared staying in Zoar, and they dwelt in a cave, him and his two daughters.

The older said to the younger, "Our father is old and there is no man in the land to come into us in the way of all the world. Let us get our father drunk with wine and sleep with him, that we may quicken with our father's seed."

So they got their father drunk with wine that night and the elder came and lay with her father. He didn't know of her lying down or her getting up. The next day the older told the younger, "Last night I slept with my father. Let us get our father drunk with wine tonight, too. You will come and lay with him so you may quicken with our father's seed."

So they got their father drunk with wine that night, too, and the younger got up and lay with him. He didn't know of her lying down or her getting up. The two daughters of Lot became pregnant from their father. The elder bore a son, whom she called Moav; he is the ancestor of the Moabites of this day. The younger also bore a son and called him Ben Ammi; he is the father of the Ammonites of this day.

What is the sin of Sodom? In a commentary on the story of Sodom, a rabbi contemporary with the one who opened this chapter suggested that the sin of Sodom was a particular form of hubris. "We don't need anyone," the Sodomites bragged, according to that commentary. "We are self-sufficient. We have food, natural resources, everything we could possibly want. Our trees are thick with leaves and fruit, our soil rich in minerals and gems. All we need is a few drops of rain. Let's cut ourselves off from everyone else. Let's forget the laws of hospitality ever existed."

Now, it is clear that this comment expands on "those who say" quoted above. This extreme isolationism is the sin of Sodom. They said, "What's mine is mine and what's yours is yours." They forgot that all humanity is interdependent, that the laws of hospitality are immutable, that protection under someone's roof is a sacred trust of ancient society. They forgot that all humans are in the image of God, are God's creatures, are beholden to the Creator for more than a few drops of rain. When they presumed on God's hospitality, the ancient rabbis propose, God repaid Sodom measure for measure. They thought all that God gave them was a bit of rain, so God rained brimstone and fire down upon them from heaven. They thought their soil and trees provided them with all their needs, so God overturned the entire plain, even the vegetation. They sought to close themselves off from all humanity, so God shut them off for all eternity.

Notice that the rabbis of old do not lean to the obvious and condemn the inhabitants of Sodom for their apparent sexual proclivities. To be sure, we'll never know if those nasty Sodomites of old were interested in homosexuality or just the brutality of raping strangers. Clearly, subsequent generations, even subsequent rabbis, have focused their homophobia on this passage. If the Sodomites were sodomites, goes the thinking, then they deserved to be destroyed. I cannot pretend that the Bible looks kindly on homosexuality, but it is clear from early rabbinic comments that there is much more complexity to the moral fabric of this story than Leviticus 18:22 and its abomination of gay sex.

If the laws of hospitality are wantonly disregarded, and this is the sin that brings destruction to Sodom, then those laws should be given some serious regard. What is it that makes the ancient commentators hold such high regard for "the protection of roof-beams"? The Bible again and again reminds the tribes of Israel, "You were once strangers in the land of Egypt," and uses this reminder as a cudgel to enforce the moral obligation of caring for the stranger, feeding the poor, housing the homeless, clothing the naked. Xenophobia is something the Bible legislates against, and the story of the destruction of Sodom is a grim reminder of how poorly God looks on those who would abuse strangers. The destruction of Sodom and Gomorrah is the most terrible act of destruction God wreaks following Noah's flood. It seems God wants to make a clear point about the inviolability of sanctuary and the sacredness of hospitality.

To be fair, the biblical book of Leviticus is replete with exclusivist themes that might make one feel a bit self-righteous about closed borders. The Israelite people have carefully wrought laws to keep them separate from other tribes. At the end of our story we are informed that Lot, Abraham's nephew, is the father of Ammon and Moab. In Deuteronomy, the law prohibits Ammonites and Moabites from entering the congregation of the Lord.

Of course, by the time the Bible gets to the Book of Ruth, it is a Moabite, Ruth herself, who mothers the grandfather of King David, ancestor to the Messiah. A complex moral is being taught here. Yes, there are exclusivist tendencies—don't we all have them, in our own nations, in our own communities, in our own families? In the end, hospitality must overturn our dislike of the other, our fear of the stranger. Unless we know we live in one global village, all the cities of the plain may yet be overturned.

Another interpretation: How ironic that Lot is saved after all of Abraham's bargaining with God. This Lot who accompanied Abraham and Sarah to Egypt during their sojourn with Pharaoh (before they became *persona non grata* for their devious scheme) seems, at least, to have learned Uncle Abraham's good points. Like Abraham, who insists that the dirty-footed travelers come sit in his shade, Lot, too, takes them into the protection (the Hebrew word literally means "shade") of his roof-beams. But like Uncle Abraham also, Lot has learned an unfortunate lesson about what to do when feeling threatened: Offer your women to those who menace you. In Abraham's case it was his wife, whom he passes off as his sister. Lot offers his daughters, whom, perhaps, he passes off as virgins.

This last point is a bit of a conundrum in the story. If these women are married, then how is it they are virgins? The commentaries, both Jewish and Christian, have a field day untangling this knot. Whether there are four daughters (two virgin, two married), two daughters who were married and are now virgins (a favorite reading of the church), or married daughters who are simply offered as virgins, the motif is the same: Let the mob do what they want with the girls, just protect the men at all costs. This is a remarkable calculation. Are women of so little worth that they may be offered in favor of complete strangers? Is the code of protecting sojourners stronger than the code of protecting the family women? Are children so easily disposable that it is nothing to offer them up to the mob (or, as Abraham did, to God)? Or did Lot know that the Sodomites really were sodomites, in which case his offer was a safe one? The crowd would rape the men if they could, but they wouldn't touch the girls.

What is it about Lot that makes him so pathetic in this story? Is he meant to be but a foil to the righteousness of Abraham? If so, he is drawn as a crude mirror, a *Doppelgänger* to his uncle. Like Abraham, he is a master of hospitality. But like his uncle also, he offers his women for sex-bait and abuses his children. This is a distressing family trait, one that bears some notice and discussion. It is a truism that abuse is repeated in families from generation to generation. It is also true that Lot spent his childhood with Abraham. What, then, are we to make of this tale? I shall return to this particular question.

For now it is sufficient to note that the end product of the sexual misadventure (if I may use a less value-laden term than abuse, for the moment) is a pair of children who are, as it were, bastard tribes from an Israelite perspective. Is this story, then, nothing more than a crude etiology, a bad joke the punch line of which is that our neighboring tribes are a bunch of *mamzers,* that is to say, they are bastards and we'll never let our kids marry the likes of them? Is the whole story just that? A dirty joke about the neighbors? If so, why the many moral lessons about hospitality to strangers? Why the polemic (at least in the commentaries) against the heinous crime of xenophobia?

I might guess that the story of Lot carries with it more than a grain of criticism about his uncle. When the Bible merely wishes to narrate the sins of Abraham, it does so without shame—that is the received tradition. But when censure of the great ancestor is called for, that is another matter. Far better to criticize obliquely, by telling the sorry story of Lot and his daughters. Sexual misadventure and child abuse lead to no good end, Genesis seems to teach us. If you have any question about where it all can lead, just remember Lot. His derelict life in a cave was dictated by more than booze or choosing the wrong neighborhood to live in. It's a story all of us, even Abraham, could stand to learn.

Another interpretation: I mentioned above that the destruction of Sodom and Gomorrah was the worst disaster God had wrought on humanity since Noah's flood. The act of God bringing "rain" from heaven to wipe out evil bears careful notice. In the case of Noah, the "natural disaster" that wreaks destruction is a rain of water that floods the earth. In the case of Lot, it is brimstone and fire that overturn the cities of the plain. Each of these stories seems to serve, in part, as an accounting for natural disasters. Both seem to teach the same lesson: Do not blame God for this tragic event—it was the sins of humanity that brought God to send forces of nature against them. God is justified in punishing the wicked.

On closer inspection we will find that there is far more similarity in the two tales than this theodicy alone. In both stories there is, as it were, a holocaust of massive proportion. Like the holocaust of our own century, the stories of Noah and of Lot involve massive evil and massive death. In each biblical tale there is a survivor and his family. In each, the survivor is faced with scenes of horror and destruction and plagued with memories of the communities and friends consumed. He turns to alcohol for solace. By then, both wives have disappeared from the narrative. In both tellings, the father ends in a drunken stupor. Finally, there is some sexual misadventure with his children. In the case of Noah, his son Ham "sees the nakedness of his father" and is cursed by him. In Lot's case, he has drunken sex with both his daughters and impregnates them.

The rabbis of old subtly compare these two survivor stories. Two sages of the early third century, Rav and Shmuel, debated what happened between Noah and Ham. The biblical account is laconic and perhaps euphemistic. Noah's imprecations seem too serious for the ostensible crime of Ham's merely seeing his father sprawled drunk and naked. So, I believe, the rabbis take a leaf from the story of Lot and presume some more serious sexual transgression to have taken place. One of them suggests that Ham actually raped his father. The second, not to be outdone, suggests that Ham castrated Noah. If nothing else, the latter opinion explains why Noah had no more children despite God's command to be fruitful and multiply following the flood.

These two rabbis are hinting at a literary motif that well mimics reality: Let us call it the survivor syndrome. Holocaust literature of our own century mirrors these stories. In works such as Jerzy Kosinski's *The Painted Bird,* tales of postholocaust drunkenness and sexual deviance seem the norm. In fact, in almost any century there is literature that reflects the horrors first reported in these biblical tales. I am tempted to credit all subsequent literature with being intertextual, with writing midrash on Genesis as they retell the horror in their own language for their own generation. Alas, here art but mirrors reality. Each generation has its heart of darkness, each its survivors who rely on unsound methods to find consolation. Like the literary character in Conrad's novel, those who survive the reality of a holocaust can only lament, "The horror, the horror."

Another interpretation: And what of a father who can offer his daughters to the mob? What is the family dynamic that could permit such an act to be contemplated? How does this event imprint itself upon the girls? Here the dysfunction seems severe, far beyond the constraints of an already difficult cycle of biblical stories. The legend of Lot is a crude, even a fun-house mirror of the Abraham cycle. How much the more so of our own lives. What passes between Lot and his daughters is for the most part unreported, but rest assured, there is a history of pathology in this family. Long before Lot offered his daughters to the crowd, something must have been very wrong. Only that could account for the outrageous offer.

Shall we play armchair psychologists for Lot at this distance? We can mention the death of his father at an early age, his adoption by his uncle, their travels and travails. Lot endured famine with his uncle, he witnessed the events in Egypt. Genesis 14 reports a war between minor clan kings in which Lot is taken captive. He is rescued from this trauma by his uncle Abraham, noble warrior.

Yet even before the war, Lot had already made some difficult and perhaps bad choices. Genesis 13 reports that upon their return from Egypt, when Abraham and Lot were enjoying the payoff of Pharaoh, conflict broke out between their shepherds. As a result of their sojourn in Egypt, they had acquired sufficient flocks that the two family members needed far more pasturage than before. Abraham graciously offered his nephew his choice of the promised land:

> "If you go left, I will go right, and if you go right, I will go left." So Lot looked up and saw the entire Jordan plain, it was very fertile (this was before God destroyed Sodom and Gomorrah); it was like the Garden of God, like the land of Egypt, heading toward Zoar. So Lot chose the entire Jordan plain and the two relatives parted, Lot traveling from the east. Abraham dwelt in the land of Canaan and Lot dwelt in the cities of the plain, encamping near Sodom. And the people of Sodom were very evil and sinners to God" (Gen. 13:9–13).

Of course, knowing what we know, we grimace at Lot's choice. Although the neighborhood is fertile, it will not always be so. The narrator of the biblical tale makes sure, with asides, winks, and nods, that we readers know of the disaster brewing. Perhaps this disaster is a punishment for Lot's lack of gratitude to his uncle. Perhaps Lot takes too much for granted. Perhaps Lot has led too secure a life despite his father's death at an early age. Perhaps Abraham has spoiled him rotten, for lack of a son of his own. As I've already suggested, perhaps Lot has learned a bit too much from Abraham, and lacking God's grace to protect him, quickly falls prey to the ethic of Sodom.

Somewhere along the way, Lot moves into the city proper, a stranger, yet with a known protector who rescues him and Sodom in the clan wars reported in Genesis 14. This gives Lot an unusual status in the city. He does have a certain grace, after all, Abraham's grace. Indeed, it is that grace that saves his life when the rest of the city is destroyed, and yet it sets him apart from his neighbors, who perceive him as an outsider ready to judge them rather than assimilate. This, despite the fact that he has married, perhaps one of their own women. Imagine Lot, with Sodomites for in-laws. Imagine the tragic history Lot's wife carries within her. Lot's daughters are presumed married to men who cannot bring themselves to leave the city, so if Lot does not actually have a Sodomite mother- and father-in-law, at least he seems to have Sodomite sons-in-law. Maybe this explains how his girls can be married and yet virgins, "who have not been intimate with men." The severe dysfunction in the family is treated, as it sadly often is even in modern reality, as a smarmy joke.

So what happens to Lot and his daughters? What has passed between them before the angels ever appear on the scene? Did the girls have to endure hearing their father rail against all the benefits Uncle Abraham has bestowed, from riches to rescue? How emasculated does Lot feel by his overpowering surrogate father, and how does he act out on those feelings? What is the girls' course before their so-called husbands take them? What can it be like to be a young woman growing up in that household? And what recourse may their mother have to stop whatever may transpire between father and daughters?

All of this psychologizing is offered with reticence. We cannot know what Lot was feeling toward Abraham or toward his own daughters. We do not know the family history beyond what is recorded in the Bible. Yet in the aftermath of the destruction, Lot's reactions beg for explanation. Why is he so passive? What precludes him from living in the small town of Zoar, which he first flees to as a halfway house on his journey to that cave in the mountains? What happened to Lot and his daughters as they arrived as refugees there? How did the folk of Zoar greet them? Did they recognize them as blessed kin of Abraham? Or did they shun them as Sodomites who should have perished in the cloud hanging over the plain? This, too, we will never know. It is sufficient that they cannot dwell in Zoar and that Lot's daughters find no men to care for beyond their father.

What guilt do all of them carry as survivors? It is well documented in this century that those who survive carry strong feelings of shame that they live while their colleagues perished. The daughters, according to the account in Genesis, are driven to despair. "Our father is old and there is no man in the land to come into us in the way of all the world." That this despair takes the form it does—drunken incest—testifies all too eloquently to their despair. The story could have ended a million different ways. Nothing necessitated the solution they settle on. They could have found partners in Zoar, could they not? They could have died childless. They could have simply turned to each other for physical comfort in the aftermath of their holocaust. Given their upbringing in Sodom, it would have seemed quite reasonable a solution.

Yet, the story tells us, the older conspires out loud and explicitly with the younger. "Let us get our father drunk with wine and sleep with him, that we may quicken with our father's seed." Whose version of the story is this? Who benefits from this telling of the sordid tale? To ask my question another way, allow me to phrase it as a woman in my study group did: "Why would they want to sleep with a drunken, broken old man?" Since no good answer can possibly present itself, let us consider the possibility that the story we read is Lot's version, his side of the sorry events. He, who offered his daughters to the mob, now would have us believe that they got him drunk and got pregnant by him, two nights running. And he, for his part, "didn't know of her lying down or her getting up." Poor, innocent survivor, Lot. You can almost feel sorry for him.

What is the tale Lot's daughters have to tell? Was their father hiding his responsibility for what he did to them in a haze of guilt and alcohol? Did he have to get drunk in order to sleep with them in the first place? Did the abuse begin when they were very small, or only later, as they matured? Were both daughters equally abused? Did they witness each other's degradations? When Lot told the mob "do with them as you see fit," was that the first time he had made such an offer? And who laughed or cried when he reported that the girls had not been intimate with a man? How could the daughters ever expect to recover from that hidden childhood of abuse? Did they develop in similar ways or did each daughter cope as best she could, in a vacuum of pain and confusion? How tempted were they to run out the door into the hands of the mob in order to escape their father?

Perhaps they had counted on their husbands to save them. If so, Lot's daughters must have been crushed when their husbands assumed it was all a joke. Can we be surprised that they abandon civilization altogether in favor of the mountain cave? And were they not sorely tempted, daily, to seek the solace that their mother taught them? Let us not forget Lot's wife, their mother, who saw only one way to cope with the grief and rage she carried for her family. Looking back, seeing all too clearly where they had come from and knowing only too well what the bleak future held in store, she made her choice. Unable to rescue her daughters, unable to conquer her own feelings of guilt and shame, unable to turn her husband away from her daughters or herself, Lot's wife made her choice on the road leaving Sodom. Shall we not read her end as a fitting testimony to her helplessness? When the mushroom cloud of Sodom vaporized all the moisture within its range, all that was left of her years of unshed tears was a pillar of salt.

Another interpretation: Shall we not marvel that her daughters, those intrepid women, were able to survive, to live on, to become the mothers of great nations? The Bible teaches powerful lessons of both hope and despair in the story of Sodom. Lot's older daughter is the mother of Moab. It is her offspring, when reunited with the seed of Abraham, that will bring the messiah.

7

ISHMAEL'S
BABY

IT IS HARD TO KNOW which way to stretch my imagination. Do I try to remember what it was like when I was thirteen, a skinny Bar Mitzvah boy starting high school? Or do I look to my own thirteen-year-old, also beginning high school? When I do look to my daughter, although the experience of adolescence is much more immediate, it cannot be seen by me except through my role as her father. When I imagine myself at thirteen, there's thirty years intervening. And, to be bald about it, I now remember myself with sympathy for my father. Trying to remember thirteen is, well, trying. The exercise of remembering does help me be sympathetic to my daughter and even sympathetic to who I've become over the years. Still, it is a stretch of the imagination. Like all stretching exercises, it's good for me, but sometimes a bit painful at first.

How much harder, then, to imagine a thirteen-year-old of three thousand years ago. He is a boy of very different circumstances. Son of a wealthy shepherd, living in a tent. He hunts rather than studies. His mother is a slave of his father's first wife. A rather complicated family, all in all. My daughter and I each have a sibling five and a half years apart from us. In my case, my sister is the firstborn; in my daughter's case, she is the elder. In the case of Ishmael, son of Abraham and Hagar the Egyptian, thirteen years would pass before there was a younger sibling. Ishmael's baby would be a half brother, sharing the same father but a very different mother.

In this chapter we try to imagine Ishmael; his mother, Hagar; his stepmother, Sarah; and finally, his father, Abraham. In every instance, we imagine only one possibility for each character. As the use of "another interpretation" in previous chapters should indicate, the readings offered here are but one possibility, only one stretch of my own imagination. For each of these four characters we could offer other possible interpretations. It is the whole point of moral education to be able to imagine being in another's position. It is usually helpful to try and imagine many different positions for each "other" we imagine, since only by exploring a subject from many different angles can we get the whole picture. Here, I have limited the exercise with one attempt for each of four characters, just to get us started. None of these readings should be considered authoritative. They are but a foil for your own imagination and debate. Try becoming Sarah, Hagar, Ishmael, or Abraham on your own. Try to be them in more than one mode. Offer as many "another interpretations" as you can, until the possibilities of the text seem exhausted. Do midrash. But first, let us read the biblical text.

God remembered Sarah as God had said. God did for Sarah what God had promised. And Sarah became pregnant and bore Abraham a child in his old age, in the very season God had predicted. Abraham named the son who was born to him, whom Sarah had borne him, Isaac *(yitzhaq)*. So Abraham circumcised his son Isaac on the eighth day, as God had commanded him. Now Abraham was one hundred years old when he bore Isaac, his son.

Sarah said, "God has delighted [*tzhoq*] me. All who hear will be delighted [*yitzahaq*] for me."

She said, "Who could have predicted to Abraham, 'Sarah will nurse children'? I have borne him a child for his old age."

The boy grew and was weaned and Abraham made a big feast on the day of Isaac's weaning. Sarah saw the son of Hagar the Egyptian, whom she had borne to Abraham, laughing *(metzaheq)*. She said to Abraham, "Drive out that slave and her son. That slave's son will not inherit with my son, Isaac!"

The incident was very grievous in Abraham's eyes, on account of his son. God said to Abraham, "Do not be grieved about the boy or your slave woman. Whatever Sarah tells you, listen to what she says, for your family name shall be carried on through Isaac. But I will also make the son of the slave woman into a nation, for he is your offspring."

So Abraham rose early in the morning and took bread and a water skin and gave them to Hagar to put on her shoulder; and the boy. Thus he sent her away. So she wandered in the wilderness of Beer Sheva. The water in the skin was finished, so she cast the boy under a shrub. She went and sat a bow shot across from him, for she said, "Let me not watch the boy die." So she sat across from him and cried resoundingly. God heard the sound of the boy and so a messenger of God called to Hagar from heaven and asked her, "Hagar, are you okay? Don't worry, for God has heard the sound of the boy where he is there. Get up and hold the boy, take him by the hand, for I will make him a great nation."

God opened her eyes and she saw a well spring. She went and filled the water skin and gave the boy a drink. God was with the boy and he grew. He dwelled in the wilderness and was an archer. He dwelled in the wilderness of Paran. His mother took a wife for him from the land of Egypt.

ISHMAEL

What a tumultuous adolescence poor Ishmael lives through. It is all too easy, after all, to imagine him Ping-Ponging back and forth from being Daddy's dutiful helper to slamming the tent flaps as he furiously storms into his room. The only thing that commands his calm and complete attention is his little brother, Isaac. Ishmael is certainly old enough to be a wonderful baby-sitter. He could change Isaac's diapers, entertain him, carry him papooselike on his back as he goes about his young man's chores. With reluctance, and perhaps resentment, he gives the baby over to old Sarah to suckle. It dawns on Ishmael that he, the big brother, might just be old enough—just—to be Isaac's father. Isaac becomes a symbol of Ishmael's budding manhood, his baby.

Ishmael is a torrent of ambivalence about everything but his baby. He resents Sarah, but she is his adoptive mother. She is the power in the house, and Ishmael, though inwardly resentful, learns to charm her. He does this, he tells himself, for the benefits it brings him and his baby brother. But it costs. It costs Ishmael to feel like a traitor to his real mother, Hagar. Now that Isaac is born, Hagar is back to being the slave. It's not pretty watching his mother be relegated to such hard labor by Sarah. All of their old rivalries resurface and are laid to rest on Hagar's back. Now that Isaac is in the house, Hagar has no status.

Ishmael's own status is more secure, but nonetheless under attack. He feels secure in Abraham's love, much as he feels secure in his love for baby Isaac. Yet the onslaught is relentless. His feelings toward the baby grow more complex, for while Isaac is his baby, Isaac is also the usurper who will supplant him. Old lady Sarah will see to that. Sarah shows little tolerance any longer for Ishmael. Whatever relationship they nurtured during those years when she played at foster mother has evaporated. Wary though he is because she holds the power of the household, Ishmael grows to resent Sarah more and more. He resents that she supplanted his mother. She did so certainly with Abraham. She tried, as well, to supplant Hagar even with him, for in playing the foster mother she tried to poison his feelings toward his birth mother. Now, worst of all, she resents his affections toward his baby and wants to supplant him there, too. Does she think at eighty-six that she can properly mother baby Isaac? It is Ishmael, not Sarah, who spends hours playing (*metzaheq*) with him. It is Ishmael who laughs *(metzaheq)* with him and can get him to laugh. It is Ishmael who hugs and fondles *(metzaheq)* baby Isaac *(yitzhaq)*. Yet the feelings Sarah's dour presence engender are no laughing matter. Ishmael worries that Sarah will go back to hitting them—Hagar, himself, and now his baby Isaac, too.

As though it were not difficult enough to be thirteen, and then to have endured circumcision at your own father's hands. Now, there's an item for the therapist! And Abraham had circumcised himself, too. The old man claimed that it would bind them. Well, thinks adolescent Ishmael in his ambivalent mode, it did make me feel closer to him, having gone through it together with him. It wasn't quite as threatening since he did it to himself, too, although, Ishmael might admit, it would have been easier to endure had Abraham's old hands not trembled quite as much. In the end, even baby Isaac got circumcised, too. So his baby and he were twins in that department. Ishmael liked to remind himself that he could have refused circumcision but underwent it willingly for his father's sake. Baby Isaac was too small and young to protest. That made Ishmael's circumcision better, did it not? And, Ishmael always added, he was the firstborn.

So Ishmael was simply not prepared when Abraham rousted him out of bed one morning after Isaac's weaning party. Abraham was remote, silent. He had that look in his eye, like he did when he cut Ishmael with the knife. Although Ishmael was a fair bit older now, it made him feel just as weak as when he had been circumcised. His knees gave out on him. He was so ashamed. He couldn't carry the water skin or the bread for his mother. Ishmael knew this was no picnic. Abraham had listened to Sarah, he was sending them away! Ishmael knew enough to read his mother's fear and consternation, too. He would protect her, if only he felt stronger.

In the end, Ishmael thoroughly embarrassed himself. He blubbered so much that his mother couldn't stand to be near him. She shoved him under a bush and squatted far away. He was so thirsty, but drinking his tears didn't seem to help. Ishmael wanted so much to be an adult then, but he was just Hagar's baby. Ishmael felt faint and frightened. His greatest worry was this: If I die here in the wilderness, who will play with my baby Isaac?

HAGAR

Hagar's status was a problem. When she slept with Abraham, he was quick to remind her that she was his wife, but since the time of God's command for Abraham to bear a child with Sarah, he began sleeping with the old lady more and with Hagar less. Hagar had always had troubles with Sarah. It was bad enough at first when Sarah turned her over to Abraham for sex, without even a by-your-leave. Well, it was the life of a slave, no better and no worse than she had it in Egypt. But when she became pregnant with Abraham's baby, Hagar felt her status change. Here was a way out of slavery! If bearing a child to the old man brought her some dignity and rest, so be it. But Hagar hadn't counted on Sarah's wrath. And then, when she ran off in despair, she was taken in by the sweet promises of that voice in the desert. Go back, be abused. What could Hagar have been thinking?

She gave Abraham and Sarah a son. As it turned out, Sarah didn't have all that much to do with sweet Ishmael, which was just fine by her. Hagar would mother Ishmael and be a real wife to Abraham. Life was good during those years. Of course, Sarah was ferocious, but it was little to endure, all in all, for the privileged status of being mother to Abraham's only begotten son. Sarah worked on Ishmael occasionally, but he was a good boy and knew who his real mother was. Hagar cared for him, whatever Sarah's status. Sarah couldn't buy her son away any more than she could beat him out of her.

But Hagar's fortunes and Ishmael's took a sorry turn for the worse when little laughingstock was born. Isaac, Isaac, Isaac—it got to where she was sick of hearing the name. In fact, it got to be so bad that when anyone even laughed she resented it. And Sarah lorded her pregnancy with a vengeance. Hagar never worked so hard in her life. She surely was reminded what it meant to be Sarah's slave, cleaning up her morning sickness during that miserable first trimester. Sarah was either nauseated or bragging. And then the commotion during labor. Oh my God, Hagar had never seen the midwives work so hard. It was as though Sarah wanted the baby but didn't want him. Sarah understood that having the baby gave her absolute mastery, but that having the baby also meant she had to relinquish her own role as baby of the household, whatever she may have made of baby Ishmael.

Isaac's bris was a day Hagar also wouldn't be likely to forget. There was more fuss over that little boy than there had been on the day that Ishmael, Abraham, and every other male in the household was cut. You'd think that Sarah had invented the penis, she was so arrogant and boastful. And when it came to feeding the baby, Sarah couldn't seem to stop bragging about the fact that her breasts gave milk. She actually offered to wet-nurse all the babies in the neighborhood, that foolish old lady. A cow, that's what she was, a stupid, fat, old cow. Hagar wondered if Sarah realized that teats with milk made her no better than a goat or cow.

As far as Hagar was concerned, had baby Isaac been born dead, that would have been baby enough for her. Hagar had no use for the brat, really. All he meant was trouble for her and even more trouble for Ishmael. Her poor Ishmael, so besotted with the idea of being an older brother, he didn't see that Sarah's Isaac would cause them endless trouble. It pleased Hagar that even though she couldn't stand the baby, Ishmael was good to him. Ishmael had always been such a rough-and-tumble kid, his bow and arrow never far from his hands, but when he was with baby Isaac, why, her Ishmael was just an angel. He burped the baby, diapered him—Hagar never would have thought Ishmael had it in him. Made Hagar think she should have given him a sibling—but that would have meant getting pregnant by Abraham again. Hagar wasn't sure she was willing to endure that whole ordeal just so Ishmael could have a playmate. Hugging Abraham and batting her eyelashes were one thing. Actually getting pregnant again, well, if Abraham wasn't disincentive enough, Sarah certainly was. No, Sarah would have killed her, Hagar realized, if she had gotten pregnant again.

What Hagar hadn't counted on was that Sarah's getting pregnant would cause Sarah to kill her anyway. Either way, another baby for Abraham spelled death for Hagar and Ishmael. Hagar wasn't even surprised that Abraham sent them off. Oh, she knew he found it distasteful. Hagar knew that if Abraham had any say at all, he'd keep her around for a cuddle and a kiss now and then. Hagar also knew that Abraham genuinely loved his older son. However distant and remote the old man might seem, she knew he was proud of Ishmael.

But there was no reckoning with Sarah. If it weren't enough that Sarah beat her, now she'd forced Abraham's hand against her, too. Hagar remembered how she had submitted to Sarah once before. Now she would pay the price for listening to the messenger's voice. That God of Abraham's was out to kill her, that's for sure. First it was "Return, be abused." Now it's "Whatever Sarah tells you, listen to what she says." Both Hagar and Abraham had word that spelled doom for Hagar, no matter what vague promises were made to her when she was pregnant. Will God remember Hagar as God had said? Will God do for Hagar as God had promised? Or did those words only have meaning when they were spoken about Sarah?

So Hagar, full of doubt, actually let Abraham save face before his son as he sent them into the wilderness to die. She let Abraham hand them a paltry skin of water and a loaf of bread. How long did he expect that to last? Hagar knew it was a sop, it would last just long enough to get them out of his sight and out of his conscience. What kind of father can send his son to die of thirst with the claim that the command came from God? What kind of father can have nothing more to say as last words to his eldest child than "Call me, Ishmael"?

Hagar was so sick with grief and disappointment that she would not allow herself to watch the boy die. The only comfort she could offer him was to put his body in the shade so that the birds might not peck at him until he was dead. And how surprised she was to hear that dreaded voice again, gently reminding her that God remembered her, too. She rose and took hold of her Ishmael. She grasped firm his hand. The water was there, for God had saved him. God would make him a great nation. Just to make sure, though, Hagar returned home to Egypt. There she found a wife for Ishmael—one of her own kind. Ishmael may well be seed of Abraham and brother to Isaac, but Hagar would never let him forget that it was his mother who saved him, who brought him down to Egypt so that he could be free from slavery.

SARAH

It's true she lied about laughing when the angels first told her and Abraham that she would have a baby. Worse still, when confronted she denied it. Well, who wouldn't laugh? It's a good thing she didn't throw them out altogether. When they told her she'd bear Abraham a child, it seemed like another cruel joke. How could she have a child? Surely she had spent the best years of her life hoping, praying, waiting for a child. Who knew the sounds of her waiting? The painful, slow drip of water into the cistern at the end of the winter months, heralding the drought. The sounds of shadows on the sand, lengthening as the day waned. The arrhythmia of her heart as her hormones overtook her and the blood stopped flowing. The rhythms of four-week cycles, once regular as the moon, first longer, then missed, then altogether absent.

It was bad enough that God had promised and years had passed and nothing, but nothing, had come forth from her womb. She withered, her body dried up in the desert heat. And she dried up to her husband as well. To be honest, it was never all that good between them. Abraham always seemed to have his mind on greater things. He fantasized about fathering a great nation—better he should have fantasized about Sarah. It was almost as though he didn't even see her.

Sarah remembered the debacle in Egypt all too well. It had been quite an adventure, not that she would have survived Pharaoh's harem very well. But she was beautiful, whether Abraham knew it or not. When the impotent coward suggested that she tell them she was his sister, well, she was. They hadn't been man and wife in any real sense in a very long time. What could happen? Some other man might take her? And what if it was Pharaoh? Would it have been so bad to go from sleeping with a grubby old shepherd to sleeping with the King of all Egypt, a man whose subjects worshiped him as god? Pharaoh would have been good. At least the preparations had been fun— the facials, the aromatherapy, oil treatments for the hair, depilatories, nail polish, kohl, henna. Sarah really was beautiful that day. Too bad Abraham's God had spoiled her fun and made Pharaoh act so righteous. But at least the episode brought them some comfort financially, enough so that Abraham tried the scheme again, in Gerar, the old fool. This time Sarah didn't even get to the makeover before God intervened. Although she must admit that the king there, Avimelekh, was a perfect gentleman. So what came of all this Avimelekh and Pharaoh business for her? A bit of self-esteem, still no child, and, yes, her very own slave, Hagar.

Sarah never could have imagined that the demure girl she brought up with her from Egypt would wind up such trouble. She did her best for the girl. Loved her like a mother, treated her like a sister. And then arranged the surrogacy contract when she found herself with child. We'll say Abraham fathered the child, no one will know. You'll have all the rights of a wife, only I will be over you in my household. How was Sarah to know that Abraham would turn his face to the little thing, let alone come to believe that the baby really was his? There were those in the household who gossiped that Abraham had fathered the child and that Sarah was a saint for putting up with it. Others, more malicious, suggested that Abraham had been sleeping with Hagar since she was barely a teen. Sarah refused to believe that. She knew about Abraham's problem in that area.

After all she did for Hagar. Then the girl played her part too well, insisting that she was really carrying Abraham's baby. Sarah was a fool for not having ascertained who the real father was in the first place. After all the good that Sarah did for her, that little ingrate expected to be waited on just because she was pregnant! And who was her slave last year? Sarah had to remind her who was whose slave. It's what all the women at the well advised. Sarah had been a fool to be so soft on her before. So she disciplined her a bit, it was only natural. Hagar was a slave after all. But the little idiot had to run away. Well, thank goodness, she came back home. Nowhere else for her to go in any case; being pregnant and black and blue didn't give her the option of prostitution.

Sarah had resolved herself to love that baby, raise him as her own, but Hagar's rebelliousness never abated. Try though she might to win the boy, Hagar reneged on the agreement. Sarah hated it when Hagar told everyone of voices in the wilderness. Who did she think she was, Abraham's wife? In fact, that's just who she claimed to be, it peeved Sarah so.

Well, Sarah showed them all a lesson. However shocked she was when those dirty men claimed she would have a child, however much she laughed at them and then lied about it, it did change her. Sarah felt hope as she hadn't in decades. And when Abraham mounted her, she almost laughed again. My God, who would have thought he could still perform? And all in all, it was rather nice. Good to be fondled, kissed, hugged, noticed. Abraham made her feel like a woman again. Even though the minute he came Sarah knew she was pregnant, she insisted he try again and again, night after night. It almost made up for the three months of constant nausea that followed.

My God, Abraham's God! It was a miracle. Sarah had been sure her menopause was fully over. No more hot flashes, no more bleeding. And instead, morning sickness. Was there ever anything as glorious as vomiting on the morning of your eighty-sixth birthday? It was almost a bonus when the droll thought occurred to Sarah to ask Hagar to clean it up. Never was a pregnancy more glorious. Every time she looked down at her swelling belly, she laughed and laughed. I'll be damned if those angels weren't the real thing. God remembered Sarah as God had promised all those many years ago. God did exactly what God promised, and Sarah delivered a baby boy.

The delivery was difficult, of course. How could it be otherwise with a woman her age? Thank God Abraham didn't have to see her like that or hear the curses she uttered about having sex with an old goat. It was worth every ounce of pain, every contraction, every moment on the birthing stool. She thought she would split apart, and when she pushed to die, out came Isaac. Was there ever a baby more aptly named? It was not just she but everyone who laughed anytime the baby came in view. What a sweet bundle. What a gift to aging parents.

Thank God, of course, that they could afford help. It was Hagar and Ishmael who got up with the baby in the middle of the night, who diapered and fed him, who kept him clean. Well, Sarah had paid her price years ago in Egypt. Sarah had waited long enough, God knows. It was sweet to watch that boy play with Isaac. Wasn't it?

On further thought, Sarah wasn't so sure that Ishmael should be nannying Isaac so much. God, now that Isaac was here, that wild boy would just have to get over thinking he was Abraham's son. He surely couldn't expect to be a son with Isaac in the house, could he? Even if he were to believe that Abraham was his father, he was old enough to understand that his mother was a slave, wasn't he? Perhaps it would be a better idea to keep him away from Isaac. And that mocking laughter! It drove Sarah to distraction. Did he think the baby enjoyed it? And the way Ishmael hugged and cooed over the baby was a bit unnatural. Unsettling. God only knew what filthy habits he might teach Isaac. Why, Ishmael probably ate limbs off living animals, the little brute. It really would be better if he was kept away from Isaac. All that hugging and kissing. Oh God, what if he turned out to be like those neighbors of Abraham's nephew? No, better not even think of that. And the boy simply had to get rid of the bow and arrow. Playing with Isaac like that. Someone could lose an eye. This kind of play can only end in tears.

Sarah had almost reached her limit. She now thought of Ishmael as that filthy boy. It didn't help her to hear him brag that his circumcision was better than Isaac's. What is he doing now? Sarah raged. Was he touching her baby? No more changing Isaac by Ishmael, even if it meant Sarah had to do it herself. And what was this talk she was hearing from the help about Ishmael being the firstborn? Firstborn slave, perhaps. "That slave's son will not inherit with my son, Isaac!" Sarah better act on this decisively. Abraham was never good at dealing with the slaves. "Drive out that slave and her son!" There simply is no other way. Enough with pretensions of both mother and child. All Sarah gets for her goodness is insolence. Even a beating didn't teach Hagar a lesson. Out with her, away! I don't care what doubts you have, Sarah says, go ask your God. And God deals kindly with her. How could it be otherwise? The same God who made her wait all these years, the same God for whom she had endured all these decades, the same God who brought her laughter, who brought her a son, how could it be otherwise? "Whatever Sarah tells you, listen to what she says, for your family name shall be carried on through Isaac."

Is it any wonder Sarah laughs?

ABRAHAM

"I would prefer not to" seems to be Abraham's mantra. He actually almost never says it out loud, but goes around chanting it to himself, like Melville's Bartleby the scrivener. It started long ago, when Haran died and Abraham was asked by his father to take Lot in as his foster son. Then God told him to go, to leave, to utterly uproot and go to what seemed all too often to be a godforsaken land and to be a stranger there. Yes, God promised Abraham property, offspring, and blessing, but Abraham would have preferred to stay in Ur, with his father and brothers. But move he must.

Abraham would certainly have preferred not to have endured the famine that cursed land of Canaan greeted them with, nor to descend into Egypt. He would have preferred not to have felt threatened into giving up his wife, even if that did turn out okay in the end. He would have preferred not to have to keep trying to have children with Sarah long after he tired of her, precisely because of her obsession to bring God's promise to fruition. And he surely would have preferred not to have to perform for that young slave girl. She actually boasted she would kill him with her youthful vigor. Well, maybe that wasn't so bad after all, showing that sweet young thing what a good teacher experience can be.

Abraham would have preferred not to have to get up in the middle of the night to tend his son Ishmael because the two women in his life were too damn stubborn to do it themselves, each outwaiting the other. He assuredly would have preferred it had God not given the command to circumcise. That day was almost as bloody as the time that he rode off to rescue Lot when he got kidnapped. What a fool-hardy thing to have ever undertaken. It's a wonder he didn't get killed.

Speaking of Lot, Abraham absolutely would have preferred not to have ceded all the good pasturage of the plains to him as an avuncular gesture. He decidedly would have preferred not to have to argue with God, only to see Sodom destroyed anyway, and was determined never to do that again. Just too risky taking God on that way, no matter what the stakes.

Abraham definitely would have preferred not to have another round of baby-making with Sarah, no matter what God and the angels promised. Although he might have admitted that that, too, wasn't as bad as he had thought it would be. He indubitably would have preferred not to go through the circumcision ritual all over again. He just hated even the thought of picking up a knife to his child. It clearly had hurt Ishmael; it had hurt him, too. And baby Isaac was so little and helpless, no, Abraham would have preferred not to circumcise Isaac.

He positively would have preferred not to listen to Sarah on the matter of Hagar and Ishmael. God certainly didn't help him out on that one. "Whatever Sarah tells you, listen to what she says"—no,

Abraham would have preferred not to listen to Sarah. He unequivocally would have preferred not to have to send them away to die.

It seemed to Abraham that everyone and God just expected far too much of him. He was raised to be a shepherd, not to father a nation. Abraham was over one hundred; he only wanted to grow older in peace and watch his two sons grow old, too. Have grandchildren, raise sheep and goats. Most of all, Abraham would have preferred some quiet. Enough was enough already, wasn't it?

8

Isaac Unbound

AND SO IT HAPPENED that after all of these things God tried Abraham. God said to him, "Abraham."

He answered, "Here am I."

God said, "Take, if you would, your son, your only one, whom you love, Isaac, and go to the land of Moriah. Offer him up there as a burnt offering on the mountain I will tell you of."

Abraham rose early in the morning and saddled his own donkey. He took two servant boys with him, along with his son Isaac. He split firewood for the offering. He got up and went to the place God told him of. On the third day Abraham looked up and saw the place from afar. Abraham said to his servant boys, "Remain here with the donkey. I and the boy will go over there, where we will bow in worship, and then we will return to you."

Abraham took the firewood for the offering and put it on his son Isaac. He took the fire and the cleaver in his hand, and the two went off together.

Isaac said to his father, Abraham, he said, "My father."

He answered, "Here am I, my son."

He said, "Here is the wood and the fire, but where is the lamb for the burnt offering?"

Abraham said, "The Lord will show him a lamb for the burnt offering, my son."

And the two went off together.

They came to the place God told him of and Abraham built

an altar there. He built a fire and bound Isaac, his son. He placed him on the altar, atop the wood. Abraham reached his hand out and took the cleaver to slaughter his son. An angel of God called out to him from heaven, saying, "Abraham! Abraham!"

He answered, "Here am I."

He said, "Do not put your hand on the boy, do not do a thing to him. For now I know that you are a God fearer; you did not withhold your only son from me."

Abraham looked up and saw a ram in back, caught by its horns in a bramble. Abraham went over and freed the ram and offered it as a burnt offering instead of his son. Abraham called that place "The Lord Will Show"; as is said today, "On the mountain the Lord will show."

The angel of God called out to him from heaven a second time. He said, "I swear—this is God's message—because you did this thing, that you did not withhold your only son, I will truly bless you and vastly multiply your seed, like the stars in heaven or the sands upon the seashore. Your seed shall inherit the very gates of his enemies. All the nations of the land will be blessed through your seed, because you heeded my voice."

So Abraham returned to his servant boys and they rose and went together to Beer Sheva. So Abraham dwelt in Beer Sheva.

Here we return to ethics: how can Abraham justify what he sets out to do? Abraham must answer to himself, to Isaac, to the two servant boys, to Sarah, to his community, perhaps even to Ishmael and Hagar, and finally, to God. Of course, it is clear that Abraham is not the only one who must provide answers following this trial. Isaac may have deeds or words to answer for. Perhaps even Sarah must justify her silence in this chapter of Scripture. Last, but certainly not least, God must answer for the terrible trial imposed upon Abraham.

Were this sparse story nothing more than the translation above, it would fill a chapter on ethics, and more. But the Binding of Isaac, or as it is called in Hebrew, the *Aqedah,* is part of a greater narrative cycle which we cannot ignore. Consideration must also be given to a phenomenon noted in an earlier chapter of this book: The family saga is but one level of drama. The story of Abraham and Isaac is also very consciously a legend about the birth of the Israelite nation.

As if this were not more than enough—an overflowing platter of interpretive elements—the *Aqedah* has a rich afterlife. Almost from the time it became part of the biblical canon, it has struck a resounding chord as religious literature. These chords, harmonics, and overtones echo through the religious literature and even the secular literature of Western culture. The *Aqedah* stands side by side with the *Odyssey* as a classic of our literary heritage. Judaism, Christianity, and Islam each have multiple readings of the *Aqedah*, some in harmony, others in dissonant cacophony.

All of this, in addition to the hundreds of volumes and commentaries that have been written on this passage, serves as a backdrop to our discussion. Yet we will try to keep our focus on the moral dilemma that the *Aqedah* constitutes. I am less interested in rehearsing what others have thought about the binding of Isaac. What I wish to provide is an opportunity for each reader to form his or her own opinions about the many issues this story raises.

Now late in his life, Abraham again hears a voice that tells him, as it did at the very outset of his journey, "go" *(lekh lekha).* The words of Hebrew no doubt ring the three promises of God in his ears, promises of a land, a blessing, and most of all, offspring. To date, Abraham has received land, even if a famine or battle had made it a harder land to inhabit than he had expected. And Abraham has had blessing. Kings, priests, and rulers have blessed him (even if they cursed him *sotto voce*). "Blessed is Abraham to God on High, Creator of heaven and earth," intones Melchizedek in Genesis 14:19. And through Abraham, Melchizedek and his confederates have been blessed, too.

Most important, perhaps, is the gift of offspring, although to be quite honest, it is hard to tell which of these three gifts of God Abraham may value most. Perhaps it would be offspring, but since the loss of Ishmael, Abraham has not allowed himself to feel either confident or fulfilled in the matter of offspring. When the Lord first told him of Isaac, Abraham had prayed, "Would that Ishmael flourish before you." Now Ishmael has been banished at God and Sarah's insistence.

God only knew if the boy was still alive. Could Abraham dream of thinking that Isaac was safe?

So perhaps the command to take Isaac was simply the other shoe dropping for Abraham, the bookend of a cruel pair of trials God was subjecting him to, for reasons unclear to the patriarch. It was grotesque, even kafkaesque, this snatching away of the son of Sarah after all the miracles that were wrought to have him. Had not Abraham given enough to God as yet? Raising the knife twice for circumcision of the boys and himself did not satisfy this God's desire for their blood. Now Isaac's life was called for, to be slaughtered like one of Noah's animals after the flood. Abraham thought briefly of drowning his sorrows as Noah had. At least Abraham had the solace of knowing that after the sacrifice of Isaac, he, the survivor, would have no offspring to lure him to sexual misadventure.

Did Abraham wonder if the *Capo del Tutti Capi* was finally collecting his due? Abraham, long a "made man," now had been given an offer by the Godfather that he could not refuse. Was this, in the end, the price of God's protection during the Pharaoh and Avimelekh capers? Was this the cost of God's cover during the war of the local bosses when Lot had been kidnapped? Perhaps Abraham understood the rules of the game from the outset. Being chosen had its costs. When the Don asked for a son, who could refuse him?

Abraham had already learned that it was fruitless to argue with God about these matters. It was grace enough that God spoke with him. It was grace, of a perverse sort, that God saw fit to test him in this way, to make such a claim on his loyalty. The last time Abraham presumed to say, "I am but dust and ashes," the end result was an entire city wasted and all the once-fertile cities of the plain reduced to dust and ashes. Could there be a clearer message from God about the value of bargaining?

In the end, Abraham would have more than he began with. Flocks and slaves beyond any expectation he ever had. Prestige, and respect from all the local bosses, even Pharaoh. A son, maybe, off somewhere—either dead in the wilderness or seeking refuge in Egypt with his mother. Lot was probably still alive, though traumatized by the terrors of Sodom and the nasty business with his daughters. Land, loads of valuable real estate, even though a deed of sale was still lacking. So he would do without Isaac. He still had Sarah, after all. Or would he if he killed the boy? She never understood the demands God placed upon him. She'd laugh, or kill him, or die herself.

These are some of the issues Abraham has to consider during the three-day period between the command and Isaac's execution. Odd, though probably accurate in the end, that refusing God was never seriously considered. Saying no just wasn't an option.

Then there is the murder itself to consider. How does a father raise his hand and put a cleaver against his son's throat? Now, I know that every parent has a moment or two, particularly with teenagers, when the thought "I'll kill them" has flitted through his or her mind. But it is a long way—three days' distance—from an angry or frustrated passing thought to the assumption that this murder is a divinely commanded sacrifice. To most modern sensibilities, that three-day journey could as well have been measured in light years. Or was Abraham simply empty by then? The *Aqedah* one trial too many for him?

One can almost see the flat affect of the depressive as he walks, zombielike, up the mountain. It takes the angel more than once to catch his attention. And when it's over and Abraham has won the greatest prize of all, he stumbles down the mountainside, not even noticing that Isaac has been left behind. Abraham dwells in Beer Sheva, far from Isaac, far from Sarah, who is in Hevron, far from Ishmael and Hagar in Egypt. In the end, Abraham is close only to God.

So now God knows. It should be immediately apparent that there is, again, a problem of theology in the story. I am not referring here to a God who might demand child sacrifice or is capricious or cruel— these matters will be discussed later. For now we must focus on what God knew and when. God's angel speaks for God following the *Aqedah* and stays Abraham's hand from harming the boy with the words "For now I know that you are a God fearer; you did not withhold your only son from me." Does this then mean that before the trial of Abraham God did not know what Abraham might do? If this is the case, then God seems a bit less cruel and somewhat more innocent. Without prior knowledge that Abraham would put the cleaver to Isaac's throat, there seems to be a reasonable chance that

Abraham would have refused. This possibility, at least, precludes the psychological discomfiture that Abraham and Isaac (and perhaps even Sarah) must endure to be tested in this way. To this extent it may be argued that an ignorant God is less cruel.

I'm not sure how much we gain by claiming ignorance. Certainly the theology is less satisfactory. As in the discussion on Sodom, we must contend here with a God who does not seem to be omniscient or omnipresent. Giving up these two attributes for a marginal improvement in ethical behavior doesn't seem like much of a trade, if theology is a measure worth consideration.

In any case, it remains an unsavory test. Could God not have devised a trial of Abraham less extreme than blood sacrifice of his long-awaited son? One could very well argue that it is precisely the extremity of the sacrifice called for that makes it a trial worth enduring. I demur. It is true that God is described in Exodus as a jealous God, but that jealousy traditionally extends to other gods, not to human relationships. That God might be jealous of Abraham's affection for his son is not something one wishes to happily contemplate. One would wish for a God who celebrates familial love rather than finds it a threat to hegemony. Of course, this God is also described as creator-master to the creature-slave humanity made in God's image. It does not help to consider God tyrannical.

Modern theologians have suggested that God's jealous test of Abraham is in response to something far more iniquitous than parental love. The claim hinges on the way in which Abraham and Sarah relate to their long-awaited child. Their behavior toward Isaac is obsessive. Professor Phyllis Trible argues the case that Sarah's protectiveness, her own jealousy, her zealous dismissal of Hagar and Ishmael borders on the idolatrous. This argument carries some weight—it goes a long way to explaining the drastic trial God imposes. Much as God did for Pharaoh in Egypt, the efficacy of the idol must be destroyed. That God spares Isaac in the end is then a symbol of God's mercy. Of course, this reading presumes that God does not confuse the fierceness of parental love with idolatry.

On the other hand, perhaps it is we who get confused. I recall the Texas cheerleader murders of tabloid headlines but a few years ago.

Parental obsession certainly can run to the psychotic. Is Sarah any better in ordering Hagar and Ishmael to their deaths? Of course, God is complicit in this act. But even assuming it is Sarah's obsessiveness that God wishes to cure, why test Abraham rather than the idolatress herself? Why is Sarah not put to the test? I suppose in an oblique way she is. Her obsession is marginalized by the nature of the *Aqedah*. Isaac, the very object of her idolatry, is taken from her completely. It is Abraham and God who hold the power of life and death over Isaac, not Sarah. Of course, in the end, it is God who holds that power. In this way does Sarah learn the lesson of appropriate mothering.

I'm still not satisfied. If Sarah was the problem, God helped cause the problem. No need for God to make Sarah wait so long in the first place. No need for God to condone her viciousness toward Ishmael and Hagar. No need for God to make Abraham the subject of the test if Sarah is its target.

It might help if we read God allegorically as the power that makes a father sacrifice children and family to outside demands. How many children have felt the force of an all but invisible boss who ruled a family ruthlessly? How many children have felt sacrificed before that absolute authority? How many wives have felt helpless, as invisible as Sarah, to the whims of an employer who requires loyalty to the company at all costs? And how rare the boss in those circumstances who prefers a ram in the child's stead?

This allegory pays no attention to the real trauma Isaac endured under the knife. One could shift the allegory to governments asking that children be sacrificed on the altar of foreign policy—this reading was popular in certain circles during my college years when the war in Vietnam yet raged. Or one could allegorize Isaac being sacrificed as a sign of loyalty to God in the face of religious persecutions. Readings such as this made the *Aqedah* a very popular motif in medieval Jewish martyrologies written in response to Jewish suffering during the Inquisition and Crusades. Here God still makes ultimate demands of life and limb, but parents seem more willing to offer their children. When the *Aqedah* serves as a paradigm for history, it takes on its greatest power as religious literature and theology. All that needs to be determined is whether the child being sacrificed by Father Abraham is meant to be understood as Judaism, Christianity, or Islam.

We shall forgo answering that question. Debate over which religion is more worthy is foreign to the open inquiry this book requires. It is of little import to me in these pages whether Judaism, Christianity, or Islam is the true child of Abraham. If anything, I would insist that all are, and that all who develop morally by studying these stories may inherit the mantle (assuming one is still comfortable wearing that particular garment any longer).

It would serve us better to contemplate Isaac, walking bewildered with his father, sensing that something is not quite right but not yet aware of how very wrong things are. It is difficult to read Isaac, to have any firm ideas of the ethical issues of his case, unless we have some clue to his age. That his age changes the ethics of the situation is clear. It is one thing for Abraham to raise a knife to a five- to eight-year-old child, yet another still to slaughter a young man of sixteen. How much different, still, to sacrifice a man of thirty-six or -seven. For each age group, it seems, a separate moral code may apply. We look, then, to see if we can learn more of the boy who was bound.

From the apparent innocence of his question, Isaac seems to be quite young. "Here is the wood and the fire, but where is the lamb for the burnt offering?" he asks. It is a naive query that makes him out to be very young. And yet "Abraham took the firewood for the offering and put it on his son," which seems to mean that he is old enough to carry some significant weight. Either we have a teenager who is a bit slow on the uptake or a very strong six-year-old. Frankly, I'd be inclined to imagine an Isaac who was neither clever nor sophisticated, especially given the subsequent events of his life. However, we could read this passage with a bit different emphasis to make him a clever enough teen who puts two and two together and sees that it adds up to himself as sacrifice. With more than a bit of consternation and even a trifle terrified, he asks, "Where is the lamb?"

Abraham's answer is not helpful in quelling this terror. "The Lord will show him a lamb for the burnt offering, my son." If I were Isaac, I'd want to know much more clearly what this "Lord will show him a lamb" business meant. Further, I'd check father Abraham's punctuation very clearly. The rabbis of old imagined the sentence to read something like "A lamb for the burnt offering = my son." But some of those rabbis of old tipped the balance of interpretation and suggested that Isaac was much, much older. Their reasoning had to do with Genesis 23, the immediate next chapter of Scripture. In it we are informed that Sarah died at age 127. If her death followed as immediately upon the *Aqedah* as did the narration of the death, then the mathematics is clear. Sarah was 90 at Isaac's birth, 127 at his near death. Ergo Isaac was 37 at the *Aqedah*.

A thirty-seven-year-old Isaac can in no sense be considered a passive participant in the event. This is one of the side benefits, if not the chief benefit, of the rabbinic math. Isaac at thirty-seven is a mature male, old enough to fight his own battles, or at least join at his father's side as an equal partner. The volition this imputes to Isaac makes it as much his trial as it is Abraham's. Indeed, his courage is as unflinching as Abraham's would need to be for him to raise the knife in the first place.

Here, if I may, I'd like to present another rabbinic story of old to illustrate the moment. For the purpose of illustrating Isaac's courage and equal measure of terror (for what value is courage if not to combat terror?), it almost is irrelevant what his age is. Isaac turns to father Abraham in this rabbinic fantasy and says, "Father, bind me really well, tie my hands and legs up firmly, for I am trembling out of fear of the knife and I do not wish that my nervousness should cause your sacrifice to be spoiled." As if there were not enough pathos in the story to begin with. But the point is very clear, it is a stark moment for Isaac. This particular midrash depicts him as not only courageous and caring of the sacrifice he is undergoing, but actually makes explicit another biblical value: Isaac fulfills the commandment of "Honor your father" when he asks Abraham to bind him.

Other possible readings of Isaac's reaction to the knife in his father's hand are offered by still different rabbis. In a classic displacement of emotion, one ninth-century source has the angels in heaven wailing and weeping, on the verge of hysteria, imploring God not to permit this sacrifice. "You who have pity on dumb animals, have you no pity on a father who binds and a son who is bound?! It is written in Scripture, 'Human and beast the Lord saveth.' Will you not, then, save Isaac?" This midrash is dear to me not only because it captures Isaac's frantic terror at the moment the cleaver is brought to his throat, but also because of the sharp critique of God's trial of Abraham. As far as this ancient rabbi is concerned, the angels themselves censure their Creator for not playing by the rules set out in the Bible.

One more midrash amply illustrates Isaac's dismay with his father's knife. Also in the ninth century, a clever rabbi suggests that when Isaac felt the knife touch his throat, at that very moment he died of fright. What a delicious irony this midrash entertains. The very son who feared invalidating his father's sacrifice and shaming him now dies on the altar, not as a sacrifice, but as a carcass, wholly unacceptable as an offering for God. The irony of this midrash continues when the medieval storyteller suggests with a wink, "When the voice from heaven said, 'Do not touch the boy,' Isaac's soul returned to his body. He unbound his ropes and stood up on his feet, exclaiming, 'Praise to you, our God, Who resurrects the dead!' "

All of these rabbinic sources and more also notice a final anomaly of the text. Abraham comes down Mount Moriah alone. Isaac is very much not with him. Although the two "went up together," they come down separate, apart from each other. Indeed, the Bible never again records Abraham and Isaac together. They do not speak to each other anymore. It must be noted here that Abraham and Ishmael also have not spoken since his banishment. Obviously, Abraham no longer speaks with Hagar, either. Ishmael and Isaac do come together in one more scene in Genesis, when together they bury their father.

Can we wonder for a moment what passed between the two brothers over that grave? Were they at the funeral to be sure that the old man was in the ground once and for all? Did either of these brothers have regrets, things they wished to say to their father and now could not? Were they full of rage? Full of love? It is certainly possible they felt both love and rage toward their father. Think how his zealousness had harmed each of these young men, what his brutal love for God taught them. And what of Abraham's love for each of them? Did they know, in the end, that he loved them? Did they mourn his passing and miss him? Or did each shovel the dirt with a barely concealed glee, inwardly satisfied to be burying their abuser? It's not a happy family that we contemplate here. For Isaac, scarred though he may be, it is a moment of liberation. He regains his beloved older brother on the same day that he loses his father. Isaac is finally unbound.

We cannot conclude this chapter without word of Sarah. Following the *Aqedah,* Abraham does not speak again with Sarah before her own burial. He returns to Beer Sheva, but she is in Hebron. What do we make of her silence in this episode? What is her relationship with God? How does she feel about Isaac's near sacrifice? What happened between her and Abraham? One might have expected that following the banishment of Ishmael and Hagar, Sarah reigns triumphant. Instead, the next we hear of her, she has died.

My student and teacher Jane Kanarek once suggested that Sarah committed an unforgivable wrong against Hagar. The betrayal of Hagar was not just one woman turning on another, it was a failure of both love and morality. In Sarah's competition for Abraham's affection, in her ruthless campaign for Isaac over Ishmael, she forgot her own relationship with Hagar. They had shared so much over the years, enough for Sarah to have wished Hagar to bear a child on her behalf. How quickly that decision destroyed their relationship, led Sarah to unrelenting abuse of her Egyptian sister. At Isaac's birth, when Sarah might have sympathized with Hagar, shared with her the pains of pregnancy, labor, and childrearing, shared with Hagar the joys of motherhood, laughed with her while watching Ishmael play with baby Isaac—at that moment the rupture was complete. Sarah banished Hagar and Ishmael.

Did Sarah suspect Abraham of keeping in contact with them? Did she worry that his affair with Hagar had not, in fact, ended, despite his promises? Did she worry that Abraham might plot to get even for his loss somehow? Or that God might punish her for her unyielding savagery, whatever support God had offered at the moment? Was Sarah, in fact, ready for the *Aqedah,* expecting it to happen all along? Did her own guilt for how she'd treated Hagar make Sarah feel the sacrifice of Isaac was inevitable?

I doubt she expected more from Abraham. A Syriac church poem of the fourth century captures her attitude toward Abraham nicely when Sarah tells her husband, "You are drunk with love for God." Unspoken is the assumption that Sarah laments Abraham's lack of love for her. We have dissected their marriage at length and, I am certain, unfairly. My constant harping on their dysfunction raises an ethical dilemma in its own right, no matter how much I may offer the justification that it is offered in a didactic rather than prurient spirit.

But still we must wonder if Abraham "rose early in the morning" to escape her baleful glare, for had she known of the impending *Aqedah,* would she have permitted her boy, Isaac, to be sacrificed? That same Syriac poem suggests that Sarah could have overcome her love for Isaac with her love for God. That she, too, could have proven herself and offered the boy. That her loyalty to God outweighed her fierce protectiveness of her son. I have to wonder about Sarah. Could she have offered Isaac? Was she sufficiently inured to beating Hagar and Ishmael that when Isaac woke her once too often or demanded her attention at an inconvenient time, he, too, might have experienced her wrath? Could we consider the possibility that this behavior repeats itself and even Isaac was not exempt from her abuse? In the end, could the *Aqedah* have been a relief to Sarah? A religious ending to an idea that just was too long in coming, so that when it came it no longer worked for anyone involved?

One is just as likely to conclude that the *Aqedah* was her final break with God and with Abraham. When Sarah realized just what Abraham had set out to do, she left him. At first, she searched for him and the boy with the intention of calling a halt to the event. When she couldn't find them, there was nothing to go back to: no son, no marriage to speak of, no husband of hers who would do such a thing, and no God who would command it. So Sarah went to Hebron to curl up in despair and die.

Two final interpretations: Sarah in Hebron matches her fate to that of son Isaac. If Abraham can offer him to God, Sarah can offer herself. She may reason that if God can demand the fruit of her womb, the life she brought forth from her own body, then she can offer womb and body in sacrifice. Or, if we may close this chapter with one last image from the rabbis of old: Sarah gets the news of the *Aqedah.* The vision of her Isaac, bound on the altar, is too much for Sarah's old and frail heart and so she dies. Faced with the sacrifice of her son by her husband, Sarah, too, is finally unbound.

9

STILL
PLOTTING

FUNERALS DO NOT NECESSARILY bring out the very best in people. Mourners in particular are susceptible to all manner of misbehaviors, although this acting out is generally excused as a manifestation of grief. It is true that grief brings emotions to the surface. Further, the anger one may feel at the departed is generally repressed as being an inappropriate manifestation of grief, so instead of raging at the corpse, family members vent their ire at one another. Siblings are very good at bickering with one another on funereal occasions. Spouses often fall out over the grave. Parents and children snipe around tombstones. Relatives, both close and distant, engage in vicious gossip. It isn't merely boredom with the rituals of death that causes this miasma to fall upon families in the face of death. It is an antipathy toward the one who has abandoned them and left them there, alone, to sort it all out.

I've observed this array of behaviors firsthand. As a rabbi I am called upon to bury people. I have learned to watch for these eruptions, identify them, attend to them, and get on with my job of burying the dead and consoling the survivors. Often the anger is directed at me. A name was omitted from the eulogy. I stopped too often or not enough between the hearse and the grave side. I did not display sufficient gravity or displayed too much and was thus untrue to the memory of the departed. Other people balk at the details I recall as I speak of the dead. Without exception these are the details that some other family member has implored me to mention. I try to take it all in stride, listening very carefully nonetheless. For the most part what I am hearing is anger toward the dead or toward God, displaced upon me, the rabbi. Better me, I think, than have the mourner lash out at a loved one, a family member, another mourner.

What fascinates me is how even in mourning, even as they assume a profoundly new relationship—that of mourner and corpse—families continue to play out the dynamic that controlled the family when it was intact. Husbands who were dependent on wives during their lives continue to act out their dependence after the wife's death. Siblings who were rivals for a parent's attention now vie for the role of chief mourner, seeking to garner the attention of the corpse. Sometimes strong families with healthy interactions can manage to continue that dynamic even as they mourn. Brothers can support one another. Suddenly single parents can still find room for their children to grow and separate.

I alluded to Isaac and Ishmael's possible reactions to each other in the last chapter when we discussed the death of Abraham, but before Abraham dies, there is an earlier death to mourn. In the biblical chapter following the *Aqedah* we learn of Sarah's passing. It is to this event and its aftermath that we now turn our attention.

> Sarah lived for one hundred and twenty-seven years, these are the years of Sarah's life. Sarah died in Qiryat Arbah—that is, Hebron—in the land of Canaan. Abraham came to eulogize Sarah and to cry for her. When Abraham rose from facing his dead he spoke to the Hittites, saying, "I am a resident alien among you. Give me deed to a grave site among you that I may bury my dead from before me."
>
> The Hittites answered Abraham and told him, "Hear us, our lord, you are a prince of God in our midst. Bury your dead in the choicest of our burial plots. Not one of us would withhold his burial plot so that you might not bury your dead."
>
> Abraham rose and bowed to the men of the land, the Hittites. He spoke with them and said, "If it please your souls to bury my dead from before me, give heed and arrange a meeting for me with Ephron, son of Tzohar. Let him offer me the double cave

he has, that which is at the edge of his field. Let him offer it to me at full price, that I may have a deed to a grave site among you."

Ephron was sitting with the Hittites and Ephron the Hittite replied to Abraham in the hearing of the Hittites. To all who passed the gates of his city he declared, "No, my lord, but hear me. I give you the field and the cave that is within it. I give it to you. In the presence of all my kinsmen, I give it to you to bury your dead."

Abraham bowed to the men of the land. He spoke to Ephron within the hearing of the men of the land and said, "Would that you but hear me! I offer silver for this field. Take it from me so that I may bury my dead there."

Ephron replied to Abraham and said to him, "My lord, but listen: a land parcel of four hundred shekels weight of silver, but what is that between me and you? Now bury your dead."

Abraham hearkened to Ephron and weighed out the silver mentioned in the presence of the Hittites. Four hundred shekels weight of silver passed to the seller.

Thus it was established as a purchase for Abraham in the presence of the Hittites and all who passed the gates of his city: the field of Ephron, which is doubled, which lies before Mamre, the field and the cave therein, and every tree in the field that is within the perimeter borders.

Only after this did Abraham bury Sarah, his wife, in the cave of the doubled field, which lies before Mamre, which is Hebron in the land of Canaan. Thus were the field and the cave therein established as a deeded grave site from the Hittites.

Abraham has come to Hebron "to eulogize Sarah and to cry for her," a noble gesture of a loving husband. What he actually does when he gets there is another matter entirely. Here we see Abraham acting out his own emotional distress in the aftermath of the death of his wife, Sarah. If we begin an accounting of Abraham's recent past (and we assume with rabbinic commentators that very little time has passed between events), we will recall that in short order Abraham has driven out his wife Hagar and his son Ishmael—this at Sarah's insistence—and then almost murdered his son Isaac. His emotional state must be fragile when he is greeted with a third trauma, his wife Sarah's death in the distant city of Hebron.

One might expect Abraham to fall apart at this point. His wife of many years is gone. Perhaps before her death she has left him, though this detail is difficult to determine with any certainty. It is sufficient to note that following the *Aqedah*, Abraham has returned to Beer Sheva while Sarah was in Hebron. Whether she went there as a result of the binding of Isaac or in the aftermath of the expulsion of Hagar and Ishmael or for entirely innocent reasons is unknown. What matters is that there she has died and there she will be buried.

We might have expected to learn details of that era's mourning customs given the introduction to the scene. Abraham comes to eulogize Sarah and cry for her. Both of these verbs seem to be technical terms. To eulogize (Hebrew root: *spd*) may have the broader sense of burial and all the attendant ritual. To cry for her (Hebrew root: *bkh*) may mean the emotional accompaniment, which is to say, mourning. Yet the latter term may mean the personal action and the former may mean the more communal, technical action. In modern parlance, "to eulogize" may have the sense of funeral and burial, while "to cry" may mean the physical rituals of the mourner. In the ancient Near East, professional mourners were known to wail, lament, clap their hands, tear their clothing and hair, and generally give voice to the grief of the community and loved ones.

Whatever the technical definitions of these terms, we are not given any further detail. Instead, there is a minute account of Abraham's real-estate dealings regarding the grave site. In one sense, we see here a bereaved husband doing the best he can for his departed wife. Unprepared for her death, he now has to assure that Sarah will have a proper burial. What I mean by "proper" is that the site itself has clear title. Abraham cannot afford to have any dispute over his wife's grave. He does not wish to contemplate that he or his children or subsequent offspring might ever have to exhume the body because of dispute over ownership of the plot.

So what we see demonstrated in this chapter is a most practical demonstration of Abraham's caring for Sarah. Despite his grief, he is careful not to accept a gift from the concerned Ephron. While all of the sons of Het and the community do everything in their power to console Abraham, he finds his consolation in the security of a deed. Though he cannot possess Sarah any longer, he can possess the land in which her body lies for perpetuity.

There may be another phenomenon at work here, which should be explored. This is also a manifestation of the displacement I wrote about above. Here, it is not anger or even grief that is displaced, but impotence. Whatever problems they may have had in their marriage, whatever circumstances they endured together, however threatened Abraham may have felt from outside forces, he and Sarah endured them together. Even at the worst moments—when, for example, Abraham gave Sarah up to Pharaoh for fear of his life—Abraham had hope of getting Sarah back, of surviving the ordeal. It gave him some feeling of control, some modicum of comfort that he was "doing something" to address the situation.

Now, in the face of Sarah's death, all of their adventures and misadventures come back to haunt him. He has absolutely no control whatsoever over Sarah's life or death. She dies far away, completely outside of Abraham's realm. One can imagine the thoughts and feelings that rush in to plague him. If only he had been with her, if only he had not taken Isaac off to Moriah, if only he had not succumbed to her insistence about banishing Hagar and Ishmael . . . No one suggests for a moment that an attack of "if only" need be rational. So Abraham is mired in doubts and beset by feelings of helplessness. He cannot prevent Sarah's death, so perhaps he can regain control by attention to the pettiest details of her burial.

This is a well-established phenomenon among mourners. Fussy attention to detail, whether the rituals of burial and mourning or the negotiations with the cemetery, is a hallmark of a mourner struggling to feel some control. Given that a loved one has died and the thing the mourner most wants to control is completely out of his hands, this reaction is understandable. I recall being at a funeral where the widow of the deceased actually stood in the street directing traffic as the cars lined up for the funeral procession. It was a feeble attempt to reassert control over a world turned topsy-turvy by death. Our view of Abraham at this moment, heatedly negotiating the purchase of a grave site, brilliantly narrates this moment of mourning.

There is a more insidious reading of this passage, however, more in keeping with the earlier portrait we have seen of Abraham. God has promised him blessing, offspring, and the land of Canaan. Thus far he has received blessing, particularly blessing from those around him. In this very chapter the reactions of both the Hittites and Ephron can be described as blessing. They are eager to please him, to assist him in his time of need, to offer him of their very own property during his grief. There is little greater blessing than a community that is supportive following the loss of a loved one. Abraham has richly received the blessings God promised him.

Abraham has also received the promised offspring. Contrary to any expectation he should have had, certainly for the first eighty-five years of his life, Abraham has fathered two children. Much as the promise has been fulfilled in the birth of each child, Abraham can hope for and even expect that the multitude of offspring will come to fruition, whether or not in his own lifetime. Here hope plays a very important role, for he is without either son at this emotional juncture in his life. The funeral of Sarah certainly takes place without Ishmael's presence, but it is essential to notice that Sarah and Abraham's son, Isaac, is also absent from his mother's burial. We will learn in coming chapters how Isaac finds comfort over his mother's death—but it is not found at the funeral standing at his father's side. Whatever sense of loss this engenders in Isaac, one must assume that Abraham is profoundly shaken by Isaac's absence at this crucial moment.

With or without Isaac at Hebron, Abraham can be assured that God has given him the offspring promised. Not only does Abraham have two sons, but each has been promised his own plentiful offspring by God. Each of Abraham's children will father a nation. Each will have a line of twelve princes. Each will have issue as plentiful as the stars in the heavens and the sand on the seashore. Indeed, if we are to count Jews, Christians, and Muslims of this century as the offspring promised to Abraham, God's promise has been fulfilled in abundance.

What remains is land. God has repeatedly promised the land of Canaan to be an inheritance for Abraham. From the time he left Ur and Kharan to go to the land, Abraham's hopes of inheriting the land have been frustrated. Famine, war, brimstone and fire from heaven—all these and more have thwarted Abraham's acquisition of real property. Although he is wealthy, his riches are in movable property. Abraham still has to receive God's promise of land. At the turning point of Sarah's death, when he is no longer encumbered by family, Abraham moves decisively to acquire the land of promise by deed in perpetuity.

It is ironic that much as he used Sarah during her lifetime as the instrument of acquisition, Abraham does so still upon her death. Redolent of his dealings with Pharaoh and Avimelech, Abraham uses Sarah's very body as the means for garnering exactly what he desires. It is as though he is determined to employ Sarah for one last ploy, for old times' sake. It is for this reason that he is unwilling to gratefully accede to Ephron's generous offer of a burial plot, for Abraham's chief interest is not the burial of his wife so much as it is the deed, the contract, the irrevocable ownership of property in the land of Canaan. In a bold stroke of negotiating, Abraham uses the pretext of burial to get a foot in the door of the Hebron real-estate market. It might have sufficed him to accept the grave offered him and buried his dead, but Abraham is after a very different end. Nothing short of outright purchase will do.

So Abraham is taken aback at the initial offer of a grave. We have seen before how it is his nature to impute base motives to others. He did so in Egypt when he assumed they would kill him. Here he rejects the generosity of their friendship and counters with a monetary offer. He knows exactly the real estate he desires and asks for a meeting with Ephron to negotiate the purchase. If this were not already a breach of etiquette, he exacerbates the interaction when Ephron offers him the land as a gift. Again, Abraham holds out for no less than purchase by deed. His motives here should be clear to all assembled, Ephron, the Hittites, and all the men of the land. Ephron, in chagrin, assents to this crass display of greed by naming a very high price for the property.

I can only guess that the four hundred shekels asked for are meant to be a signal from Ephron to Abraham that negotiations of this type, under these circumstances, are grossly inappropriate. One must presume that faced with such a high asking price, a reasonable bid would then seem paltry. The only honorable response is to drop out of the bidding. Realizing that he has insulted Ephron, Abraham should beat a hasty retreat in his quest for a deeded burial plot. Instead, Abraham meets the offer. There is no further negotiation required. Ephron has only the dubious satisfaction of having garnered enormous profit at the expense of a friend in need.

Abraham has a much better end. He can feel aggrieved, having paid far too large a price for his purchase. As well, and most important, he now has what he has set his sights for, property in the land the ownership of which is beyond dispute. He has a deed, has paid for the plot, and has purchased the double cave and field at Qiryat Arbah, which is Hebron. By his own initiative he has bought the promise God has given him.

These three varied readings of Sarah's funeral seem at odds with one another. In the first two, Abraham appears to be a loving husband, trying his best to give his wife a proper burial. In the first, he is sure to provide a permanent resting place for his beloved wife. In the second, he acts out his own sense of frustration and impotence in the face of the chaos that has overtaken his life. In either of these two readings, Abraham is more or less sympathetic.

In the last reading, we have offered a much more Machiavellian character. Abraham plots to open a wedge into the Canaanite real-estate market. Willing to pay any price, he ruthlessly exploits Sarah's death, much as he may have exploited her in life, to gain his desired goals. In this latter reading Abraham once more uses Sarah as the means to the next transaction. It hardly matters whether the end achieves God's promise. The crass exploitation of sad circumstance seems morally repugnant.

But need we set these readings in such stark opposition to one another? Is it not possible to be both a loving husband and a sharp businessman? Must we censure Abraham for taking advantage when the situation provided the means he sought? After all, it is not as though he has cheated Ephron the Hittite. Quite the contrary, while Abraham acquires the real estate he desires, Ephron turns a tidy profit. The silver shekels go a long way to repaying the kindness that Ephron has offered. At the very least, one may argue, funerals are funerals and business is business.

Does it make a difference if funerals and business intersect? Is there a necessary border between bereavement and profit? Can people not function on more than one level simultaneously? Abraham has been repeatedly revealed as an extremely complex character, like most of us. Surely we should be able to imagine a situation in which Abraham can bury his wife, act out his own anxieties about control of his life, and make sensible, if aggressive, business decisions. CEOs are called upon to make such decisions all the time. We pride ourselves on not letting family matters get in the way of our business lives. What happens in the home should not affect what goes on in the office. So why need we censure Abraham for functioning as a businessman and husband at the same time?

I suppose one of the questions that needs be asked is whether business decisions are, in fact, amoral. Are there ever mitigating circumstances that dictate an inappropriate environment for business? Is the bottom line the only factor worth considering? Is good will a real commodity in business, and if so, may one trade in it as one would any other commodity? Are there fixed rules that govern this type of conduct or must we engage in debate every time such a situation arises?

The negotiations over the plot at Hebron raise many moral questions. Abraham's dilemma is one that speaks with surprising eloquence to the modern business and even political environment. Has Abraham breached some invisible boundary by insisting on a purchase deed in place of a gift of a funeral plot? Does his action guarantee that he will always remain alien, a stranger in the land promised to him by God? Is it any wonder that we continue to anguish over the rights to Hebron to this very day?

10

SARAH'S SON
FINDS COMFORT

BOY MEETS GIRL, GIRL meets boy. It's a very old plot. In the 1990s they meet cruising the Internet, in the 80s in business school, in the 70s in a bar, in the 60s at demonstrations. In the 1950s they met cruising for burgers. The scene changes, the plot stays the same: Boy meets girl, girl meets boy. Boy and girl fall in love. There are some obstacles thrown in the way, boy and girl overcome obstacles. Girl and boy marry and live happily ever after. If we follow this plot far enough back in time, we find it in Genesis. There, the scene is set at the village well.

Genesis 29, for example, has just such a scene, worth peeking at for a second just to be reminded how stock even the Bible can be: "And so it happened that when Jacob saw Rachel, daughter of Laban, his mother's brother, with the flocks of Laban, his mother's brother, that Jacob approached and rolled the stone off the mouth of the well and watered the sheep of his mother's brother, Laban. Then Jacob kissed Rachel . . ." (Gen. 29:10–11). Thus begins one of the most famous love stories in Israelite history. Oh, and did we mention that Laban was Jacob's mother's brother?

Kinship or marrying-in is a motif that is melded to the romantic-type scene to produce a plot repeated again and again in Genesis. Even Abraham claims kinship with his wife, Sarah! The propriety of tribal offspring becomes a powerful indicator of the covenantal promise. Making sure that the promise goes to the correct offspring is also a plot motif established in Sarah and Abraham's generation. Parents worrying about who their children marry and those children falling in love continues to be the formula, yea, even unto this very day. It's not so much that our universe is so biblical on this point as it is that the Bible is so universal on this particular.

As we saw in the first paragraph of this chapter, or in the two verses of Genesis quoted above, the story can be told in a very few words. We have also observed, when reading the *Aqedah,* that Genesis is exceptionally good at relating high drama with minimalist brush strokes. The entire narration of the binding of Isaac, from the opening call to Abraham until the sacrifice of the ram in Isaac's stead, takes but thirteen verses. Given the conjunction of biblical brevity with the terseness of the boy-meets-girl motif, we should expect that when Genesis narrates Isaac's marriage, shadow of a character that he is, the telling will be so laconic as to be as stunted as Isaac himself. The effect is comic, then, like a long-winded vaudeville joke, when the telling of Isaac's grand romance runs for sixty-seven verses of Scripture, followed by another eighteen verses of epilogue.

In the translation that follows, I have eliminated some of the repetitious retelling of plot that both the biblical narrator and the voluble servant engage in. What follows is, then, an accurate, only briefer, rendition of Genesis 24.

Abraham was old, getting on in years. God had blessed Abraham in all things. So Abraham told his servant, the senior member of his staff who had charge of everything, "Put your hand under my thigh so that I may adjure you by God, Lord of heaven and earth: Do not take a wife for my son from among the daughters of our Canaanite neighbors. Rather, travel to my land, my birthplace, and take a wife for my son, for Isaac."

The servant asked him, "What if the woman does not desire to follow me to this land? Shall I then bring your son to that land which you left?"

Abraham replied, "Beware not to return him there! God, Lord of heaven, Who took me from my father's house and from the land of my birth, Who spoke with me and swore to me, 'I shall give this land to your offspring,' will send God's angel before you that you may take a wife for my son from there. If the woman does not desire to follow you, you are clean of this vow. Just do not return my son to there."

So the servant placed his hand beneath Abraham's thigh and made the vow about this matter. Then the servant took ten camels of his master's camels and left, taking of all the good things of his master, and went to Aram between the rivers, to the city of Nahor. At evening, he knelt the camels outside the city, at the well, when the women came out to draw water.

He said, "God, Lord of my master, Abraham, please let this happen to me today, and show your love for my master, Abraham. I will station myself by the well when the daughters of the city folk come out to draw water. Let it be the case that if I say to a girl, 'Please tip your pitcher so I may drink,' and she says, 'Drink while I water your camels,' that that be proof that she is the one for your servant Isaac. Thus will I know that you have shown your love for my master."

He had barely finished speaking when Rebecca, who had been born to Betuel, son of Milcah, wife of Abraham's brother, Nahor, came out with her pitcher on her shoulder. The girl was very pretty, a virgin whom no man had known. She went down to the well, filled her pitcher, and came back up. The servant ran to her and said, "May I please have a bit of water from your pitcher?"

She said, "Drink, m'lord," as she hurried to lower her pitcher to her hand and offer him a drink. When she had finished giving him water, she said, "Let me draw water for your camels, too, until they have had enough to drink."

Quickly she emptied her pitcher into the trough and ran to the well to draw water for all the camels. The man stared at her in silence, wondering whether his mission was successful or not. When the camels had finished drinking, the man took a gold nose ring worth a *beqa* and two bracelets worth ten gold coins and asked her, "Tell me please, whose daughter are you? Does your father's house have a place for us to lodge?"

She told him, "I am daughter of Betuel, son of Milcah, whom

she bore to Nahor." She added, "We have straw and plenty of fodder as well as a place to lodge."

The man knelt and bowed to God. He said, "Praise be God, Lord of my master, Abraham, who has not denied true love from my lord! God has placed me in my travels in the home of my master's brother!"

The girl ran to report these things to her mother's household. Now, Rebecca had a brother named Laban and he ran out to the man at the well when he saw the nose ring and the bracelets on his sister's arms . . . He said, "Praise God, come, why stand outside when I have made room in the house?" . . .

They offered him food, but he said, "I cannot eat until I have delivered my message."

They replied, "Speak."

He said, "I am servant to Abraham. God has abundantly blessed my master and he has prospered. God has given him flocks and cattle, silver and gold, slaves and servant girls, camel and donkeys. Sarah, my master's wife, bore a child to my master after she had aged, and he gave the boy everything that was his . . . so now if you wish to show true love for my master, tell me, and if not, tell me, so I may depart either right or left."

Laban and Betuel answered, "The matter comes from God. We cannot speak either good or ill. Rebecca is yours; take her and go, that she may be a wife to your master's son, as God has spoken." . . .

He said, "Send me off to my master."

But her brother and her mother said, "Let the girl stay with us for ten days or so, then she will go."

He said, "Do not detain me when God has made my mission successful. Send me on my way to my master."

They said, "We will call and ask the girl herself."

So they called Rebecca and asked her, "Will you go with this man?"

She said, "I'll go."

They sent Rebecca, their sister, and her nanny and Abraham's servant and his party. They blessed Rebecca, telling her, "You are our sister. May you become thousands of myriads that your offspring inherit the gates of their enemies."

Rebecca and her maidens mounted the camels and followed the man. The servant took Rebecca and left.

Now, Isaac was coming from a visit to the well of the Living One Who Sees. He was dwelling in the Negev. Isaac went out into the fields at dusk to urinate and looked up to see a caravan of camels arriving. Rebecca looked up and when she saw Isaac she fell off her camel! She asked the servant, "Who is that man? The one walking in the field toward us?"

He replied, "He is my master." So she took her shawl and covered herself. The servant recounted to Isaac all of the things that he had done. Then Isaac took her into his mother, Sarah's, tent. He took Rebecca and she was a wife to him and he loved her. Thus Isaac found comfort after his mother.

Abraham took another wife. Her name was Keturah. She bore him Zimran and Yoqshan and Medan and Midyan and Yoshbak and Shuah . . . Abraham gave everything that was his to Isaac. Abraham gave gifts to the children of the concubines he had and sent them away from Isaac; while he was yet alive, he sent them eastward. Abraham lived one hundred and seventy-five years and died at a ripe old age . . . Isaac and Ishmael, his sons, buried him in the double cave, in the field of Ephron, son of Tzohar the Hittite, facing Mamre. This was the field Abraham had bought from the sons of Het. There Abraham and his wife, Sarah, are buried. After Abraham's death the Lord blessed Isaac, his son, and Isaac dwelled at the well of the Living One Who Sees.

These are the generations of Ishmael, son of Abraham, whom Hagar the Egyptian, servant girl to Sarah, bore to Abraham . . . twelve princes of as many tribes . . .

This is a really long story, more than twelve hundred words in the very abbreviated version I have just related. I recount it without the garrulous servant's repetition of the plot and *sans* the detailed genealogies of Abraham and Ishmael's offspring that serve as the supplement and provide counterpoint. I nonetheless recall it here at length because there is so much nuance in the telling. It is remarkable how far away it strays not only from the brevity of style elsewhere in Genesis, but from the bare-bones narration of the boy-meets-girl type scene reported for Jacob, Isaac and Rebecca's son.

In fact, this telling plays very strongly against type. To begin with, it does not appear to be a boy-meets-girl fable at all. Quite the contrary, it is the story of an arranged marriage. To make matters worse, the match is not even arranged by the parents of the couple. On the one hand, a foolish servant serves as suitor. On the other, there is a mother, a father, a brother, and the girl herself, all involved in the negotiations. Usually, if the telling is of arranged marriage, this itself would be the plot obstacle for the couple—they would have chosen on their own and would have to overcome the parents' arrangements for a different spouse. Here, after all the endless repetition that leads to the choice of Rebecca, when boy does meet girl, they do fall in love with the chosen partner.

The test set to determine what girl is the right one for Isaac was recognized by the rabbis long ago as being ghastly inappropriate. "What if the woman who watered the servant's camels had been a slave or a prostitute?" they asked in horror. Yet the foolish servant blithely goes his merry way and is guarded by God against error. Further, the servant dangles images of riches before the eyes of the girl's family, rather than the sterling qualities of character one might have hoped for. It makes one wonder about Isaac.

When we do meet up with Isaac and the couple first sees each other, there are hardly violins welling up in the background. Against the pastoral setting, he is urinating in the field and she tumbles from the camel. I confess my translation of this passage is open to debate, as many different translations will offer as many differing renderings of the scene. In some traditional readings, Isaac is out walking in the field, in others contemplating, in still others praying. Yet the fact remains that the Semitic root behind the word I translate as "urinate" also means what I say it does. Here, too, the narrator has gone for the ribald, preferring the guffaw to the high romance of love at first sight. And yet, despite every attempt to play against type, boy meets girl, girl meets boy, and they do fall in love.

Even here, the storyteller resists a happy ending, adding a disconcertingly Freudian note to the tale. Now Isaac, a man on his own with a wife of his own, takes her into Mommy's tent and is comforted for the loss of Sarah. I wonder how that information sat with Rebecca. I am certain it was no comfort to her that like Isaac's mom, she, too, had trouble getting pregnant.

And then there is father Abraham, "getting on in years" and presumably wishing before his death to see his son settled. He does not speak with Isaac; indeed, Isaac is not even on the scene when Abraham calls in his nameless servant. Why does Abraham not send Isaac off to the village of Nahor? Is he so fearful that Isaac will never return? Is Abraham unable to consult Isaac or urge him to undertake the journey because Isaac will not speak with him? And yet, in the end, Isaac accepts his father's mail-ordered bride without demurral.

Where was Isaac while father Abraham was doing all this arranging? Why, at the well of the Living One Who Sees. It is comfort that God sees to Isaac's future, but we should not overlook the irony that this well, where Isaac settles with Rebecca, is the very well Hagar names when she has angelic revelation that Ishmael will be born to her. It seems that perhaps young Isaac is off visiting his banished brother, Ishmael. This certainly goes a long way to explaining why Isaac and Ishmael are together for father Abraham's funeral at the story's denouement.

And the aged patriarch was very busy himself during his waning days. After packing off his servant on the find-a-wife-for-Isaac mission, Abraham finds a new wife for himself. With barely a blink he fathers six more children and they many more in their turn! Now, the narrator is careful to remind us that Abraham has given all his property to Isaac and only gifts to the children of his concubines (a plural? Is Hagar counted now as a concubine or are there even more women we are not told about?!). The fact of their multiple births remains a stark contrast to the difficulties Sarah had in bearing Isaac, and to Isaac's wife, Rebecca's, own barrenness.

If all of this were not startling enough, there's still Ishmael to contend with. He, too, has plentiful offspring—twelve princes—in virile fulfillment of God's promise. Isaac's older brother may not have been

Sarah's favorite, but he is blessed with abundance by Abraham's God. The rabbis of a fifth-century midrash serve up the mischievousness of the passage with a piquant suggestion of their own, that the woman Keturah, whom father Abraham marries in old age, is really Ishmael's mother, Hagar, resuming her rightful place in Abraham's tent in Sarah's absence. So the first wife to bear him offspring and her now-plentiful children attempt to reassert themselves. No wonder poor Isaac needs some comfort.

Up to this point, we have concentrated on the literary motifs of the narrative. This is a tempting approach because of the short-story nature of the narration. It could stand as a virtually self-contained unit, a tale to be told around the campfire. Good story line is enhanced by piquant characters (i.e., the silly servant), family conflict is offset by God's grace. But strong art and divine protection need not preclude our recognition that there are dilemmas in this story that demand consideration.

Since the story takes such pains to focus on characterization, drawing with such care the buffoonish servant, we may ask what character traits Genesis seems to value. Since the three characters who are central to the plot—Abraham, Isaac, and Rebecca—are also briefly sketched, we can see how the narrator draws them.

Abraham appears concerned for the welfare of his son and the continuity of his covenantal lineage. Yet he is not sufficiently concerned to carry out himself the job of finding his son a wife. Rather, he spends his time finding himself a new wife and fathering another half dozen children. This may indicate his zeal at assuring continuity. It may also, however, indicate a selfishness which values his own comfort over that of his son.

Isaac for his part is barely characterized. Here I fear the narrator has given an all-too-accurate drawing of the next in line. Isaac should be the protagonist of this tale; if not that, then the antagonist. Instead, there is no *agon* whatsoever. He wanders around in the field and accepts whatever the servant hands him. Granted, Rebecca is a pretty girl, but his love for her is so tied up with his love for his dead mother that it does not bode well for their marriage or the nation's future.

Finally, there is Rebecca. We have already experienced two strong women—Hagar and Sarah—who have complex relationships with God, Abraham, their sons, and each other. We are immediately given another such woman in Rebecca. On the surface she appears innocuous, if pretty. Your typical virgin whom no man has known. A child who is swayed by rings and bracelets. Yet at closer examination we see that she is gracious, self-sufficient, and independent. She greets a stranger, offers water to him and his caravan, arranges lodging for them at her home, and agrees to leave her family at once. When she spies her future husband, she inquires after him before she knows who he is—a risky business that—and falls for him at once. She is either strong or impulsive or both. These character traits will be more decisively drawn in coming chapters.

Rebecca's family, who are, after all, Abraham's nephew, his wife, and their children, also merit some discussion. How can they be measured? Are they quick to see God's hand at work in the events that unfolded at the well? Or are they simply quick to evaluate the jewelry, the other gifts the servant offers, his caravan of ten camels, his tales of Abraham's riches, and his assurances that all of this will belong to Isaac, the proffered husband? Can they have both piety and greed? What are we to make of their attempt to keep Rebecca with them after the deal has been struck? Are they protecting their virgin daughter from going off with a caravan of slaves and camel drivers? Are they reluctant to part from their sweet young Rebecca? Or are we to detect the beginnings of fraud here, which the wily servant (perhaps not so foolish after all) is swift to debunk? The lessons Rebecca learned in Aram will reappear as she raises her own family. As she reproduces her own mothering, Rebecca—far more than Isaac—will mold the fate of the nation of Israel.

And what of the conflict between Isaac and Abraham? Is Isaac still traumatized by the *Aqedah?* Does the knife his father wielded continue to haunt him? Is Isaac simply overwhelmed by the powerful patriarch to the point that he has very little of his own character? Isaac could only cope under the watchful eye of Sarah. When she died he was bereft. Now he wanders the fields, waiting, searching. When Rebecca comes he finds comfort, a surrogate, someone to give him direction. The conflict played out between father and son, Abraham's aggression and Isaac's passivity, is an age-old motif. It dominates great literature much as it dominates many people's real lives. For Isaac, resolution of his conflicts never comes; the comfort he finds with Rebecca perhaps precludes it.

But we would be remiss if we did not note that this story includes some very powerful possibilities of resolution. Abraham, though he fathers other sons, finally leaves Isaac alone. By dying, Abraham grants Isaac a certain immediate freedom, even if he leaves Isaac with a wife he engineered and ghosts to battle. Ironically, Abraham also leaves Isaac with a brother who shares those ghosts. The clues the story provides, the well of the Living One Who Sees and the brothers' joint presence at the burial, offer up the possibility that one avenue for resolution of parental-child conflict is through sibling coopera- tion. But all we get are hints, never full-blown cooperation between Isaac and Ishmael, at least not for three millennia. This lack of reso- lution between father and son or between brothers makes it perhaps inevitable that the story of Isaac and Rebecca's children provides us with one of the classic sibling rivalries of Western culture.

11

Rebecca's Twins

THIS IS THE STORY of Isaac, son of Abraham: Abraham begat Isaac. When Isaac was forty years old, he took as wife Rebecca, daughter of Betuel the Aramaen from Paddan Aram, sister of Laban the Aramaen. Isaac entreated God on his wife's behalf, for she was barren. God treated Isaac well and Rebecca, his wife, became pregnant. When the children struggled inside her, she said, "If so, why me?"

She went to inquire of God. God told her, "There are two nations in your belly; two peoples shall part from your womb. One people shall gain strength from the other and the elder shall serve the younger."

When she was at the end of term, it was clear she was carrying twins. The first was born red and all covered with hair, so they called him Esau. Then his brother was born, his hand grasping Esau's heel, so they called him Jacob (heel). Isaac was sixty when she bore them.

The boys grew. Esau was a man who knew the hunt, a man of the field, while Jacob was simple, dwelling among the tents. Isaac loved Esau because of the game he fed him, while Rebecca loved Jacob.

Once Jacob was making stew when Esau came in from the fields, exhausted. Esau asked Jacob, "Gimme some of that red stuff, okay, 'cause I'm just exhausted." It is for this that they call him Edom (Red).

Jacob said, "Sell me your birthright today."

Esau replied, "I'm dyin' here, whadda I need a birthright for?"

Jacob said, "Swear to me today." So he swore to him and sold Jacob the birthright. Then Jacob gave Esau bread and lentil stew. He ate, drank, rose, left. So Esau degraded the birthright.

It's hard to decide who's the bigger jerk, Esau or Jacob. What kind of a brother sells brunch to his sibling? On the other hand, what kind of fool is so hungry that he agrees to such a ridiculous proposition? The birthright is not a small thing by any measure. According to biblical law, the oldest inherits a double portion. For the twins, that means that Esau gets two thirds to Jacob's one third of Isaac's eventual estate. One would have to be awfully famished, or awfully stupid, to give up half of a potential inheritance for a bowl of lentil stew. Could Esau really be so cavalier or Jacob so avaricious?

In order to understand what brings the brothers to this sorry transaction, we should fill in the difficult family history that precedes it. That history itself is a minefield of moral dilemmas, carefully laid out over two generations. We have spent many chapters writing of Esau and Jacob's paternal grandfather Abraham and uncle Ishmael, mother Rebecca and her family in old Aram. Now is the time to consider the history of the immediate family in their own generation, as much as does our passage from Genesis 25:19–34, translated above.

As the Bible says, it is the story of Isaac, who at forty years of age takes himself a wife. Here already we can learn something that eluded us in the last chapter. Isaac's mother, Sarah, had been dead for three years when the nameless servant went off on his matchmaking mission. When Rebecca came to the well of the Living One Who Sees, at least three, if not thirty years had passed since the *Aqedah*. Isaac was not a young man; he was as fully formed an adult as he could become. Still living under his father's thumb, he and Rebecca tried and tried to bear children of their own.

Abraham and Sarah had gone ten barren years before Hagar was offered and Ishmael borne. Another thirteen had passed before Isaac came upon the scene. It is interesting to note how much like father Abraham his son Isaac turns out to be. He, too, goes decades and more without child. Unlike his father, though, Isaac learns to pray for his wife. His entreaty to God is answered and after two decades he has offspring. To compare Rebecca for an unkind moment to Sarah, Isaac's wife delivered a baby three years ahead of Sarah's schedule—after twenty years of marriage to Sarah's twenty-three. Rebecca surpassed Sarah in yet another way as well. Sarah had to contend with a rival wife for Abraham. Rebecca only had to compete with Sarah's memory for Isaac's attention.

For his part, Isaac had enough with one wife and a very active father. The mathematics bears this out. Abraham was one hundred when Isaac was born and one hundred and seventy-five at his own death. Therefore, when Abraham died, Isaac was seventy-five and already married to Rebecca for thirty-five years. Further subtraction reveals that Esau and Jacob were fifteen when Grandpa Abraham died. He must have been a real, if largely absent, presence in their young lives, too. Broad is the thumb that can quash two subsequent generations. One cannot help but feel for Isaac, still overshadowed by his father. How might post-*Aqedah* Isaac have looked upon his father's third wife, six new children (more half brothers!), and Abraham's overbearing interference with Isaac's own sons?

Of course, that last bit, about Abraham being a meddling grandfather, is no more substantiated than Rebecca's father, Betuel, being a meddler or her brother Laban or the boys' uncle Ishmael. But of Betuel and Laban, more later. For now we can but ruminate on just whether Abraham and Isaac spoke with each other again after the *Aqedah*. Or, if Isaac adamantly refused to have anything to do with his father (who certainly meddled in his marriage affairs), did Abraham then not reach out to Isaac's bride (the very one he arranged) and his own grandchildren? Surely Grandpa Abe would not be denied the pleasure of his grandchildren. Did he dote on Jacob? Dandle Esau? Did Abraham favor one over the other? Did the twins warm to the grizzly old man? Did they prefer him to their father? All this and more we can only conjecture, we'll never really know. The only clue we have that Abraham had some say in Jacob and Esau's lives is their future successes with trickery and the evidence of the mathematics, offered above.

Still, the continual presence of Abraham took its toll on Isaac, particularly as the years passed and Rebecca remained childless. What an unspoken rebuke Abraham offers to the son who after triumphantly surviving the *Aqedah* cannot sire the offspring necessary for the promise. Did Abraham mention that he was a fool to listen to Sarah and bank on Isaac? Did Abraham imply that he would have been better off relying on Ishmael or Yokshan or Zimran or Yoshbak or Grumpy or Sneezy or Bashful, one of the seven half brothers of Isaac? Was it Abraham's unspoken or, heaven forfend, spoken rebuke that taught Isaac to entreat God on his wife's behalf?

My entire generation of Yuppies is intimately familiar with being sandwiched between long-lived parents and our own children. The parents grow ever more demanding as time goes on. Our children, born to us late in life, reap the benefits of both our own success and of grandparental attention. As for us in the middle, competition with and from the parents only increases the stress. Our generation faces the unenviable possibility of not surpassing our parents' achievements—which, of course, makes us hell-bent to do so. And as our parents age and grow infirm, financial burdens from their needs and care conspire to assure that we will not overtake them. In the end, their shadow falls on what we have for ourselves and what we can give our children. This was territory that Isaac and Rebecca knew well.

Isaac and Rebecca were also like our baby-boom generation in having children later in life. I was thirty and thirty-six when I fathered my Leora and Alexander. Most of my friends were the same age or older—some are still fathering kids, well beyond Isaac's age of forty. Others of my friends are struggling, like Rebecca, with infertility. Husbands entreat God, visit the clinic, consider adoption. In an earlier chapter I wrote of parents eager to adopt and was not sufficiently sensitive to their needs, for I was focused on the loss suffered by the biological mother. But the hunger for children is a very real one and the pain of childlessness psychologically as stark as the pains of labor.

Did Rebecca, like some of my friends, suffer pregnancy loss? It is a bitter blow, indeed, even to couples who already have a child. In a universe where we continue to ask whose fault it is when someone dies, explaining the loss of an innocent fetus is extraordinarily guilt engendering. It is heartening, then, that Genesis does not engage in this type of theodicy. In both Sarah's and Rebecca's cases the Bible merely reports that they were barren. No blame, no guilt—just a sorry fact of everyday life, and yet a fact that bears within it the seeds of hope. Pray to God, you may yet be rewarded. As with many women who battle infertility (especially those who engage in the battle using modern pharmacology), when Rebecca does conceive, it is with twins.

But like many women who have suffered miscarriages, her pregnancy is difficult, fraught. In a poignant moment she utters five words of Hebrew which I've translated above as "If so, why me?" Here, Rebecca does engage in the theodicy question. "Why me?" implies "What did I do to deserve this? Why not someone else who is more deserving of this difficult pregnancy?," forgetting for a moment that it need not be a zero-sum game. No one deserves a difficult pregnancy, not they or Rebecca. Nevertheless, she asks and God answers. The answer presages the future of her offspring—they are in conflict in the womb and will remain so during their lifetimes and, apparently, beyond. It very much turns out to be a self-fulfilling prophecy. It's a good thing that modern birthing facilities do not include oracles among their amenities. For Rebecca, at least, the prophecy will haunt her and affect the boys' destinies in profound ways.

Which brings us back to the boys. Esau is born hairy and seems to have been vigorous from birth. Jacob, mere seconds younger, clings to him in an apparent attempt to hold him back from primogeniture. Perhaps that was what all the wrestling in the womb was all about— who would see the light of the world first. It is sibling rivalry in its most profound and innocent sense. I cannot help but wonder what it might have been like had Rebecca lived today. What might the sonograms have shown? What would those hazy first snapshots have revealed? Would they teach us what God's oracle could not? Might Rebecca have been convinced to abort the pregnancy based on the scientific evidence? I am dubious that any obstetrician would tell a mother, "There are two nations in your belly; two peoples shall part from your womb. One people shall gain strength from the other and the elder shall serve the younger." These days it's incredible enough to learn that the one in the womb is two. I wonder if Rebecca told Isaac that they'd both be boys?

Their names are a window to their souls, unlike the name of "Laughter" *(Yitzhaq)* for their dour father. Esau sounds hairy and after the brunch incident simply gets nicknamed Red. Innocuous enough, except we must remember that Edom (Red) is a tribal neighbor and not a very friendly one at that. In later times the rabbis would dub Rome Edom, casting Italy as a red menace centuries before our own. As for Jacob, well, it's a good thing he later gets renamed Israel, for in Hebrew *Yaakov* means heel, and toward his older brother, that he was.

One cannot help but compare these twins to Abraham's offspring, even if those boys (Isaac and Ishmael) came from different mothers and were born thirteen years apart. Ishmael, we will recall, was a wild ass of a man. He was a bowman, much as Esau turned out to be the hunter living in the fields. Red and Uncle Ishmael were two of a kind, their affinities for each other uncanny. Were Ishmael not raising a family in Egypt, I would imagine him to have become very close to his nephew, indeed.

Is it any wonder, then, that in the absence of older brother Ishmael, Isaac transfers his affections for the macho man to his rough-and-tumble son? Esau feeds him fresh-killed game. Poor Isaac, blinded to just about everything going on about him, does not even know that he might die from the cholesterol if not a broken heart. One way or the other, his affection for Esau will kill him.

What amazes me is not so much Isaac's shortsighted preference for the son who brings home the bacon, so to speak, it is that given his own father, Abraham's, apparent evenhandedness between his sons, Isaac does not in some way reproduce it. Instead, he mimics his mother with fierce bias toward one of the two. Of course, this analogy is more than inexact, for Sarah simply preferred her own child, while both boys are Isaac's offspring. This invidious preference of one child over another is something that Jacob himself internalizes and reproduces. As for why Isaac prefers Esau over Jacob, well, all we have to go on is what the Bible tells us, and it's pretty thin. A good dinner should not suffice. Which brings me back to wondering about Isaac liking Esau because of his resemblance to Ishmael. A fetid triangle, that. Maybe it really *is* better to think that Isaac would choose one son over another because the elder is a better cook.

And what of Rebecca's choice of Jacob? Is she a mother who sees her husband's choice and then compensates by preferring the younger son? Or was there something in her upbringing back in Aram that might have caused her to commit such an egregious breach of mothering etiquette? Again, the evidence is very thin, though the Bible does offer a clue: "Jacob was simple, dwelling among the tents." I'm not very sure what this description of Jacob really means. The Hebrew for "simple" *(tam)* may also mean pure, as in the pure lineage Noah boasted (see Genesis 6:9). If that word is difficult, the phrase "dwelling among the tents" eludes me almost entirely. I understand that he did not go hunting. But what, then? Did he farm? Stay home among the women? Was he a mama's boy? Or was he versed in the gossip and politics of the tents, a bureaucrat who understood the intrigue of an enclosed society? Was it at Rebecca's knee that Jacob gained his later talent for deception? Or, finally, did Rebecca prefer Jacob simply because he reminded her, in his simple naïveté, of his father, her husband, Isaac?

All this was the legacy of the boys practically from birth. Is it any wonder that they will try to cheat each other at any opportunity? Is it not clear why Jacob envies Esau's easy status with his dad? Would that Jacob could feed him game and gain his favor. But Jacob sits home and boils lentil stew, a granola-eating hippie of three thousand years ago, furiously plotting to overtake his burly devil-may-care twin. What a pair. It's hard to see them and not think of Cain and Abel. Or Stallone starring as Esau and Woody Allen as Jacob. Or perhaps this should be played with Schwarzenegger and DeVito as twins.

Now, on to brunch. Esau returns from the hunt famished. He might be expected to have caught something, shot it, trapped it, whatnot. In any case, there he is, sweaty and tired from a hard morning's work out in the field. He cannot be expected to come home and cook. He expects his meal, on the table, now. Jacob has spent the morning at the stove, sautéing onions and garlic, simmering tomatoes and the remnants of last night's red wine, reducing it all to a proper roux before adding the lentils he has sorted and soaked in preparation for this vegetarian treat. Esau enters, treating his brother's gourmet cooking like some ground beef. Jacob takes offense, spoiled chef brutalized by his elder sibling's positively philistine tastes.

Perhaps this scenario is a bit too precious, too late-nineties, too much Manhattan's Upper West Side. The point's the same in any case, the chasm between the brothers' cultures is virtually unbridgeable. Whatever the distinction between hunting in the fields and dwelling among the tents, Jacob pretends to a refinement that Esau is not only lacking, but does not even notice. This is not my invention, for the Bible is careful to characterize Esau as a boor. The verbs are everything in this sketch. The first, which I attempt to capture as "gimme," is a Hebrew verb generally employed in the Bible for the act of providing fodder to animals. As for the latter, Esau does not exactly savor his meal. Rather, Genesis reports with four brief Hebrew words, "He ate, drank, rose, left."

This crudeness must serve as a goad to wily Jacob. How can this boor, he thinks, have any clue what primogeniture means? He probably cannot even spell it. What will Esau do with all that capital, invest it in nets and traps? Jacob would invest in the right portfolio, perhaps with a somewhat aggressive ratio leaning to high-tech stocks. In a slightly earlier era he'd use the double portion of the birthright for risk arbitrage or floating junk bonds. Clearly, Jacob deserved the bulk of their father's estate, not this lug, no matter whom Father favored.

What place does blood or brotherhood have in business in any case? Business is business, the bottom line has nothing to do with bloodlines. If Esau cannot delay gratification, then he deserves to lose. Timing is everything, brunch is for wimps. Never mind that Jacob can only eat lentil porridge because his stomach is too knotted with worry and intrigue to digest anything like Esau's game.

As for Esau, he knows his survival skills are intact. Forget the birthright, he's hungry now. Why wait around for the old man to die? He's not looking to get rich and he is not eager to inherit; he likes having Pops alive and sharing meals with him. Enough of intrigue, investment, hanging around the tents. If Jacob needs the birthright so much, Esau doesn't mind. Let him have it if it makes him happy. One third share is plenty for Esau. He is as generous and easy of spirit as a man of the fields. Hell, he *is* a man of the fields. Jacob can have what he wants, Esau will still eat venison.

It's hard to say who will succeed in the end. It is clear that Jacob cannot abide his older brother. As for Esau, he has the natural ease of a born athlete and with that ease a hard-to-provoke love for his sibling. Yet Jacob will provoke it, he will bank on that. Siblings quarrel; it is the way of the world, and a very powerful way in Genesis. "The elder will serve the younger," Rebecca is told. It may as well be the narrator (or the Author) telling us what the central family motif in the book will be. Abraham is not the oldest, yet he among his brothers gets the promise. Isaac supplants Ishmael. Now, through the expedient of a bowl of porridge, Jacob supplants Esau. So it shall continue, with Joseph and his brothers, David and his brothers, until Shiloh comes.

This motif, of course, that the little brother comes to be the inheritor of the covenantal promise, goes a long way to explaining the minor nation Israel's survival in the ancient Near East. It is for this reason that the tales of Genesis are so popular on one level (the national) while ringing true on another (family dynamics). I confess I find the motif appealing since I am the younger of two children. In my greedy moments I like to think that I will inherit the mantle while my big sister falls prey to the plague of being the firstborn. Of course, upon reflection I feel that as siblings we must share and share alike, even generously, if the family is to survive. Our parents raised us that way, neither Mom nor Dad favoring one of us over the other (although I wonder if my sister saw it that way from her end). Now that our parents have died, we do our best to maintain parity. It bodes well for our future as siblings and as parents to our own children.

Jacob and Esau didn't work out quite that way. There was the literary motif working against them. There was Isaac's love for beef. And, perhaps, Rebecca took the oracle of her pregnancy to heart. Maybe her very piety, her belief in God's promise, caused her to tilt to Jacob. She felt it her mission to assure that "one people shall gain strength from the other." In so doing, she condemned her family to decades of separation and strife. Her favorite son would leave home, never to see her again. Brothers would part in enmity, never to fully forgive each other. All this is yet to come. For now, over brunch, the die is cast. "Esau degraded the birthright." Yet he could not have done so had Jacob not degraded his brother, and with him, the family of Isaac and Abraham.

12

Isaac's Sons

An old friend of mine from New Jersey was describing to me in excruciating detail her eight-bedroom house. She is the mother of five children, married to a physician, and her aged, ailing mother is living with them at the moment. Given those statistics, the house didn't seem to be all that big, even though I know there are families of eight who get by on far less space. "In the end," she commented, "it doesn't make all that much difference how many bedrooms we have. We spend all of our time in the kitchen. Yeah, there's a living room and a dining room, but everybody always crowds around the kitchen table."

I didn't doubt for a minute the essential veracity of this report. The kitchen table is to our culture what it has been to so many others—the hearth, the central locus, the gathering point around which family exchanges joy and sorrow, good news and bad. It is the place where our kids, with any luck, learn some culture. Where we bring our guests for dinner. Where we celebrate holidays, birthdays, anniversaries. It is a place of song and laughter, good smells, good food, fellowship, and love.

In my own Manhattan apartment, my kitchen has a long counter, suitable for eating, but not very conducive to conversation. Often this suits my children just fine, but for Sabbath and holiday meals and any time we have company in the house, we eat at the dining-room table. No matter how crowded, it is there that extended dialogue takes place. We talk, we laugh, we sing, we celebrate, and when it's called for, we commiserate. We are blessed with having friends who are clergy, Jewish and Gentile, who are writers, artists, musicians, composers, archaeologists. At my dining-room table my children are exposed to friends who travel the world, who make and report on the culture in it. Businesspeople, attorneys, philanthropists, foundation presidents, professors of this and that, all have sat with us. I try very hard to share all of my extraordinary acquaintances with my children at our table. I also try to impress upon my kids how very fortunate we are to break our bread with such company. Any company, really. I want them to know how wonderful it is to share a meal in friendship.

When it's just the three of us, I catch up with my children on school and adventures, gossip about our friends, share takeout pizza or serve up a dinner cooked by my own two hands. Sometimes I can coax my kids into helping with the meal, even preparing it on their own. I'm always pleased when this happens, not only because I do not have to cook, but because I am raising my children to be independent, capable. There is a great deal of pride expressed for my children at these moments, no matter what the flavor of the dish placed before me. It's not the quality of the food that counts.

As children growing up in the fifties, my big sister and I sometimes cooked, my father, never. It was Mom who was the homemaker. Dad worked and came home to sit down at the table for supper. That's just the way things were. In my own home, when I was still married, we consciously sought to break the paradigm of that division of labor. In the family we were raising in the enlightened eighties, both parents worked (in fact, both our mothers also worked, but that didn't count in the fifties), both parents cooked, both parents raised the kids. If anything, the assignment of traditional male and female roles was anathema. We did not wish to encourage the kind of scheming and playing one family member off the other that is often learned with rigid parental role expectations. We meant for our dinner table to be a happy place where children and guests could eat the fruits of true marital equality.

When Isaac had grown old and his vision had dimmed, he called his older son, Esau, and said to him, "Son?"

He replied, "Here I am."

He said, "Now I'm getting old, I don't know when I'll die. Now take your stuff, your quiver and bow, go out to the fields and hunt me some game. Make me some tasty dish like I used to love. Bring it to me to eat so that my soul might bless you before I die."

Rebecca heard Isaac speaking with his son Esau. Then Esau went to the field to hunt game to bring home. So Rebecca said to her son Jacob, "I heard your father speaking with your brother, Esau. He said, 'Bring me game and make me a tasty dish to eat and I will bless you before God before I die.' Now, my son, listen to me and to what I am telling you. Go, please, to the flock and bring me two nice goats. I will make them into a tasty dish like he loves. You will bring them to your father and he will eat so that he will bless you before he dies."

Jacob said to his mother, Rebecca, "But Esau is a hairy man and I am smooth. What if my father should feel me and then he will see me as though I am trifling? I will then bring upon myself a curse and not a blessing!"

She said, "Your curse be on me, my son. Just listen to me. Go, bring me." So he went and he took and he brought to his mother, and she made tasty things that his father loved. Then Rebecca took her elder son, Esau's, favorite clothing that she had in the house and clothed her younger son with it. The skins of the goats she draped on his arms and on the exposed portion of his neck. She put the tasty food and bread into the hands of her son Jacob.

He went to his father and said, "My father?"

He replied, "Here am I. Who are you, my son?"

Jacob said to his father, "I am Esau, your firstborn. I have done as you asked me. Come now, sit up and swallow my game so that your soul may bless me."

Isaac asked his son, "How did you find it so fast, my son?"

He answered, "God made it happen for me."

Isaac then asked Jacob, "Come near, my son, that I may touch you. Are you my son Esau or not?"

So Jacob moved close to Isaac, his father, who felt him. He said, "The hands, they are Esau's hands, but the voice, it is Jacob's voice!"

He could not recognize him because his hands were hairy, like his brother, Esau's, hands. So he blessed him. He asked, "You are that one, my son, Esau?"

He said, "I."

He said, "Come here. I'll eat my son's game so that my soul may bless you." So he served him and he ate and he brought him wine and he drank. Isaac, his father, told him, "Come near and help me drink, my son." So he approached and helped him drink. He smelled the scent of his clothing and blessed him, saying, "Behold, the scent of my son is like the scent of a field blessed by God. May the Lord give you dew from heaven and the fat of the land, an abundance of grain and corn. May nations serve you, peoples bow down to you. Be mightier than your brother. May your mother's sons bow to you. Those who curse you, may they be cursed! Those who bless you, blessed!"

When Isaac finished blessing Jacob, he left him. It was then that Esau entered from his hunting. He, too, had made tasty foods which he brought to his father. He said, "May my father rise and eat his son's game, that your soul might bless me."

Isaac, his father, asked, "Who are you?"

He replied, "I am your son, your firstborn, Esau."

Isaac's entire body trembled as he asked, "Who was it, then, who hunted and brought me game and fed me before you came? I blessed him and blessed must he be!"

When Esau heard his father's words, he shouted loud and bitterly to his father, "Bless me—me too, my father!"

He said, "Your brother came deceptively and took your blessing."

He said, "So is his name the Heel, he has tripped me up now twice. He took my birthright and now he has taken my blessing." He asked, "Haven't you anything left for me?"

Isaac answered, telling Esau, "I have made him mightier than you, I've given him all his brothers to serve him, I invested him with grain and corn—so what can I give to you, my son?"

Esau asked his father, "Have you but one blessing, Father? Bless me, too, my father." Then he wept out loud.

Isaac, his father, responded to him, "Here, may your dwelling be of the fat places of the earth, of the dews of heaven above. May you live by your sword, yet serve your brother. And when he rules over you, may you break his yoke from off your neck."

Esau begrudged Jacob the blessing his father had blessed him with. Esau said to himself, "Just let the days of mourning for my father draw near; then I will kill Jacob, my brother."

Rebecca was told the words of her elder son, Esau, so she called in her younger son, Jacob, and told him, "Here, your brother Esau is finding comfort in plotting to kill you. Now, my son, listen to me. Get up and flee to my brother, Laban, in Kharan. Stay with him a few days, until your brother's anger passes, until your brother's fury departs and he forgets what you did to him. I will send for you and take you from there. Why should I be bereft of you both in one day?"

So Rebecca told Isaac, "I'm at the end of my rope with these Hittite girls. If Jacob takes a wife from these Hittite girls, these local girls, why should I live?"

Isaac then called Jacob and blessed him and commanded him, "Do not take a wife from among the Canaanite girls. Rise and go to Paddan Aram, to the house of Betuel, your mother's father. Take a wife from there, of the daughters of your mother's brother, Laban. May our God, El Shaddai, bless you, make you fruitful and multiply, that you be a confederation of tribes. May God give the blessing of Abraham to you and to your offspring, that you may inherit the land where you dwell, which the Lord gave to Abraham." So Isaac sent Jacob, to Paddan Aram, to Laban, son of Betuel the Aramaen, brother of Rebecca, the mother of Jacob and Esau.

When Esau saw that Isaac had blessed Jacob and sent him to Paddan Aram to take a wife, that he blessed him and commanded him not to take a wife from the girls of Canaan, and

that Jacob had obeyed his father and his mother and gone to
Paddan Aram, then Esau realized how bad the girls of Canaan
looked to Isaac, his father. So Esau went to Ishmael and took
Mahlat, daughter of Ishmael, son of Abraham, she the sister of
Neviot, into his harem as a wife.

Not a very happy dinner table. Nor a very happy family. What we
have just witnessed is a disaster motivated, perhaps, by the best of
maternal intentions, which nonetheless destroys a family and in so
doing fulfills God's plan for the people Israel. Since I ended the last
chapter by raising the possibility that Rebecca was acting out of piety
in her scheme to garner Jacob the blessing, that is to say she does
what she has to in order to bring God's oracle about her sons to fulfillment, this may well be the juncture to raise the thorny question of
the double-leveled drama we are reading. Let me explain. Jacob will
go off with father Isaac's blessing to become a nation. Esau will become a nation in his own right, and his personal pique causes him to
ally with his uncle Ishmael. Since Ishmael, too, is a nation, a confederation of princes, we are talking about the formation stories here of
the ancient equivalents of NATO and the late Warsaw Pact, as it
were.

As political history, our narrative is not very satisfying. It's far too
personal to constitute any but a narrow and skewed version of how
these alliances really came into being, even from an Israelite perspective. But if we concentrate on the interaction of the personal and political, particularly in an attempt to justify the actions of Rebecca,
then the moral question of individuals acting in the national interest
is actually finely focused. To what extent can personal morality be
put aside for a greater goal? May one act unjustly toward one's children in order to further a religious or partisan cause? Is it permissible
to deceive your husband if it furthers God's plan for history? Is it
okay to teach one son to cheat in order that the blessing be enacted?
Can one cut another out of his fair portion, indeed out of the family,
if purity of lineage is at stake?

If God has spoken—and let us remember the *Aqedah*—is there,
then, any need to justify what otherwise seem to be unethical actions?

How does one know when it is God's oracle and not merely the rumination of a very pregnant belly? Is religion a cause for immoral action? This doesn't sound right, does it? And yet the history of Western religion (I'm writing here only about those religions that claim to be derived from the very document we are studying) may well be characterized as persecution of tribe after tribe, nation after nation, race after race in the cause of "fulfilling God's blessing." And need we be reminded, the history of Western religion is, in essence, the political and military history of the West. For those of you who demur and say that political history, at least in this twentieth century, is a separate phenomenon from religious history, I merely retort, Look again.

I write these words because I am all too familiar with the two thousand years and more of war that have been waged in God's name, on the one hand, and the frequent justification of Rebecca's actions as the fulfillment of God's will, on the other. Either hand leaves some children of Abraham outside the pale of covenant. Either reading justifies exclusion, intolerance, and even murder. In this most fratricidal of centuries I write this book as a very small attempt to encourage readers to see where these justifications can lead, before they lead there yet again. That's the whole point of moral development. A messianic vision, if you will, but one that I am constrained to nonetheless. If the study of Genesis cannot lead us to consider both individual and national moral action, then I cannot imagine why we should ever read the book again. We do not need more soap opera. What we do need is a happy dinner table, and a happier family of humanity. Here endeth the sermon.

The dangers of the nationalistic interpretation of the Bible are clearly rung. The exclusivism of biblical tribalism, whether in Jewish, Christian, or Muslim political structures, is very well known. I do not wish to lose sight of it as we read our story, for this very exclusivism helped shape the tale. But I would prefer if this book were not wagged by the nationalist tale, so I will invite us back to the family table and the dilemmas we encounter there. The rabid dog of nationalism will have to be content with the meager scraps just offered.

It is hard not to be sympathetic to Esau, who goes in but a few verses from being his father's favorite to feeling he no longer has a place at the table. Esau is an interesting character; his growth is carefully charted by the book of Genesis and we will see yet more of him in Chapter 15. In our last chapter we saw him to be a quintessential boor. His interest was so focused on food that he willingly swore to give up his birthright. He was not very articulate when he was young, and he ate like an animal. A man of action, a bowman, a man not conditioned to the intrigues of the tent. Yet Esau grew up secure in his skills as a hunter and in the father's love which that brought him.

How dismaying to watch such a hale and hearty fellow reduced to tears. He cannot comprehend the enormity of his brother's deception. It was one thing to deal with Jacob's pretensions—Esau could never take his brother very seriously—but for Esau to see Jacob's machinations actually come to fruition and deny him his father's blessing, that was something very serious indeed. I suspect that even here, if it were simply blessing (if there were such a thing), Esau might be sanguine. But when his father, Isaac, shortsighted shadow that he is, informs him that there is no other blessing to offer, Esau's natural stolidity is roused to ire. He sees red, his blood lust boils. Only now can he articulate the thoroughness of his little brother's perfidy: "So is his name the Heel, he has tripped me up now twice. He took my birthright and now he has taken my blessing."

The real blessing Jacob has robbed from Esau is his father. " 'Have you but one blessing, Father? Bless me, too, my father.' Then he wept out loud." Esau cries for his own loss of innocence here. He cries for the loss of his father, who appears to be an all-too-willing party to this deception. He cries for the lack of a mother's love. He cries as he realizes that whatever blessing he may wrest from his father, it is time to leave home, it is no longer his. For the first time, Esau experiences the insecurity that is Jacob's daily companion and that led the younger brother to deceive him. Like all insecurities that are bred from the basic unfairness of daily life, it breeds rage. In Esau's case, after so many years of betrayed trust, the rage is murderous. Esau said to himself, "Just let the days of mourning for my father draw near; then I will kill Jacob, my brother." In that moment Esau wishes both his father and his brother dead. How must he feel about himself?

As Rebecca plots to remove Jacob from his older brother's lethal reach, Esau finds himself again betrayed. His father, who had to be coerced to give him a blessing that promised "May you live by your sword, yet serve your brother. And when he rules over you, may you break his yoke from off your neck," now finds yet a second blessing for Jacob. Damn Jacob! Damn Isaac! Damn his mother, Rebecca, and her entire family! At this moment boorish Esau would have been in complete agreement with the sentiments of the twentieth-century British poem "This Be the Verse," by Philip Larkin, who wrote, "They fuck you up, your mum and dad."

Still, Esau had always been his father's son. It was hard for him to break completely, to transfer his affections wholly elsewhere. He wished to lash out, to hurt his family. He certainly did not wish to have anything to do with Rebecca or her Aramaen family from Paddan Aram. Leave that to his heel of a brother, Jacob. When Esau heard his mother lament those Hittite girls, he knew exactly how to wound them. No better way to break up the family than by marrying out. This, too, is a motif not unknown in our own world. Children can just break their mother's heart by marrying someone from another religion, another race, another tribe.

But Rebecca's lament also has a modern ring to it. After all, it was she who chose to live among the Hittites. It was her father-in-law, Abraham, who was so eager to buy property among them. When it came to purchasing the field of Ephron, the Hittites were certainly good enough. Why not marry Canaanites if Canaan is to be the promised land? Here Esau stumbles headlong into the swamp of chosenness. Abraham and Isaac have been chosen by God to live in this chosen land, yet the daughters raised therein are anathema to his mother. She would rather die than see, at least, Jacob intermarry among them.

And so, after all of Abraham's warnings to his servant, adjuring him not to let Isaac live in Aram, Rebecca and Isaac send their blessed Jacob to live there—ostensibly to preclude his marriage to a Hittite girl. Didn't Isaac or Rebecca remember the flow of traffic that brought her to Isaac in Canaan for the sake of marriage? Could they not have sent a servant to Aram once again to try their luck at finding Jacob a bride? Alas, it seems the worry about intermarriage was no more than a convenient excuse to conceal their other familial sins. Here, too, the story sounds very modern. Jacob is sent away, to the very land Abraham dreaded his son Isaac might ever return to.

And Esau, the wronged son, the one not of the covenantal line thanks to Rebecca's plotting and thanks to God's oracle, Esau stays in the promised land and looks for a wife from among the Hittites and the girls of Canaan. Surely they will be a vexation of spirit to his mother and father. Esau, in finding a wife, will find a way to hurt his father, much as his father has hurt him. How ironic, then, that when Esau chooses a local, she is the daughter of his uncle Ishmael, his beloved father's brother. Esau is no one's fool. He finds a way to hurt his mother back, while signaling to his father that their tie is strained yet unbroken. Esau takes for his wife Mahlat, daughter of Ishmael, binding his fate ever more firmly to the sons of Abraham.

Isaac, for his blindness, both figurative and literal, is bereft of both his sons in one fateful day. Much like his Esau, his hunger leads him to degrade his blessing and offer it to the wrong child. Worse, Isaac is incapable of righting the wrong he has done to his favorite, Esau. Having eaten Rebecca's tasty meal, Isaac is too full to think of a way to bless Esau, too. So he loses Esau to his own brother, Ishmael. It must have seemed inevitable to the weak Isaac that his powerful son would wind up in the family of his powerful brother.

As for Isaac's loss of Jacob, well, he certainly did not see that coming. He knew all too well his own father, Abraham's, anathema of Aram. And now he was sending off a blessed child to live there, God only knew for how long. All blind Isaac had left to himself was his Rebecca, sweet wife who bore his children and fed him the tasty dishes that tickled his palate and almost made up for his loss of sight.

Is it really possible that Isaac can be such a fool? We have speculated in earlier chapters about the long-term effects of the trauma of the *Aqedah*. Isaac is a shadow of a man, wholly passive, given only to feeding himself without any vision of the consequences of his hungers. He has already grown up in a household where sons are banished, sent away to live elsewhere. Why does he tolerate Rebecca's machinations? Could he really not see that both sons would leave home as a result of this venture?

Or did it appear to Isaac that their departure was inevitable? The boys were at an age when leaving home was what was called for, and if he could arrange that they do so with his blessing, so be it. Perhaps Isaac could think of no better way to marry off that sneaky Jacob than to send him to Rebecca's homeland and his uncle Laban and grandfather Betuel. Jacob would feel right at home with those wandering Aramaens and their tent-bound schemes. As for Esau, he would fend well for himself wherever he wound up. His skills were honed, he was a lovable and well-balanced boy. That Esau married Ishmael's daughter, Isaac's niece, Mahlat, was mete. It would keep him close by, in the family and in the company of other hunters. Let Rebecca think she had had her way with him again. Isaac wasn't nearly as blind as everyone thought. Things that were blessings were invisible to the eye; Isaac knew that—it said so in the Talmud.

Isaac is certainly hard to figure. On the one hand, he appears a blind old fool. On the other, one could make a case that he is as cunning as his father or his younger son. Isaac learned long ago, as a kid, really, his neck stretched beneath his father's knife, that passivity was often the best course of action. If you kept your eyes open, passive behavior could get you just about everything that you wanted. Oh, sometimes you had to play the fool, pretend you could not see what was right in front of your very eyes, but in the end it worked. You got to eat what you wanted, twice over, and you got the boys settled in the right way after all. Yes, game was tasty, but we are not giving away blessings for game; blessings are the fate of the people Israel.

Isaac may well have learned that the way to his son Esau's heart was through his own stomach. Esau wasn't one with whom he could sit and study or even gossip much. Esau carried great pride in his physical achievements, in his hunting skills. So Isaac ate his game and loved him. Had Esau been an athlete, Isaac supposed, he would have had to shoot hoops with the boy. At least this way he got a good meal. And Esau certainly would never have stood still for what he might have thought the silliness of blessing. So Isaac let him think that he would bless him for a good meal. Sometimes you just had to speak your child's special language. If that was what it took to bless the boy, amen and so be it.

In the end, he gave Esau exactly the blessing he had intended to from the start: fields, dew, sword, and the very apt warning that brother Jacob would attempt to dominate him. It is not easy for a father to give his son permission to overthrow the attentions of a more wily brother, but Isaac had achieved that for Esau in his blessing, too. He as much as told Esau, Don't let him rule you. If he tries to yoke you, shrug him off. Isaac felt good about the blessing he gave Esau, even if it cost a bit of deception. Could Esau have thought for a moment that he had only one blessing? Could Esau, for that matter, have thought that he would not give a major blessing to Jacob?

As for that blessing to Jacob, did they really think Isaac was so stupid that he could not tell his own sons apart? That he wouldn't know the difference between goat meat and venison? That goat hair felt anything like Esau's strong arms? It's just that Jacob was always so damn cocky, plotting with Rebecca. So be it, if he wanted the blessing, let him earn it. And let him know that his plotting would cost him his brother, that neither Esau nor Isaac were endlessly patient, that one plot too many could cost him his life. It was good to teach Jacob a lesson as he gave him his blessing. Good, too, to send him away for a bit, out of Rebecca's reach. Toughen him up with her tough family, force him to work instead of sit in the tent and gossip.

Isaac was very satisfied with his little ruse. He enjoyed toying with Jacob, asking him again and again, "Which one are you?" Did Jacob have no sense of shame that he could lie like that to his father? Was the blessing so essential? Hadn't he already cheated Esau out of the birthright? Isaac knew of all this and more, but it was better to pretend to blindness. With dim eyes he could accomplish all he wished to for his boys and leave Rebecca with the illusion that she had the upper hand.

Ah, marriage, even to just one woman, was not an easy thing. Isaac sometimes envied his father his ability to control his women, though come to think of it, father Abraham also played blind for Sarah on occasion. Were it not for that, his brother, Ishmael, might have turned out differently. But then again, Sarah certainly turned a blind eye to Abraham's continued involvement with Isaac's brother. Maybe a little blindness was good for marriage, after all. It certainly made for a happy dinner table.

Rebecca, as it turned out, was anything but blind. She refused to admit blindness into her repertoire. Too many women turned a blind eye or played passive. It almost hurt her that Jacob was so versed in that passive-aggressiveness, but she knew that he had learned it from a master, his father. Rebecca had a mission and she would actively seek to fulfill it. Ever since she was a little girl in her father's house back in Aram, she had felt that sense of mission. Nothing would deter her from her own greatness or from raising her sons, both of them, really, to their destinies.

I will give her the maternal benefit of the doubt here, on Esau. Let us assume that she knew Jacob needed her attention while Esau was secure in his own prowess and his father's love. So she determined that the best course of action for Esau was benign neglect. Let the boy be a boy, let him hunt his game, feed his father, grow up sound, if uncultured, a dependable and unthreatening brother to her younger son, little Jacob.

She identified with Jacob, much as she had once felt that strong pull toward Isaac. They had so much of the feminine about them, it was hard not to be sympathetic, to want to gossip with them, to bustle through the tents with a sense of purpose. Jacob reminded her of, well, herself when she was young in Aram. She remembered her determination the day that servant showed up with the caravan. She just knew it would be her day, he would change her life. All it took was a bit of charm and some determined water drawing. Why, Jacob could handle both of those, and cook, too, thank you. She had made sure Jacob was competent in the ways of the tent. And when the servant, flashing all that gold, asked whether she would come along with them to parts unknown, she had defied her father's and brother's warning glances and said, Why, sure, why not?

She knew she had been expected to demur, to wish to stay in Paddan Aram, down on the farm. The result would have been that her family would have kept the gold and she'd still be available for resale to the next traveler. But Rebecca felt the pull of God. Even her father and brother admitted to it. And so the great adventure began. It was excellent, really. She had come to Canaan, lain eyes on Isaac, and practically swooned. Well, it wouldn't do to lament what she actually got when they were finally alone in the tent after what she had seen on display that day. What she got was talk of mother Sarah. Is it any wonder that they didn't have children for twenty years? Even if Isaac had been more vigorous, all that talk of Mommy would have jinxed them.

But sex was only an instrument for her destiny with God, so she had Isaac pray and she herself consulted oracles. She thought she wouldn't survive that pregnancy. Every day for nine months she was in pain and in fear of losing the babies after all. She thought she'd just die. Well, it was a story she had taught the boys often enough. She was sure that each of them had a clear sense of what they owed her. It just had not occurred to her that Esau would be so cunning as to try and garner the blessing without consulting her first. It was a good thing she kept a clear head and a sharp ear out. Otherwise her little Jacob would have been left out in the cold with Esau taking everything: hunting skills, physical stature, father's love, and the blessing.

Sometimes you just had to take charge of a situation. She whipped Jacob into shape. He understood the stakes. He understood what she sacrificed for him. He understood that he had to read his lines very carefully for the ruse to work. It's a shame, really, that the boy didn't take better account of his brother. A bit of finesse with Esau could have saved them both a load of trouble. Well, never mind. It wouldn't hurt Jacob to spend a little time with her family. They could teach him to sharpen his skills a bit, make him a bit more wily. Maybe he'd even find a nice girl, now wouldn't that be something? If nothing else, it was a way to sell the trip to Isaac without bringing up the touchy matter of the blessing again.

Things had turned out well, Rebecca had to admit. Esau was well launched. Even though he thought he was spiting her—and he was a bit—he had married more or less in the family. More than she had expected of him, really. As for herself, she felt fulfilled. Her destiny had been met and conquered by diligence and perseverance. She had taken some risks and they'd paid off. Now she could settle down with Isaac, sweet old thing. If the stratagem for the blessing taught her anything about her old husband, it was this: What he couldn't see didn't hurt him. There were worse ways to get along in a marriage after all these years, weren't there? She'd just have to be sure to feed him those dishes he really loved. It would make for a happy dinner table. And a quiet one, too, now that Jacob was on his way to her family in Aram. It looked to Rebecca as though everything was working out just fine, exactly as she'd planned it. In the end, her vision was as dim as Isaac's.

13

Jacob Climbs
the Marriage Ladder

Jacob left home with a dubious legacy. From his father he had learned a dangerous passivity, a blindness that came with the feeling of being overshadowed. His brother, Esau, bore him an enmity earned by Jacob's continual undermining of his elder brother's inherent good nature. And from his mother, Rebecca, Jacob carried with him an outlandish notion of destiny, a sense of privilege that was his to have at any cost. The manipulations and deceptions that his mother taught him would carry him directly to her father's house. There, Jacob would find love and deception in his own turn, without Rebecca to protect him. There, he would play the victim for almost two decades until he had suffered sufficient penance for the sins against his own family he committed throughout his youth.

What started as a battle in the womb never left Jacob during his childhood. His uncanny sense was that his twin would have more than him if he did not grasp firmly to Esau and keep him from getting too far ahead. Like Plunkett of Tammany Hall, Jacob had seen his opportunities and he took 'em. He might be excused for youthful ardor when he cheated Esau out of the birthright, although his zeal was apparent even then. It was not enough to buy the birthright for a bowl of porridge, he had to have Esau swear an oath. In later life, Jacob is more passive but no less conniving.

The deception Rebecca suggests to him regarding the meal is a stunning display of Jacob's morals. He does, indeed, question his mother about her plot, yet it is not the morality of the ruse that he queries, rather its practicality. He is not worried about deceiving his father or cheating his brother, he is worried about getting caught Red-handed. Isaac calls his bluff when he intones, "The hands, they are Esau's hands, but the voice, it is Jacob's voice!" To this very day there is no more derisive portrayal of hypocrisy in rabbinic vocabulary.

Even so, Jacob is a victim. His father toys with him and makes him sweat before giving him his blessing. Surely Isaac can tell the difference between Jacob and Esau, yet once he decides to accept the ruse, he cannot resist punishing the boy with fear of discovery. Again and again Isaac asks his son, "Which one are you?" He goes so far as to bring the boy near to sniff at him. Isaac knows just how corrupt Jacob is as he exclaims, "Behold, the scent of my son is like the scent of a field blessed by God," from which we are to understand, perhaps, rich in natural fertilizers.

Jacob is also victimized by Rebecca. She wishes, he thinks, for him to have a blessing. When the plot goes awry and Esau is finally provoked to rage, Rebecca lays the blame at Jacob's feet: "Flee to my brother Laban, in Kharan. Stay with him a few days . . . until your brother's fury departs and he forgets what you did to him." Jacob must be dumbfounded at this suggestion. It has two parts, and the part he notices first is the latter, "what you did to him." Jacob must think, What I did to him? Where were you, Mom? Wasn't this all your idea? Wasn't it you who said, "Your curse be on me"? So now that it's Esau and not Isaac doing the cursing, how come I'm the one who has to flee?

Jacob cannot for the life of him understand why his mother will not intervene yet again on his behalf, until the first half of her statement sinks in and he realizes that she has indeed sentenced him to exile. This little trip to Kharan to Uncle Laban was part of her plan all along! Oh my God, she's hell bent on getting me married off, thinks Jacob, and she means what she says about the local girls being the death of her. No, my father's brother's daughter will not satisfy her. Only her own Aramaen bloodline will fulfill her sense of destiny. And that means Jacob is but another rung on the ladder of Rebecca's ambition, will he, nil he, on his way to Kharan.

*   *   *

Jacob left Beer Sheva and traveled to Kharan. As the sun was setting, he struck camp at a certain place. He took some of the stones there and set them beneath his head, and slept in that place. He dreamt, behold, a ladder set upon the earth with its top reaching the heavens. Behold, angels of the Lord going up and down upon it. And, behold, God appeared to him and said, "I am God, Lord of Abraham, your father, and Lord of Isaac. I give the land upon which you are sleeping to you and to your offspring. Your offspring will be like the dust of the earth. You will spread seaward and eastward, northward and down to the Negev. Through you and your offspring will all the families of the earth be blessed. Behold, I am with you. I shall guard you wherever you go and I shall restore you to this soil. I shall not abandon you until I fulfill all that I have promised you."

Jacob woke from his sleep and said, "It is so, that God is in this place and I did not know it." He was frightened and said, "This place is awesome. It is the House of God, and this, the Gate of Heaven!"

Jacob rose in the morning and took the stone that had been beneath his head, set it up as a marker, and poured oil over it. He called that place House of God, although it had been called Luz before this. Then Jacob swore an oath. He said, "If the Lord is with me and if God guards me on the path that I am traveling upon, if God gives me bread to eat and clothing to wear, and if God restores me in peace to my father's house, then God will be my Lord. Then let the stone that I have placed as a marker be the House of the Lord and I will tithe a tenth to You of all that You give me."

We'll pause here with Jacob at the outset of his momentous journey and observe him briefly on his own, before he gets embroiled in the household of his mother's brother. Jacob, now out of the tent, has his first encounter with God in the form of a dream vision. This ladder has been the subject of centuries of commentary and a number of years ago got me into trouble personally. When I was running my writers' group, the Genesis Seminar, we were visited by a reporter from *The New York Times*. She happened to visit us during the session that we discussed this text. Since I was the founder and director of the group, she had conducted an extensive interview with me well before the group's Wednesday-evening session. Like anyone who has been interviewed by the media, I was already wondering just how I'd look in the press. What quotes of mine would she use?

I forgot about the reporter as our discussion of this passage grew intense. Various interpretations of the meaning of Jacob's dream had been offered when a thought occurred to me. "The ladder is a lovely phallic symbol," I blurted. "Just look, even the message God gives Jacob confirms that the ladder is phallic, for God tells him his seed will burst forth and be plentiful." Of course, as soon as the sentence was out of my mouth, I knew exactly what words of mine would be quoted in the *Times*. And so it was.

A few days after a really complimentary article about my study group appeared in the paper, a very pious senior colleague pulled me aside in the mail room of the seminary where I teach. From the stern expression on his face, I knew he was not going to offer me congratulations. "Burt," he intoned, "you should not be quoted saying such things about our patriarch Jacob, may his memory be blessed. Why, a nice Jewish boy should not even think thoughts like that about our ancestors." I stood there red-faced, happy that my rebuke had been mercifully short when he added, "In fact, a nice Jewish boy should not think about such things at all." What can I say? I still think the ladder is a classic phallic symbol, and I still deeply respect my senior colleague for offering me his opinion. He has my respect, just not my agreement.

But thinking that Jacob's ladder is phallic is not yet thinking about it in terms of moral discussion, except for this: Sexuality is often a cause of moral dilemmas in adult behavior. Even repressing sexuality, as my senior colleague suggested, is a cause for moral dilemma. One cannot have read the stories we have discussed in Genesis thus far without realizing that sex plays a role in our adult moral behavior. Nor, I suppose, can we actually have much in the way of adult behavior, moral or not, without that realization. As Jacob begins his adult life and faces his first encounter with sex, this realization looms large for him. Because he is not prepared to think morally about his sexual behavior (although a fair case may be made that Jacob is not prepared to think morally, period), the folks in Aram will use his newfound interest to his distinct disadvantage.

But young Jacob is not in Aram yet, and he is but at the cusp of sex. First he must encounter God, an event with life-changing potential. While I realize that my reading of Jacob's dream combines his revelation with his budding sexual potential, we will see that Jacob experiences his encounter with God in a still-adolescent manner. Let's begin with God's side of the interchange between them.

God offers Jacob unconditional blessing: "I am God, Lord of Abraham, your father, and Lord of Isaac. I give the land upon which you are sleeping to you and to your offspring. Your offspring will be like the dust of the earth. You will spread seaward and eastward, northward and down to the Negev. Through you and your offspring will all the families of the earth be blessed. Behold, I am with you. I shall guard you wherever you go and I shall restore you to this soil. I shall not abandon you until I fulfill all that I have promised you." There is the usual promise of land and offspring, much as God has made to Isaac and Abraham, both clearly identified in this passage. But there appears to be something new in the blessing Jacob receives, something God has not yet articulated to the previous patriarchs: protection.

God has, in fact, already protected the patriarchs. God did so for Abraham in Pharaoh's court and God did so (after a fashion) for Isaac during the *Aqedah.* Yet God has not until now actually made such an unconditional promise of protection: "I shall guard you ... I shall not abandon you." Given Jacob's fears of Esau's fury and his understandable nervousness about what lies ahead of him on the road to Kharan, it is exactly the message he wants to hear. But it is such an expression of unrequited love (quite unlike what Jacob had experienced from Isaac or even Rebecca) that its effect is infantilizing. It's as though God has said to Jacob, No matter what you do, darling, I'll be there to bail you out. The effect is to unlink behavior from consequence, to encourage amoral thought and behavior. By the book of Exodus, God learns to link reward with behavior and so encourage moral action. Here, however, Jacob reads the promise as an invitation to irresponsibility and reacts accordingly. With his track record, how could he do otherwise?

Like any seasoned negotiator, Jacob senses his advantage and pushes it. He responds to God with a series of "if" clauses, causuistically linking God's relationship to him with God's own behavior! Since God set no conditions for Jacob, Jacob himself sets conditions for God. The absurdity of this reversal is apparent, its inappropriateness obvious to all but Jacob. Only a fool could so misread the balance of power. In demeaning God this way, Jacob has opened the door to disaster. Because God keeps promises, Jacob and the subsequent people Israel will be protected, but not before Jacob personally experiences some shrewd bargaining himself.

So Jacob moved on and came to the land of the Easterners. He saw there was a well in the field and three flocks of sheep were gathered about it, for it was from this well that the sheep were watered. There was a huge stone atop the mouth of the well. When all of the shepherds gathered there, they rolled the stone off of the well and watered their sheep, then they rolled the stone back into place.

Jacob asked them, "My brothers, where do you hail from?"

They replied, "We are from Kharan."

He asked, "Do you know Laban, son of Nahor?"

They said, "We know him."

He asked, "Is he well?"

They replied, "Very well, and that's his daughter Rachel coming with the sheep."

He said, "There's still a fair amount of daylight. It's not yet time to gather in the cattle. Water the sheep and go graze."

They said, "We cannot until all the shepherds have gathered to roll the stone from the mouth of the well. Only then can we water our sheep."

He was still speaking with them when Rachel arrived with her father's sheep, for she was a shepherdess. When Jacob saw Rachel, daughter of Laban, his mother's brother, and the flocks of Laban, his mother's brother, then Jacob went over and rolled the stone off the mouth of the well and watered the flocks of Laban, his mother's brother. Then Jacob kissed Rachel and he wept aloud. He explained to Rachel that he was kin to her father, the son of Rebecca. She ran to tell her father. When Laban heard her tell of Jacob, his sister's son, he ran to greet him. He hugged him and kissed him and brought him to his home . . . Laban told him, "You are my own flesh and blood!" So Jacob stayed with him for a month.

Laban said to Jacob, "You are like my brother. Shall you serve me for free? Tell me your wage."

Now, Laban had two daughters. The elder was Leah and the younger, Rachel. Leah had weak eyes, while Rachel had a fine figure and was very pretty. Jacob loved Rachel, so he said, "I will serve you seven years for Rachel, your younger daughter."

Laban said, "Fine. I'd rather give her to you than to another man. Stay with me."

So Jacob worked for Rachel for seven years, but they seemed like but a few days, such was his love for her. Jacob said to Laban, "Give me, now, my wife, for my time is up. I wish to sleep with her."

So Laban gathered all the men of that place and made a banquet. That night he brought his daughter Leah to him and he slept with her . . . Then in the morning, behold! It was Leah! He said to Laban, "What is this you have done to me? Did I not serve you for Rachel? Why did you deceive me?"

Laban replied, "We don't do that in this place, giving the younger before the elder. Finish up this week and I'll give you that one, too, provided you serve me for seven more years."

Jacob did so and finished up the week. And he gave him his daughter Rachel for a wife . . . He slept with Rachel and he loved Rachel much more than Leah. He worked with him for seven more years.

Love-struck Jacob finally knows that there is someone in the world besides himself. Coming to Kharan, he meets his match in love and his match in deceit, one the daughter, the other her father, his mother's brother. In the most stunning five weeks of his young life, Jacob learns about his mother's origins and the ability of relatives to kiss you while they cheat you. On the heels of his flight from Esau, Jacob runs headlong into a honey trap that will cost him twenty years of his life.

The scene, already alluded to in Chapter 10 above, is classic boy meets girl. Jacob, moseying into Kharan after his dream vision, is full of confidence and bravado. The action for the scene is set as we learn the custom of all the herdsmen gathering to roll the giant stone off the mouth of the well. It poses an interesting challenge to the type scene of "watering at the well" we saw earlier when Abraham's servant set his own test for finding the right girl for Isaac. Then it was the girl who drew the water. Here, that possibility is precluded by the size and weight of the stone that covers the well.

The narrator of Genesis sets his scene artfully, building Jacob's confidence at his blessed, select state, much as he builds readers' expectations. Jacob learns in short order that the shepherds know his uncle, Laban, and that he is well. Much as in the case of Abraham's servant, while he is still speaking the heroine arrives onstage. Coyly, the narrator neglects to tell us what he will reveal later: Rachel is stunning, a beauty, fine of figure and very pretty. Instead we learn, along with Jacob, that she is his uncle's daughter. I suppose at that moment Jacob forgave his mother all her conniving. His young loins stirred, he rolls the enormous stone off the well and waters the flocks himself. This is a delightful reversal of the earlier watering scene and not without its own Freudian overtones. The scene is capped by a kiss and tears as Jacob reveals to Rachel that they are kinfolk. Boy meets girl, girl meets boy.

The scene is even more subtle in its reportage, for Jacob does not only notice Rachel's beauty, he also notices Laban's flocks. It is a small but telling point. The last time someone came from Canaan looking for a girl, it was he carrying the gold to Kharan. This time Jacob, fleeing Canaan, counts Laban's wealth in flocks. One can almost imagine Jacob thinking that he will do just fine here with all these unsuspecting shepherds to fleece. Little does he suspect, when greeted by Uncle Laban's kiss and hug, that he himself is being frisked and cased. As the rabbis said it many centuries ago, "When Laban kisses you, count your teeth afterward." Had Jacob only known that he was literally in the hands of the master trickster who would requite all of Jacob's own deceptions.

It took but a month of propinquity to bait the trap. Jacob was so blinded by love, he set the terms of his own entrapment—seven years' labor for a wife. Like his father, Isaac, before him, Jacob was blind to the machinations of others. The irony is underscored by what would have been Leah's Coke-bottle glass lenses were this story being filmed as a fifties romance. Her eyes are weak, but Jacob's are weaker—how fitting that these two wind up together. Jacob is so love-blinded by Rachel that he falls for the classic bait and switch. He's so blind to his sexual desire that when the time comes to consummate it, he does not even see who his partner is.

One imagines him groping in the dark, like his father, Isaac did once, inquiring plaintively as to which sibling he was stroking. Isaac, for his part, expected the firstborn and got the younger. Jacob is avenged when he yearns for the younger and gets the elder in her stead. One can hear frontier justice at work in Laban's snappy rejoinder to Jacob's charge of deceit: "We don't do that in this place, giving the younger before the elder."

Perhaps Jacob can finally understand the power of love to blind us. Perhaps Jacob can understand what is fair and what is not. Perhaps Jacob can understand the value of hard work over deceit and the crushing injustice of theft. However Jacob must have felt about Laban in that moment, he understood that this was a small measure of what his own brother, Esau, felt toward him. Of course, Jacob's fury is somewhat mitigated by two factors Esau did not have for consolation. The first was that in Jacob's case, Laban could offer a blessing even after the deception—there was still Rachel, albeit for a small price. The second consolation was the twisted nature of Jacob's heart. Even as Laban cheated him out of the woman he loved, Jacob could not help but admire the man for his cunning and guile.

It was, perhaps, in this mixture of fury and admiration that Jacob first determined that he would get even with Laban. Even at his moment of defeat, when he was finally on the receiving end of deception, Jacob had no sense of recompense, only outrage. It did not dawn on him that this deception was nothing more than justice for his own past actions. Rather, with the smooth guile that characterized Laban and the younger Jacob, this older, wiser man agrees to serve another seven years, expecting all the while to get even. It cannot have yet dawned on him that he will suffer all the same stratagems and jealousies his grandfather Abraham had experienced with Hagar and Sarah. Or that Laban has exacerbated the tensions by providing each daughter with a maidservant—a Hagar of her own.

Jacob will spend the next twenty years getting even with Laban and raising a family. Unfortunately, along the way those two goals will become inextricably linked, so that Jacob's offspring derive from a slough of despondent amorality and dysfunction. It is to the narrator's credit that even as he spins a national saga, he spins a series of family dilemmas that serve as a beacon for ethical education and moral development for millennia to come.

14

HUSBANDRY

As a child I suffered the blessing of being the youngest of the grandchildren. This made me an easy target for my Grandma Mary's cooking. She could bake a sponge cake with the density of lead and matzo balls that could double as baseballs in a pinch. Since I was skinny in those good old days, I endured repeated cajoling to "eat, eat," every time we visited her. I remember one evening, sitting at dinner with my own family, when Grandma Mary called my father on the edge of hysteria. "Meyer, come quick," she wailed, "your father is dying." By then my grandfather was ninety-two and had either divorced or buried three previous wives. But Grandma Mary was a very big, buxom woman in her early eighties and my grandpa was as skinny as me. So my father didn't wait to hear her tale of woe but rushed out the door and jumped into his car to drive off and rescue his dying father.

My dad came home about an hour later, and when he walked in the door, there were tears streaming down his cheeks. I assumed that my grandfather had really died, but my mom knew better. "Nu?" she asked. "What was the story this time?" Through his gasps of laughter, the actual cause of his tears, my father explained that when he arrived, his own father was calmly sitting and eating a bowl of chicken soup. Grandma Mary dragged my father into a side room and explained in hushed tones that it had now been three nights running that her man had not been interested in having sex with her. The only logical explanation she could offer for this heretofore unprecedented lack of interest was "He must be dying."

My grandfather finally died at ninety-seven and Grandma Mary died, we assume of a broken heart, but two months later. His funeral, the first one I recall attending, was a crowded circus of the extended Visotzky clan. There were cousins, stepcousins, half cousins—every permutation of relative conceivable. Before my eyes I saw not only my extended family but the flesh-and-blood evidence of a long life and four wives. Grandpa Ben, may he rest in peace, was the closest thing to a biblical patriarch I will ever know.

Of course, today, when marriage, divorce, remarriage, adoption, surrogacy, and paternity and palimony suits abound, we are more accustomed to mob scenes at family funerals, weddings, bar mitzvahs, christenings, and the like. We have television shows with biblical-sounding names like *Dynasty* that celebrate such complex family trees. Characters such as Alexis or Krystle are much more glamorous than my uncle Hokey or cousin Jerome. But we all know of real families in which both husband and wife are on at least spouse number two and of households in which children of three marriages (his first, her first, and theirs together) abide in an uneasy blend under one common roof.

God saw that Leah was hated, so God opened her womb. But Rachel was barren. Leah became pregnant and bore a son, whom she called Reuben, for she said, "God has seen my affliction. Perhaps now my husband will love me." She became pregnant again and bore another son, for she said, "Perhaps God understands that I am hated, so God has given me this one, too." She called the child Shimeon. She became pregnant and bore a son, saying, "Now, this time my husband will lean my way, for I have borne him three sons," so they called the child Levi. Once more she became pregnant and bore a son. She said, "This time I thank God." They called the boy Judah. She ceased to bear.

Rachel saw that she had not borne children for Jacob, and Rachel envied her sister. She told Jacob, "Give me sons. If not I will die!"

But Jacob got angry with Rachel and said, "Am I God? Was it I who have kept the fruit from your womb?"

So she suggested, "Look, here is my maidservant, Bilha. Sleep with her as my surrogate so I can be built up through her." She gave him her maidservant, Bilha, as a wife, and Jacob slept with her. Bilha became pregnant and bore Jacob a son.

Rachel said, "God has judged for me, heard my voice, and given me a son." They called him Dan. Then Bilha, Rachel's maidservant, became pregnant again and bore Jacob a second son. Rachel said, "I have fiercely contended with my sister and prevailed." She called the boy Naphtali.

Leah saw that she had ceased to bear, so she took Zilpa, her maidservant, and gave her to Jacob as a wife. So Zilpa, Leah's maidservant, bore a son for Jacob. Leah said, "It is fate," and called the boy Gad. Then Zilpa, Leah's maidservant, bore a second son for Jacob. Leah said, "It is my fortune. I have been enriched among women," and they called the boy Asher.

Reuben was out during the wheat harvest and found some aphrodisiac fertility roots in the fields. He brought them to his mother, Leah. Rachel said to Leah, "Give me some of your son's roots."

Leah retorted, "It's not enough that you took my man, you also want my son's roots?"

Rachel said, "Fine. He can sleep with you tonight in exchange for the roots."

When Jacob came in from the field that evening, Leah came out to greet him. She said, "You come to me tonight. I've hired you with my son's roots." So he slept with her that night and God attended to Leah and she became pregnant and bore Jacob a fifth son. Leah said, "The Lord has given me my reward for giving my husband my maidservant." She called the boy Issachar. Leah became pregnant yet again and bore a sixth son for Jacob. Leah declared, "God has bestowed a good gift upon me. My husband is so fertile through me, I have given him six sons." She called the boy Zebulun. Then she bore a daughter, whom she called Dinah.

Now God remembered Rachel. God attended to her and

opened her womb. She became pregnant and bore a son. She said, "God has erased my shame." She called the boy Joseph, saying, "May God add one more son for me."

How utterly astonishing. Jacob, having fled his family due to his passive acceptance of his mother's machinations, walked right into Laban's crude manipulations of his desire for Rachel. In his youthful ardor to bed her, he winds up, instead, husband to her weak-eyed sister, Leah. When he meekly protests to Laban, he is put off with a smirking "We don't do that in this place, giving the younger before the elder," which plays upon Jacob's own guilt feelings about his deception of his brother. So he submits to Laban's plan of another seven years of labor in order to have Rachel as his second wife. As a marriage gift, Laban offers his daughters each a maidservant, Bilha for Rachel and Zilpa for Leah. Young, outmaneuvered, foolish, but in love, Jacob settles in for at least a fourteen-year stint (it winds up being twenty) under Laban's thumb.

What is astonishing about all of this (as though the plot just described were not astonishing enough) is that young Jacob finds his metier. He turns out to be very fertile, fathering children, especially sons, left and right. It seems that every time he even looks at Leah, she becomes pregnant. In rapid succession he is father of four strapping sons. What is not clear is just how good a husband he is during this stretch of years (let us assume at least three and a half). The clues the text gives us about his relationship with the mother of his sons directly contradicts the evidence of her continual pregnancies.

Leah is as bitter as she is shortsighted. Each birth becomes an occasion to emphasize that bitterness as she names her child. For the first she indulges in pathos—"God has seen my affliction. Perhaps now my husband will love me"—as though this type of acting out might make a difference in Jacob's affections toward her. Leah is the one whom Jacob bought under false pretenses. He may service her vigorously, as he did on that first night when he thought she was her sister, but he will not love her. At the birth of her second son, she comments, "Perhaps God understands that I am hated." She sees the deterioration of Jacob's pretense. A bitter pall hangs over their home, for Leah is fruitful while Rachel is not. Who can imagine what Jacob thinks as he fathers sons with his hated wife?

Leah does not give up hope, so long as Jacob sleeps with her. When a third son is born, she declares, "Now, this time my husband will lean my way." Perhaps Jacob does, a bit, for he fathers a fourth son, and Leah seems to stop being entirely dour as she declares, "This time I thank God." But perhaps her thanks come too soon, for she ceases to bear children to Jacob. Without sons, it is difficult to imagine how Jacob will react to her. Will he continue to come into her bed? Or will his hate for her flare as he turns his attentions solely to his beloved Rachel, Leah's less-than-beloved little sister?

What could Laban have been thinking when he fooled Jacob into marrying Leah? What did he tell the girls? How did they ever consent to the madness of such a scheme? Did the ruse Laban worked on Jacob destroy years of love and friendship between the sisters? Or had they always hated each other, elder Leah envying Rachel her good looks and competence as a shepherdess? Did Laban consider his daughters in the least as he bought another seven years of indentured servitude from Jacob, or did he just count the cash, as it were, without counting the cost to his daughters? It is hard not to pity Leah, despite her surface bitterness. Barefoot and pregnant is a bad enough formula, but despised, barefoot, and pregnant must have been unbearable.

It is a wonder that her four sons (and three more children later) turned out to be the tribal leaders of stature that they did. On the other hand, when we recall the actions of her three eldest sons recounted later in Scripture, perhaps we can only shake our heads and comment on the inevitability of such behavior, for Shimeon and Levi become vicious killers, presumably defending baby sister Dinah's honor, and Reuben and Judah become dubious defenders of Joseph's life. Reuben has yet one other performance in Genesis 35:22, which serves as elegant, if execrable, counterpoint to his appearance here as a root gatherer.

There, immediately following the report of Rachel's death while giving birth to her second child, Benjamin, Reuben surfaces briefly in the text. At this point in the family saga the brothers have not yet sold

Joseph (Rachel's firstborn son) or told their father, Jacob, that Joseph was killed by wild animals (more in Chapter 17, I promise). Benjamin is small consolation to him for the loss of his favorite wife following the loss of his favorite son. And then in one half verse Genesis reports, "Then Reuben went and bedded Bilha, his father's concubine, and Israel [Jacob] heard . . ."

That's the whole story, the entire report. Rachel's servant, Bilha, who bore two children to Jacob as her surrogate before Rachel herself delivered children—Bilha, too, is now lost to Jacob. It is as though the entire Rachel side of the family tree is jeopardized here: Joseph disappears, Rachel dies, and Bilha is bedded (raped? It isn't exactly what the Bible says. Maybe seduced?) by Leah's eldest son. One might imagine the unreported verse of Scripture, "And Leah heard what her eldest son had done and she said, '*Hah!*' "

So there is Leah, bitter, baby ridden, feeling perpetually sorry for herself and hating her sister for her good looks and ability to attract their joint husband's affection. Enter a much younger Reuben, innocently offering up a handful of roots to his mother with the childlike "Mommy, Mommy, look what I found for you!" Now, a great deal of speculation has gone into wondering just what were these roots or fruits or vegetables that Reuben found. The Hebrew term, *duda* (plural: *dudaim*), demands that I have Leah sing, as she takes them from her son, "My, oh my, what a wonderful day!" But we know no more about the plant than we did before. I follow most translators and commentators, as well as the necessities of the plotline, in my translation "aphrodisiac fertility roots." It's not an elegant translation, but the point is clear. Certain commentators suggest that the roots by their very shape depict their function.

If the latter suggestion is true, and ancient listeners knew just what a *duda* was, then the narrator is skating perilously close to slapstick as he sets this scene. Whatever little comedy may be offered is quickly dashed when Rachel is lured by the secret of the roots into asking for them. Leah explodes at her, the one and only evidence we have of sister-to-sister enmity in the entire saga. All in all, Leah has kept the lid on pretty well (except for naming her children). But here again the text has given us a tantalizing clue to the workings of a complex marriage. By the time the *dudaim* appear in this story, both Rachel and Leah have engaged in their rivalry by using children as the field of battle. Each has offered Jacob her maidservant as a second in her stead. Rachel's girl, Bilha, has borne both Dan and Naphtali for Jacob. As a countermeasure, once-fecund Leah feels constrained to offer Zilpa. She, in her mistress's stead, bears Gad and Asher. Leah, now that she is but one of four women vying for Jacob's attention, quickly assesses the opportunity those roots offer her. She knows that Jacob still prefers the barren Rachel to any of his other bedmates, so she strikes a bargain with her sister and rents her husband for the night.

All of her doubts, all of her pathos, is brought to the fore, not by this act of desperation, but by another comment she lets slip when naming her subsequent child: "The Lord has given me my reward for giving my husband my maidservant." With these words we see deeply into Leah's embittered soul. How lowly must she feel to have wrapped up her identity entirely in her ability to bear children to a husband who otherwise appears to hate her? How frantic must she be to keep an edge over her pretty sister that she would offer her own maidservant to her husband to match her sister's desperation? How pathetic must she feel to pay for an evening with her own husband, and to pay for it with the very instrument that might bring her sister offspring of her own?

How sympathetic of God to restore Leah to fertility at this terrible juncture in her life. Without it she might have no hold on her husband and see no future for her own life. Her feelings of reprieve are evident in the names she gives sons five and six. She feels God has rewarded her. Now, it is clear that Leah, whatever virtues she may have, is not a liberated woman in any modern sense of the word. Her entire identity is bound up in having children.

Neither she nor Rachel ever bother to recall what happened to their grand-matriarch Sarah when she offered a maidservant to her husband. Neither bothers to foresee consequence in this action. Yet perhaps Leah knows she has reached the limits of her self-respect. Perhaps her relief and delight at the birth of Issachar are evidence of a turning point for her. The close birth of Zebulun and Dinah thereafter indicate a rapprochement between Jacob and Leah, an easing of their relations. Having surmounted Jacob's adventures with not one but two maidservants, Leah can go back to worrying about just one other rival wife—her sister, Rachel.

Rachel has more than aphrodisiac fertility roots in her repertoire to try and mother sons to Jacob, but like her sister, and despite Jacob's obvious preference and love for her, she, too, defines her status as a woman almost wholly by her ability to bear children. In the end, it will lead to her unhappy death. But at the outset of this tale, Rachel only knows that she is barren while her sister turns out children with startling regularity. Rachel is curiously ignorant of her foremothers. Neither she nor her sister seem to worry that what happened to Sarah might happen to them. Further, Rachel does not take solace in her barrenness by likening herself to Jacob's mother, her aunt, Rebecca. Had she done so, perhaps she might have learned the power of prayer. Instead all she can do is harp at Jacob, "Give me sons. If not I will die!"

Jacob, for all his celebrated love for pretty Rachel, is anything but sympathetic to her. I suppose he cannot understand why, if he lavishes her with attention and love, she cannot be satisfied. Let Leah bear the babies, let Rachel keep her girlish figure. So when she nags him, his response is boorish: "Am I God? Was it I who have kept the fruit from your womb?" Even the rabbis of old, who were not famous as feminists then or now, are shocked at Jacob's insensitivity. He could have said so many things to soothe her. Instead his callous reply brings her, like Sarah before her, to offer a surrogate in her stead. So Rachel is reduced to offering her husband yet another woman to warm his bed. I am certain that in her depressed state it was not her intention to up the ante, as it were, in her competition with Leah. But let us make no mistake that she was competing with her sister. For when maidservant Bilha bears a first and then a second child on her behalf, she crows, "I have fiercely contended with my sister and prevailed." Whew!

Here, too, the tiny crack opened by this suprising verse of Genesis lets in just enough light to illuminate a dark corner of Rachel's soul, for despite Jacob's love for her, despite his attentions to her, despite sister Leah's constant whining about how he likes Rachel more, it is not enough. Rachel not only envies Leah her ability to bear children, Rachel envies her Jacob's place in Leah's bed. It galls Rachel every time that Jacob sleeps with her ugly older sister. And it especially galls her, though she may not have mentioned it for many years now, that Jacob slept with Leah first. Goddamn her, goddamn him, and goddamn their father, Laban, who gave Leah to Jacob in the first place. Beautiful Rachel, tortured soul—the little we do see of her is not always very pretty. As I said in an earlier chapter of this book, no one ever has a clue about what really goes on inside a marriage.

When the sisters ran their course of serving up their maidservants to Jacob's service, Rachel was still at her wit's end. She needed to give him children from her own body. Her need to appease Jacob was strong and her own baby hunger stronger. It was fun and all playing with Dan and Naphtali, even diapering them wasn't so bad, but they weren't hers. And Leah had six if you counted Zilpa's, too. So when that cocky Reuben showed up with the *dudaim*, Rachel had to swallow her pride and beg for them. Had she been a bit quicker, she could have charmed them from Reuben; he was always looking at her funny. Or she could have sent Bilha to get them from him. He would have gone for that ploy, too, but not without it costing Bilha a bit. Well, it was probably better she had been slow about it and had to face Leah.

But Rachel hadn't imagined the depth of her sister's rancor. My God! She was so angry! And what for? She had four sons, two more by Zilpa, and more of Jacob than she ever had any right to expect. Didn't she have any sympathy for her sister's plight? Leah just lashed out so bitterly. Well, what did it matter if she gave Leah a rare night with Jacob? No one could hold his attention like Rachel could, she was sure. Let Leah have her fling; it was a fair price for the *dudaim*, if the damn things worked.

Of course, we will never know if it was the *dudaim* that brought Rachel her baby, Joseph, or whether it was God's desire that she finally have her own son. The narrator of Genesis is coy in this regard, interrupting Rachel's purchase of the roots with three more children for Leah. When Rachel's turn finally does come, after all those stratagems and all those years of waiting, it comes with a flourish: "Now

God remembered Rachel. God attended to her and opened her womb." This is the kind of portentous language that announced Isaac's birth and will precede the birth of the prophet Samuel, some centuries later. But then, Rachel always knew that if she had a son, he would be special. Even so, she could not completely satisfy the various itches that barrenness and sister rivalry had set her scratching: "She said, 'God has erased my shame.' She called the boy Joseph, saying, 'May God add one more son for me.'"

Even in her moment of triumph, she remembers her years of shame at being childless. Even with a newborn baby in her arms, a child as beautiful as she is, that memory of her shame and her sister's triumph causes her to wish for yet one more child. We wince as we hear these words, for we have read ahead and know that the baby in her arms, destined though he is for greatness, will cause his family untold anguish. And we know that the fulfillment of her wish for another child will be the cause of her death. In the meanwhile, now that Rachel has borne her long-awaited son, Jacob can leave off his husbanding of four various wives and turn his attention to animal husbandry.

When Rachel bore Joseph, Jacob told Laban, "Release me so that I may return to my own place, my own land. Give me my wives and my children. I've worked for you on their behalf; now we will go. You know how I've worked for you."

Laban said, "If I may find favor in your eyes, I have benefited and God has blessed me due to you. Fix a wage and I will pay you."

He replied, "You know how I've worked for you and how your flocks fared with me. What little you gave me flourished. God blessed you on my watch. When may I do the same for my own household?"

He asked, "What shall I give you?"

Jacob said, "Don't give me a thing but this: Let me watch your flocks. I will pass through the flocks today and single out any spotted animal: any dark sheep or any spotted goat. These will be my reward. My righteousness will be attested tomorrow, for I will come with my wages before you and anything that's not spotted among the goats or dark among the sheep may be considered stolen by me."

Laban said, "All right, let it be as you have spoken." Then Laban removed the spotted she-goats and speckled he-goats and the dark sheep from his flocks and gave them to his sons to keep at a three-day distance from Jacob. Jacob was left shepherding the remainder of Laban's flock.

So Jacob took staves of fresh poplar and almond and plane saplings and cut white strips into them by exposing the white of the staves. He placed the staves he had peeled in the watering troughs that the flocks drank from nearby so the flocks would come to heat when they were drinking. The flocks were in heat nearby those staves, and as a result gave birth to spotted animals. Jacob separated these spotted goats and dark sheep from among Laban's flocks. He kept them in his own enclosures and did not mingle them with Laban's flocks. Any time the strong animals of the flocks were in heat, Jacob put those staves in the troughs so they could see them, so they would be in heat near the staves. Jacob did not take the weak of the flocks. The weak ones went to Laban and the strong to Jacob.

Jacob grew very abundant, with manifold sheep, maidservants and slaves, camels and donkeys. He heard what Laban's sons were saying: "Jacob has taken what belongs to our father. He made all of this great wealth from what belongs to our father."

Jacob observed Laban's looks and, indeed, they were not as they had been in times past. God said to Jacob, "Return to the land of your ancestors, to your birthplace. I shall be with you."

Jacob is even more adept at producing flocks than he is at producing children. Even Laban, always with an eye on production, grudgingly admits that Jacob has brought him benefit and blessing from God. And Jacob, taciturn though he may be with his many wives and children, is secure enough after those years of shepherding in Paddan Aram to make certain demands of Laban. There is a certain diffidence in his request, as though he is all too aware that entering negotiations with his father-in-law is fraught with difficulty, like pasturing in a minefield.

Jacob actually asks three things of Laban and does so with an admirable sense of precedence. First, he asks to go home. Second, he asks leave to take his wives and children with him. As for the first, it is reassuring to see that after so much time has passed—far, far more than the "few days" his mother had predicted it would take for his brother Esau's wrath to abate—Jacob still considers Canaan his home. Jacob knows that his future is in the promised land of Canaan and not among his mother's relatives in Aram. It is a matter of curiosity whether Jacob calculates that he will be better off away from Laban or better off near Esau. Either way, it is a difficult choice Jacob makes, for uprooting and traveling with a large family, and leaving a steady job and a secure income cannot be easy. Yet Jacob's sense of destiny, the very same sense that forced him to Aram in the first place, now leads him to return to Canaan.

Possibly Jacob even has some sense that God will provide for him as well or better in his homeland as he was provided for in Aram. In any case, he tells Laban that it is time for him to go home—and only then does God reassure him that it was a good decision with the promise "Return to the land of your ancestors, to your birthplace. I shall be with you." This brings us back to that conditional agreement Jacob made with God so long ago, a series of "if" clauses that included guardianship on the path, bread, and clothing. So far, so good—it looks like God has lived up to the conditions that Jacob imposed. Perhaps it is this that gives Jacob the confidence to propose separation from Laban, for the last clause in the covenant Jacob proposed to God was "Restore me in peace to my father's house."

The second request he has made of Laban is for his wives and sons to leave with him. This is a harder request, one more likely for Laban to deny. Now, it seems unreasonable to us in the twentieth century that a father-in-law would deny his son-in-law the right to his own wife (wives) and children, but Laban is not in the twentieth century nor is he the average father-in-law. His daughters have remained under his roof for this entire period. They have not established any separate identity as Jacob's wives by the physical act of traveling away to his ancestral home. Further, their maidservants, Bilha and Zilpa, were gifts from Laban to his daughters. His ownership of these two slaves, now Jacob's lesser wives or perhaps concubines, may well allow Laban to expect that full rights to them and their offspring—Dan, Naphtali, Gad, and Asher—will revert back to the original owner.

Jacob is sensitive enough in this regard to inquire of Rachel and Leah both whether they will join him in his return to his homeland, a place they have never seen. They are in surprising agreement with each other and answer him in one voice, "Have we yet either portion or inheritance in our father's house? We are considered like strangers by him. He has sold us and utterly consumed our silver. Whatever wealth the Lord has rescued from our father belongs to us and our children" (Gen. 31:14–16). Here, they show themselves to be both Laban's daughters and Jacob's wives. This is all about money, inheritance, silver. They view themselves as their father's property, now appropriately transferred with God's blessing into Jacob's safekeeping. He will assure that they and their children get their fair share.

It is, of course, surprising for moderns to read of this attitude in ancient women. They actually regard themselves as property to be shunted from domain to domain, rather than as independent women. I cannot condone the attitude, but will point out that it certainly, if sadly, was in keeping with their times. If nothing else, it sets a most appropriate backdrop to the competition these two women had over producing the most babies for Jacob. We may invoke Rachel and Leah as matriarchs to this very day, but it does not make them models for our daughters in the late twentieth century.

Which brings us to Jacob's third request, that he be allowed to take some fair wages for his many years of labor on Laban's behalf. The etiquette of this transaction is fascinating, for twice now Jacob has requested wages of Laban by not requesting them. It is hard to know whether this diffidence on Jacob's part stems from an inability to actually request payment or, more likely, from a keen understanding of how these transactions are negotiated. When he first arrived in Aram, it was Laban who asked him, "Tell me what your wage should be," and Jacob requested Rachel. Now, again, Laban notes the flow of the interchange and suggests, "Fix a wage and I will pay you." Jacob should have remembered that the last time he and his father-in-law had a conversation of this sort it cost him an extra seven years of his life.

This time, too, it costs Jacob precious time, six years by his own reckoning, for when Laban chases him and his family on his way to Canaan, Jacob rebukes his father-in-law, "I spent twenty years in your household. I served you fourteen years for your two daughters and six years for your flocks. You switched my wages ten times" (Gen. 31:41). Indeed, Laban, as before, agrees exactly with what Jacob suggests and then promptly turns around and with the connivance of his sons tries again to cheat Jacob. So Jacob spends six years getting even, much as he spent the previous fourteen waiting to get even. Those years of fathering have prepared Jacob for this encounter. No sooner does he make a bargain for the spotted goats and dark sheep than Laban culls them from the flock. And no sooner does Laban cull them than Jacob sets about selective breeding, increasing the number and strength of the spotted and dark flocks.

I confess I have no idea just what it is that Jacob does in his specialized program of animal husbandry. I do not know how peeled saplings of any trees, let alone poplar, almond, and plane, influence the genetic pool of the herds. Nor am I even sure that the trees are the three I've just listed; I follow conventional translations from this century and pretend no more expertise with botany than I have with herds. Finally, I confess that I am not secure about imputing to Jacob that he selectively breeds for the strength of the animals in the flock. This, too, is a difficult translation and I have consulted centuries of commentaries and translations before coming to my own version of the breeding program offered above. What is clear to me is that Jacob, with God's help, is now a match for his trickster father-in-law.

Jacob is now ready to leave Aram, return to Canaan, confront Esau, and take his place in the line of patriarchs. Yet we still know little of what motivates Jacob, what moral compass he uses to find his way. If he has learned anything during his time in Aram, it reinforces his sense that ruse and deception lead one to success. Jacob yet has sleepless nights ahead of him and a great deal of wrestling to do in order to become the man he needs to be. When he does so, he will be Israel, father of twelve tribes who become a mighty nation.

15

Homeward
Bound

So Jacob went on his journey and God's angels met him. When Jacob saw them he said, "This is God's encampment," and he called that place Two-Camps. Jacob sent messengers ahead of him to his brother, Esau, to the land of Seir, at the fields of Edom. He commanded them, "Say this to my lord, Esau: 'Thus says your servant Jacob, I have dwelt with Laban, tarrying until this time. I have oxen, donkeys, sheep, men servants and maidservants. I send this message to tell you thus that it may find favor with you.' "

The messengers returned to Jacob and reported, "We went to your brother, Esau, and he is coming to meet you along with four hundred men."

Jacob felt very frightened and besieged, so he split the populace and the sheep, cattle, and camels into two camps. He said, "If Esau comes and strikes the first encampment, then the second encampment will survive."

Jacob prayed, "God of my grandfather Abraham and of my father, Isaac, God Who said to me, 'Return to your land and your birthplace and I will do well by you,' I am minuscule compared to all the acts of love and truth that You have done for your servant, for I crossed this Jordan River with but my staff and now, lo, I am two encampments. Save me, please, from the hand of my brother, from the hand of Esau. I am terrified of him, lest he come and strike me, mother, and child. You promised I would do very well with You, that You would make my offspring like the sand at the seashore, uncountable in number."

He encamped there that night, taking what was at hand as an offering for Esau, his brother—two hundred goats and twenty kids, two hundred ewes and twenty rams, thirty nursing camels with their young, forty cows and ten bulls, twenty donkeys and ten asses—which he gave to the charge of his servants, each herd separately. He told his servants, "Cross before me and put some space between each herd . . . and tell him these are a gift sent to my master, Esau, from his servant Jacob, who is following behind you." For Jacob explained, "I will assuage his face with the gift that precedes me and afterward he will see my face. Perhaps he will save me face."

The gift passed before his face and he slept that night encamped. He arose during the night and took his two wives and his two concubines and his eleven children and crossed over the Yabok crossing. He had them and that which was his cross over.

So Jacob remained alone and a man wrestled with him until daybreak. He saw he could not overpower him, so he pressed his hamstring so that Jacob's hamstring was strained as a result of wrestling with him. He said, "Let me go, for it is daybreak."

But he replied, "I will not let you go unless you bless me."

He asked, "What is your name?"

He said, "Jacob."

He replied, "No longer will they say your name is Jacob, but rather Israel, for you have contended with the Lord and with men and have prevailed."

Then Jacob asked, "Pray, tell me your name."

But he replied, "Why do you ask my name?" And he blessed him there. Jacob called that place, "Peniel, for I have seen the Lord face-to-face and my soul has been saved." The sun shined as he passed Peniel and he limped on his thigh.

They say you can't go home again, but the trip home for Jacob both is and is not a trip home. He returns to the land and he returns to his father, but his mother, Rebecca, is now dead and buried. Never again will Jacob have to contend with the ambitions and plots of his mother. This is all well and good, he has ambition and plots enough of his own. Even the father he returns to is but a shadow of his former shadowy self. As if Isaac were not passive enough in all the narratives previous, the only appearance of Isaac in the remainder of Genesis is when he is buried, "old and abundant in days" at the age of one hundred and eighty, by his sons, Jacob and Esau.

The real home that Jacob has to face, then, is neither mother nor father, but his dreaded brother, Esau. It was Esau whom he had cheated of the birthright when he sold his hungry brother a bowl of porridge. It was Esau he deprived of blessing when he deceived his blind father and took for himself what was meant for his brother. It was Esau he feared when he fled to Aram for "but a few days." It remains Esau he fears as he turns now, away from the deceptions of Laban and Aram, homeward bound.

Jacob is bound by a web of guilt, covenant, commitment, and responsibilities. He remains wracked by guilt, two decades later, for his treatment of Esau. This much is to Jacob's credit—he has a deeply refined sense of guilt. It is hard to understand just how such guilt develops. Psychologists galore have written volume after volume on the origins of guilt. I will not impute to Jacob here desires to kill his father and/or marry his mother. It is enough that he repeatedly cheated his brother. When he left Canaan, the sentence of his guilt was ringing in his ears, and it was a death sentence from Esau's own mouth. Is it possible after twenty years of not speaking, after a series of wrongs best not spoken of, for brothers to reconcile? This is Jacob's question, and it remains to be discussed just how seriously he asks it.

For there is reconciliation and there is reconciliation. If Jacob has grown, if he has changed during his twenty-year stint abroad, fathering children and amassing a fortune, then he may well seek real reconciliation. Now a father of a tribe, he may really wish for a brother. Esau might understand his responsibilities, his problems. If Jacob can go home to forgiveness for his youthful deeds, he may find, well, a brother. At this juncture in his life, especially after the successive frauds of Laban, Jacob may be ready for the comfort of family in a home of his own.

But if Jacob is still the same boy who cheated Esau in the first place, all he will seek upon return to Canaan is a truce, forgiveness for his sins without his own repentance. Jacob will wish to be off the hook of Esau's anger but free to perpetuate his deceptions, albeit not against Esau. Jacob will not seek his brother's love, any more than he might be capable of offering his own. If Jacob has not changed, the only love he can demonstrate is for himself, Rachel, and Joseph. Now, this itself is worthy of note, particularly for one as egocentric as Jacob. But he will be unable to see beyond that tight little triangle of his own interest. Jacob will still be incapable of imagining what Esau might feel, let alone what anyone else might feel. Without that essential sympathy for another being developed, Jacob can only return home to strife and sorrow.

He is bound to return home by covenant, too. God has sent him on this journey with promises of protection. It is ironic that the short-sighted Jacob cannot see beyond his fear of Esau to realize that he may need God's protection beyond his brother. But God sends Jacob on his way home and Jacob sets off, accompanied on the way by God's angels. He is returning to his homeland, his birthplace, the land God promised to his father and grandfather before him. With wives from Aram just like his own mother to comfort him, Jacob will settle the land of Canaan.

His wives and children, of course, complete the web of commitment and responsibility that binds him to settle Canaan. He is not a young man any longer. He can no longer trip from trick to trick, deception to deception. He has four wives, twelve children. He has possessions, herds, employees. Even a modest dinner of just the immediate family requires a table set for seventeen! He can no longer stay in Aram; he must return to Canaan to meet his commitments and responsibilities to his nuclear family. Jacob, God help him, is middle-aged.

So he begins his journey, surrounded by angels, at the place he calls Two-Camps. One camp, we presume, is his own; the other, God's encampment. The parallel of this journey portended by a camp of angels and his previous outward-bound journey is striking. Both going from and coming to Canaan, Jacob has company. On the trip out, his angels ascend and descend a ladder. In this trip they are merely there, although we will wonder in a bit just whom Jacob wrestles with. The first band of angels was a sign of his fruitfulness. I suggested that the ladder was a phallic symbol and its interpretation, offered by God, was that Jacob would have plentiful seed and spread out over the land. But what of this Two-Camp send-off? This time there is no dream vision, just the angels themselves. Are they a sign of blessing? Do they really mean that Jacob's camp has a parallel encampment of God's nearby protecting them? Or is the second camp a sign of Jacob's duplicity, his essentially two-faced nature? Does the presence of the angels portend that Jacob will never have the peace he seeks upon return to Canaan? Does this second camp mean that there will be opposition wherever he pitches his tent? Is Jacob destined to have a secret-sharer to underscore the heart of darkness he will bear?

Jacob's own double nature is constantly surfacing as he returns to wear the mantle of patriarch. With all the wealth and family he has acquired, he could not be more accurate when he sends his message to Esau, "I have dwelt with Laban." The rabbis of old play with this verse of Genesis and use it to illustrate our hero's twofold nature. In the Hebrew of the Bible, "I have dwelt" is but one word, *grty*. Using a technique of reading that in our society is associated with a tabloid newspaper Jumble, the rabbis scramble the letters and have Jacob say, "I have dwelt with Laban, but I observed all six hundred thirteen commandments." In Hebrew, every letter has numerical value and six hundred thirteen comes to *tryg* when written alphabetically. Try *Grty*, "I dwelt," equals *tryg* six hundred thirteen, the number of commandments rabbinic Judaism presumes God gave the people Israel. For the rabbis these two concepts are, as it were, at war within Jacob. On one side is Laban, on the other God's commandments.

Just what message does Jacob suppose Esau will hear when he learns his brother has spent the last twenty years with the family of the mother who shunned him? What will Esau imagine Jacob learned at the feet of the master deceiver Laban? Can Esau rejoice at the news that his long-lost brother has returned from that place? It would have been far better had Jacob stayed and intermarried with the girls of Canaan. Jacob's apprenticeship to Uncle Laban might seem to Esau a very sad piece of news, a very high price to pay to prevent assimilation. It might have something to do with the four hundred men accompanying Esau as he intercepts Jacob. But, like Jacob, we will have to wait until we actually meet Esau face-to-face before judging his intentions.

For Jacob is not, in fact, estimating Esau's intentions. Rather, he is projecting his own guilt and assuming the worst of Esau. In some way, even after all these years, Jacob has not changed. He thinks the worst and acts precipitously to prevent it, whether it's destined to happen or not. It does not dawn on Jacob to try to judge the possible consequences of his own actions. He did not think about Esau's resentment when he sold him the porridge. He did not think of Esau's enmity when he stole the blessing. He did not imagine the envy of Laban's sons when he undertook his stock-breeding program. And now he does not foresee consequence to dividing his family in half, essentially preferring some children over others.

We will return to the long-term effects of dividing his family. Suffice it for now to note that Jacob has just, in psychiatrist Nancy Chudorow's words, reproduced his own mothering. Just as he had grown up in a family where the parents played favorites, now he does the same to his own children. This tendency will become grossly exacerbated with young Joseph, but even now, especially now as he returns to the scene of his own rearing, he divides his children and shows his preferences. Twenty years with Laban were not sufficient to teach him not to place the younger before the elder. But then again, had he learned that lesson, we might no longer be in Genesis.

One thing Jacob does seem to have learned over the years is how to pray. He invokes his father and grandfather, as he recalls God's command to return to the land promised to them. This is formulaic and does not, in fact, reveal much of Jacob except his ability to remind God that it was God who had sent him on this journey. But then Jacob has an unaccustomed attack of modesty. "I am minuscule compared to all the acts of love and truth that You have done for your servant," Jacob prays. He who boasts to his brother, Esau, of all his wealth and possessions realizes that in the face of cosmic proportions, he is but small. Jacob also modestly realizes that it is God he has to thank for the protection and blessing that have brought him thus far, "for I crossed this Jordan River with but my staff and now, lo, I am two encampments." The end of this line is double-edged. On one side his wealth, granted by God, is sufficient to be divided into two parts. On the other side, it is at risk—for that is why he has divided it. Finally, Jacob addresses his fears: "Save me, please, from the hand of my brother, from the hand of Esau. I am terrified of him, lest he come and strike me, mother, and child."

A healthy catharsis, this prayer. It might help him reason what his next step should be. Perhaps he might reason that he should admit these fears not only to himself and God, but to Esau as well. Perhaps he might develop sufficiently to understand that for the catharsis to be wholly effective he must confront his past sins with his brother; only then might the air be cleared. But Jacob, for all his self-exposure during prayer, is unwilling to risk exposure to Esau, so instead he placates him, thinking that gifts of wealth, rather than spirit, will mitigate his guilt.

To his credit, Jacob sends an impressive gift. The narrator of Genesis is almost tongue in cheek as he suggests that the gift came from what was "at hand." All that Jacob possessed was at hand; he had nothing else to offer. But nevertheless, he sends this circus parade of animals off to Esau as a propitiation. As we see the animals marching, we expect elephants, lions and tigers and bears. As is, more than five hundred and fifty animals are counted—a stunning display of both Jacob's wealth and his feelings of guilt.

Genesis makes very clear that this gift, indeed this entire reunion, is all about what the Orientals call "face." I have preserved the effect of the Hebrew with a rather awkward translation into English: "I will assuage his face with the gift that precedes me and afterward he will see my face. Perhaps he will save me face. The gift passed before his face . . ." You can add to that the word I translated as "precedes," which may equally be rendered "goes before my face." In short, Jacob sends a huge offering to Esau in an effort to increase Esau's face, for Jacob has stolen face from Esau back when they were children and now Jacob must offer face to Esau in an effort to save his own face.

Indeed, when their confrontation is over, Jacob will admit to Esau, "Seeing your face was like seeing the face of the Lord." Gifts or no gifts, the brothers must try to reconcile face-to-face.

It is when Jacob recognizes this inevitability that he makes his crossing. Here, too, the Hebrew is laden with the term for "crossing," in case the reader didn't quite get that some transformation was to take place. Jacob crosses a line—in fact, a river—on his return to Esau. The limnal moment should indicate a profound change, a shift in Jacob's character and moral development. As he crosses the border to return home, he crosses some stage of development. The crossing is heavy-handed here, for Jacob not only passes over the river, but like all of us, spends a restless night.

During this night of crossing, Jacob wrestles with a man. Generation after generation of commentators have asked the obvious, "Who is this man that Jacob wrestles with?" Is it God? An angel? Does Jacob wrestle with himself? His "secret-sharer" or *Doppelgänger?* Or is it Esau or Esau's angel that he wrestles with in a prelude to their match on the morrow? The text itself gives us a bewildering variety of signals as it calls the wrestler a man, yet he is one who bestows blessing. Vampirelike, he flees at the break of day, which may mean he is a demon or angel. He refuses to reveal his name to Jacob and so to us as well. But his parting blessing includes the news that Jacob has wrestled with both man and God.

Does this mean Jacob literally wrestled with both or only figuratively? We are no closer to knowing who it was that Jacob wrestled with than we are to knowing who the demons are that we ourselves fight in the gray hours before the dawn. Jacob, at least, earns a change of name, even as he also suffers a wound. He becomes Israel, the God wrestler. Although he limps from the scene, he has received what Homer scholars like to refer to as an enabling wound. Do the new name and the new way of walking indicate a new Jacob? Has he grown during the past two decades? Has there been some moral development in his life? Is he ready to meet his twin brother?

Jacob looked up and beheld, here came Esau with four hundred men. So he split his children among Leah, Rachel, and the two maidservants. He put the maidservants and their children first and then Leah and her children behind them. Rachel and Joseph were last.

Jacob crossed ahead of them, bowing to the ground seven times, until he reached Esau. Then Esau ran to greet him and he hugged him and he threw his arms around his neck and he kissed him and they wept. He looked up and saw the women and the children and asked, "Are these yours?"

Jacob replied, "They are the children God has graced your servant with." The maidservants came closer with their children and they bowed. Then Leah, too, came closer with her children and they bowed. Finally, Rachel and Joseph came near and bowed.

Esau asked, "What was all this camp that met me?"

And he said, "For my lord's favor."

But Esau said, "I have plenty, my brother, let what is yours be yours!"

But Jacob insisted, "But please, if it please you to show me favor, please take my gift from me. It is because seeing your face was like seeing the face of the Lord, and you have received me. Take with my blessing what has been brought to you, for God has been gracious with me and I have everything." And he persuaded him until he took it.

Esau said, "Let us travel on. I will go alongside you."

But he demurred, "My lord knows the children are frail and the sheep and cattle a worry to me. If I press them one day too many, the sheep will die. Let my lord pass before the face of his servant and I will lead at my own pace according to the pace of the work I have and the pace of the children, until I come to my lord at Seir."

Then Esau suggested, "Let me appoint some of my people to accompany you."

But he countered, "Why bother? I but wish my lord's favor."

So Esau returned that day on his journey toward Seir and Jacob traveled to Sukkot. He built a house there and pens for the livestock, which is why they call that place Sukkot. Then Jacob came in peace to the city of Shekhem in the land of Canaan. He had arrived from Paddan Aram and camped facing the city. He bought that portion of the field where he had pitched his tent from the sons of Hamor, father of Shekhem . . .

Again, the text informs us that Esau has a retinue of four hundred men. Again, we see the threat that Jacob perceives in these troops accompanying Esau. His fear is manifest in his division of his family into front, middle, and rear lines. He sets them out in reverse order of preference so that if Esau's intentions are for ill, those in front will be slaughtered first while those behind may be rescued. Thus he regrettably repeats the preferential division of family he had already articulated before his wrestling: "If Esau comes and strikes the first encampment, then the second encampment will survive."

What can Gad and Asher, Dan and Naphtali think when Jacob so exposes them to danger? Does he not remember how he felt when Isaac showed preference for Esau? Can he not imagine a better form of defense than making clear to his sons that they are but so much cannon fodder? Even Leah's children, Reuben, Shimeon, Levi, Judah, Issachar, Zebulun, and the uncounted Dinah, are all put in peril. Only Rachel and Joseph are protected in the closing ranks. In this moment, Jacob determines Joseph's fate with his brothers and plants the seed of Shimeon and Levi's lethal protectiveness of their sister.

In this moment Jacob also reveals that despite his wrestling, despite his sleepless night, despite his very name change, he remains the same craven lad who fled from Esau decades earlier. His cowardice is well represented in his bowing and scraping his way to Esau. At least he moves to the front of the family formation instead of hiding in the rear guard with Rachel and Joseph. His perceptions of Esau, a good mirror of his self-perception, will reflect the lack of moral development in Jacob as the narrative unfolds both here and in subsequent chapters of Genesis.

But what of brother Esau? Has he changed or does he remain the boor whom we saw at the outset, crude and ruddy, concerned only for his stomach and the moment at hand? It appears that Esau has forgiven and forgotten the slights and injuries Jacob inflicted upon him when they were children. Graciously he runs to greet his brother with kisses and hugs. He weeps at the reunion and asks, in the best fraternal spirit, about the wives and children Jacob has brought with him. One can sense Uncle Esau warming to the role. If he had leave, he would get down on all fours and play horsey with the youngest of Jacob's offspring. He would be the one to teach hunting and archery to the boys, take them camping and to ball games when their father was too busy. And the four hundred men? Why, an honor guard, the best he could muster to pay homage to his long-lost brother.

As Jacob's clan is set to muster, bowing successively before Esau, he is baffled by the gifts Jacob has set before him. Perhaps he really has forgotten what looms so large in Jacob's guilty conscience. He cannot imagine what he would do with all these herds of animals: "I have plenty, my brother. Let what is yours be yours!" Esau is the brother who has grown over the years. He has grown rich. He has raised a formidable family from his marriage alliances among the Canaanites. He has learned to forgive his brother. Although we are not told, one might assume he has also reconciled with his father and returned to bringing him Sunday dinners, as in the good old days. One can see in Esau a man of vision, high moral purpose, and generosity toward his family.

Another interpretation: The preceding two paragraphs go against the grain of almost two thousand years of rabbinic reading of this tale. Esau a good guy? He's the bad boy of Scripture; it was not for naught that when the rabbis looked at Esau, they saw the Roman oppressor. Esau comes with four hundred warriors. Jacob is absolutely correct to be on his guard. And even the Bible gives us a clue that Esau's greeting was not all that it was cracked up to be. If Laban's kiss was suspect, Esau's kiss was a thousand times so. When Genesis writes out in Hebrew, "he kissed him," scribes put a series of dots above the word. This practice goes back at least a millennium and a half—and those dots are a warning sign, signifying that all is not as it should be. In other words, the very text of Scripture tells the reader to be wary of Esau's kisses.

One final clue to make us rethink Esau's purported moral development: When he first refuses Jacob's generous gifts, he reasons, "I have plenty, my brother. Let what is yours be yours!" We already learned in Chapter 6 above how to evaluate this moral reasoning. "One who says, 'What's mine is mine and what's yours is yours'—this is the ethic of Sodom." So let us not make Esau out to be such a moral exemplar. If he has grown, it is only in strength and guile. All that does is make him more dangerous than he had been. Jacob is quite right to be wary.

So in the end, Jacob shows no generosity to his brother, Esau, even as he bribes him with gifts. He presses him to accept the flocks he has sent ahead, as though that will clean the slate of past wrongs or make them even somehow. Whether Esau has changed or not, Jacob is still the same—a deceptive trickster who can only assume the worst about those around him. His suspicions of his brother, Esau, effectively push him away and preclude any real reconciliation between them.

He resorts to all of his old ways as he successively lies to Esau about the frailty of his children, his cattle, his pace, and his destination. All Esau wishes to do is spend some time with his brother. But Jacob, believing he has kissed and made up, is eager to be on his way, on his own. He cannot even countenance Esau's gracious suggestion that he send some guides along to ease their journey. If they were in the modern world, Jacob would be ushering him out the door with a plastic smile pasted on his face and a "Thanks for coming, have a nice day" as his mantra. As it is, he comes perilously close to suggesting to Esau that when he catches up to him in Seir (something he has no intention whatsoever of doing) that they do lunch together. At the last moment, he remembers: Been there, done that. It's time to move on.

And move he does, away from Esau but into the heart of the promised land. First he stops at Sukkot, where he builds *sukkot,* pens for his animals. This is a bit of ironic foreshadowing since the Israelites wandering in the wilderness after the Exodus from Egypt will also build *sukkot.* They, however, will dwell in them themselves—perhaps a clue to us of just how good Jacob has it without having a clue to his blessed state himself. Nothing seems to move him to moral development. No dilemma in his life finds resolution through growth, only through more deception and cowardice. It does not bode well for Jacob's future.

His final stop in this journey is to settle the land, purchasing property just outside Shekhem. One cannot help but compare Abraham's protracted negotiations for land with this simple transaction. But then, it should be simple, should it not? For no matter how complex Jacob may be as a person, no matter how convoluted his family life, his intentions in this matter are pure. He and his offspring should be able to abide near Shekhem for generations to come, happily working the land and grazing their herds. After all, Genesis tells us explicitly, "Jacob came in peace to the city of Shekhem in the land of Canaan."

Peace, alas, is only as firm as the foundation it is built upon. In our very next chapter that peace will be shattered by rape and murder. Before the generation has passed, Jacob and his sons will be exiled from the promised land, awaiting enslavement in Egypt.

16

SEX AND
VIOLENCE

EVEN WHEN YOU PAY very close attention, they can just vanish right
before your eyes. I'm referring here to the women of Genesis, who
play an increasingly diminished role as the book moves along. In the
beginning, man and woman got equal billing, both created in the image and likeness of their Creator. From that point onward, women
seemed to get a shorter and shorter end of the stick. By now we have
seen strong matriarchs, women who talk with God, women who get
their own promises. We've seen active women who are willing to beat
and banish others. We've seen women who are not afraid to pull a
fast one to insure that the covenant will pass on to the right member
of the family. But by the time we come to Jacob, father of the people
Israel, there are more and more women who play less and less a role
in the fate of the nation.

It is almost as though the crowded stage of Jacob's tent, with four
different women coming and going, demands that their speaking roles
are accordingly attenuated. Sarah and Hagar each managed to occupy
the entire stage when it was their turn to speak, and when they had to
share a stage, Sarah beat Hagar until she relinquished the spotlight.
Rebecca basked in the limelight—with no women to share the stage,
she not only got all the good lines, she also played the director for the
other characters. But when Rachel, Leah, Bilha, and Zilpa all have to
vie for Jacob's attention, each simply gets less airtime. It is as though
there is but one allotted woman's role and this, then, must be divided
among them. As it is, Rachel gets most of the speaking lines and these

are very few—relating only to her barrenness and her menstrual period (Genesis 31:35).

It comes as little surprise, then, that by the time we get to Jacob's
daughter she vanishes. And she does so in a way that is especially demeaning. When Leah, her mother, has her second wind of birthing,
we are given the courtesy of an announcement that she had a daughter, Dinah. But when in our last chapter (Genesis 32:23) Jacob fear-
fully transferred his family to the other side of the river during the
night before his meeting with Esau, we are informed, "He arose during the night and took his two wives and his two concubines and his
eleven children." What is so galling about this is not simply the fact
that Jacob has twelve children at this point, eleven sons and Dinah,
but the Hebrew word for children is less gender bound ("children")
than the usual "sons," and even so, Dinah goes uncounted.

It is true that there will yet be women who crop up in Genesis, but
they do not have very happy roles. Most often they are sex objects.
We will see Judah's daughter-in-law, Tamar, in Genesis 38. She is ac-
corded the judgment of being "righteous," but only after Judah has
threatened to kill her for playing the harlot, which she does in order
to force his family to honor her levirate marriage agreement. And
then there is the wife of Potiphar in Genesis 39—the one who sexually
harasses poor young Joseph by repeatedly asking him to sleep with
her and then when he refuses accuses him of attempting rape. Finally,
there is Joseph's wife, Asenath, who doesn't do much of anything at
all, except mother Joseph's two sons. All in all, the passing of the matriarchs was not very good for the women of Genesis, so is it any
wonder that Jacob's daughter, Dinah, went looking for companions
among her new neighbors? And is it any wonder that her doing so
leads to deep trouble?

Dinah, daughter of Leah, whom she bore to Jacob, went out
looking for companions among the daughters of the land. But
Shekhem, son of Hamor the Hivvite, prince of the land, laid
eyes on her. He took her, he had sex with her, he raped her. Yet
his soul cleaved to Dinah, daughter of Jacob; he loved the girl
and spoke to her heart.

Shekhem said to his father, Hamor, "Get me this girl as my wife."

When Jacob heard that he had defiled Dinah, his daughter, his sons were with their cattle in the field, so Jacob stayed dumb until their return. Hamor, Shekhem's father, came to speak with Jacob. When they heard, Jacob's sons came from the field. They were hurt and very angry. He had disgraced Israel by having sex with the daughter of Jacob. It just wasn't done.

Hamor said to them, "My son has lost his heart to your daughter. Please give her to him as his wife. Marry with us: Give us your daughters and take ours as yours. Dwell with us; the land will then be before you. Settle, do business, take hold of it."

Shekhem said to her father and brothers, "If I might find favor in your eyes, whatever you tell me I will give. Set a high dowry and gift price. I will give whatever you tell me, if you but give me the girl as my wife."

Jacob's sons answered Shekhem and his father, Hamor, deceitfully—speaking so because he had defiled their sister, Dinah. They said, "We cannot do it. We cannot give our sister to one who has a foreskin; it is a disgrace to us. But this could bring us to agreement with you: if you were to have every male circumcise himself and be like us. Then we would give you our daughters and take your daughters as ours; we could dwell with you and be one people. If you cannot agree to circumcise, then we will take our daughter and be on our way."

These things seemed good to Hamor and to Shekhem, son of Hamor. The lad did not hesitate to do it, for he so desired Jacob's daughter. And he was most honored of all his father's household.

So Hamor and his son, Shekhem, came to the gate of their city and spoke to the men of their city, "These men wish to make peace with us and dwell with us and trade with us. Now the land is broad, stretching out before them. We shall take their daughters as our wives and give our daughters to them. This one thing is required for their agreement to dwell with us and be one

people, that each male among us circumcise, as they are circumcised. Their cattle, their possessions, all their livestock will be
ours if we reach agreement with them and they dwell with us!"

All those in attendance at the city gate agreed with Hamor
and Shekhem, his son. All those in attendance at the gate of the
city were circumcised. When they were in pain on the third day,
Shimeon and Levi, Dinah's brothers, each took his sword and
came to the city armored and killed every male. They slew
Hamor and his son, Shekhem, by sword, and they took Dinah
from Shekhem's house and left. The sons of Jacob despoiled the
city and the corpses, because they had defiled their sister. Their
sheep, their cattle, their donkeys, everything in the city and the
fields they took. All their soldiers, their children, and their
women they took captive and despoiled, in addition to what
was in that house.

Jacob said to Shimeon and Levi, "You make me look bad, destroy my reputation among the inhabitants of the land, the
Canaanites and Perrizites. I am but few in number. They will
gang up on me and strike me. I and my household will be destroyed!"

But they replied, "Should our sister be made a whore?"

One imagines the princes of nearby tribes gazing upon the shattered
ruins of the city of Shekhem the next morning and exclaiming,

> A glooming peace this morrow with it brings.
> The sun for sorrow will not show its head.
> Go hence, to have more talk of these sad things;
> Some shall be pardoned, and some punished;
> For never was a story of more woe
> Than this of Dinah and her Shekhem, Oh!

My quote from Shakespeare here (it's really Juliet and Romeo in the
last line—his name does rhyme better) is meant to raise a point in our
reading of the story of Dinah. This story is an archetype of the "girl and
boy from opposing tribes fall in love" tale. My citation of *Romeo and*

Juliet makes a radically revisionist assumption about the tale: Dinah was not an unwilling partner to Shekhem; rather, they were star-crossed lovers.

This last presumption is radical, even outrageous. I declare myself a feminist on the Dinah issue, but I confess there is an element of apologetics in this assertion. I do not know how women feminists will react to my taking a story presented as a rape and in crude essence reading it as though it were saying "she was asking for it." That reading is hardly feminist, and hardly the one I wish to promote. But I want to defuse these charges at the outset so we can get on with the discussion. I am not suggesting that we ever read rape as anything but rape. I am, however, suggesting that we read the story of Dinah's rape as something that might not be her version of the story.

I am inclined to this radical reading because of the brothers' rhetorical question, the answer of which had lethal results for those of Shekhem. "Should our sister be made a whore?" they ask. To which I reply, "Well, gentlemen, did it dawn on you to ask Dinah what she thought about all of this before you set about slaughtering the men of the city and rescuing her?" What offends me here—beyond the carnage, which I'll return to below—is the very invisibility, the inaudibility of Dinah. In the same book of Genesis in which matriarchs have such strong voices, Dinah is utterly denied any voice of her own whatsoever.

The idea that Dinah might be a Juliet to Shekhem's Romeo was first planted in my reading consciousness by a college senior who was busy planning her own wedding. I am not sure whether her identification with Dinah came from wedding plans or from some earlier boyfriend whom her parents disapproved of, but her idea was really simple: The rape never happened. Dinah, who "went out looking for companions among the daughters of the land," found her companion in Shekhem. They were young, they were in love, they had sex. "His soul cleaved to Dinah, daughter of Jacob; he loved the girl and spoke to her heart." But no one asked Dinah what her opinion in the matter was, because she did not matter. All the Israelite men could think of was that their "daughter" had gone off, without their consent, and consorted with a Gentile neighbor. They ask, "Should our sister be made a whore?" They mean, How is it possible for one of our women to have sex outside of our system of supervision? The only tenable answer is rape, which is to say: The girl has no volition; therefore we blame the outsider, the Shekhemite males. The whole scene is conceived *mano a mano* with nary a thought to Dinah, her opinion, her desire, her safety, or, for that matter, her virginity—except as it reflects on the men of her tribe. She vanishes before our very eyes. What is left after the vanishing act is the carnage of Shekhem.

Another interpretation: Dinah *was* raped. Shekhem still fell in love with her and held her captive. If he was perverse enough to rape her in the first place and if he was perverse enough to hold her captive, then he was also perverse enough to believe that if he struck a bargain for her with her family, she would eventually come around to loving him in return. I think this is still called the Patty Hearst syndrome— she identifies completely with her oppressors. But even in this reading, Dinah still has no voice. Her brothers rescue her violently. See above.

Another interpretation: The story is her point of view as well as that of the male narrator. She needs no voice because her loyal brothers, Shimeon and Levi, speak on her behalf while Shekhem brutally holds her captive. Dinah has not quite disappeared, but she is in the hands of Shekhem and her voice is the voice of Shimeon and Levi. She has, however, been raped. There is no moral ambiguity whatsoever in her situation. She is utterly a victim who is valiantly defended by the males of her clan. Therefore, her dilemma needs no discussion, for she is wholly sympathized with by author and readers. Only the interchange among the men merits discussion here as a dilemma.

I'm nonetheless still interested in hearing what she has to say. If Mrs. Potiphar can falsely accuse Joseph of rape and gets a voice in the biblical telling of it (although thanks to my colleague Phyllis Trible, I now have to wonder just what her voice would have sounded like had she been the narrator of the tale), then is it not all the more so imperative that Dinah, too, should be heard?

I think, by now, I've made my point painfully clear regarding Dinah's dilemma. Perhaps it is time to move on to the other issues this disturbing drama raises. Rape is the foremost of these. We are reading of a society that was appreciably different from our own on the issue of rape. The Bible has carefully delineated laws of rape, the most telling of which is that a rapist who is caught in the act is required to marry his victim. While this may seem like a deterrent and a punishment to rapists, it certainly does not seem like a sympathetic solution for the victims.

It was a society in which the victim's shame had to be accounted for, and marriage did erase the shame attendant upon loss of virginity. But this is shame of an emphatically male construction and stunningly lacking in sympathy for the woman victim. There is little face to be gained from the dubious honor of marrying your rapist. At least Dinah's brothers agree with this last point, if not with how I arrived there. Feminist critique was not widely appreciated during the biblical era. As a matter of fact, it is little appreciated in our own era. That any society, whether Hivvite or Israelite, could countenance rape in any measure seems to me morally unacceptable. Had Dinah's brothers asked, "Shall our sister be raped?" I still would have been queasy about their violent reaction to the rape. But I do not believe rape was an issue for them. Shame and control were their buttons. Rape is one of ours, and in reading and discussing this story, the rape buzzer must sound loudly. Consider these last eight paragraphs that buzz.

There are yet other pressing issues to be raised here, if not wholly vented. For instance, how could Dinah's father, Jacob, have heard and yet stayed dumb? Dinah was held captive in Shekhem's house and Jacob stayed dumb! How can a father hear of such outrage and not react? Of course, it must be recalled that when Reuben, Jacob's son, sleeps with Bilha, Jacob's concubine, his reaction is similar. Well, maybe similar—the Bible is very laconic in its account of that episode. After it reports that Reuben bedded Bilha, Genesis merely adds two words, "Jacob heard," and then discreetly changes the subject. One assumes the narrator is simply too embarrassed to continue reporting this ignominious action. Still, we are left with a clear impression of Jacob's inaction on the matter.

So perhaps Jacob is as passive when regarding sexual transgression against himself as he is when regarding it against his daughter. But there is a flaw in the reasoning of this assertion. It was Bilha who had sex with Reuben, not Jacob. Which is to say that if there is a sexual transgression, it is against Bilha and not, in fact, against Jacob. Or, if we do wish to consider Reuben's bedding of Bilha a transgression against Jacob, then Shekhem's bedding of Dinah, daughter of Jacob, is equally a transgression against Jacob. Either way, focusing on his honor or on the physical assault on women under his "domain," his passivity is unconscionable.

The dilemma here is not only one of passivity, but its opposite, naked aggression, for if Jacob is one side of the equation, then Shimeon and Levi are the other side. Their reaction to the rape and abduction is violent and premeditated murder. Before we weigh whether passivity and aggression must be judged as an either/or choice of reactions, we should examine some of the nuances of the brothers' response.

First, again using a feminist measure, let us note that Shimeon and Levi have reacted tribally. They, like Dinah, are "children of Leah." They protect their sister, as it is the obligation of klansman to protect the women of their tribe who are the chattel of the tribe. These women are not to have sex outside the domain of the tribal males' permission. This raises all of the same issues that our discussion of Jacob's passivity above did, at least as far as the moral dilemma is to be construed as a male-female issue.

The other area where Shimeon and Levi's violent reaction should be juxtaposed with Jacob's is in regard to the deceit they practiced on Shekhem and his tribe. Here it is high irony that Jacob should so worry about his reputation in the neighborhood—what shall he fear, that he will be rumored to engage in deceit? That was already Jacob's reputation, almost from the first moment we met him. All we can say regarding Shimeon and Levi's tactics is that they come by deceit "honestly."

Here we should also wonder about Jacob as a father again. We reiterate the question raised earlier: How can a father sit silent when his daughter has been raped and/or abducted? The corollary to this question is: Does Jacob care more about his reputation than he does about his family? Asking the question in this fashion gives it an appropriately contemporary ring, for even in families where nothing of this violent and tragic nature has occurred, business and community demands often cause fathers to ignore the needs of their families.

It is a dilemma of our society that the paterfamilias often finds himself trapped between demands of his family and of his community or work. What they might think of him at work/synagogue/church/the club is often pitted against what the family needs. This is a sad dichotomy primarily because it is unnecessary for it to be an either/or choice. One can learn to mediate between family demands and communal image. One can learn to meet both family demands as well as communal image. One can learn to cultivate communal image precisely by teaching a community about the value of meeting family demands. Of course, this is more readily accomplished when the issues are less pressing than rape and kidnapping. Given the Dinah scenario, average everyday tensions between family and "reputation" seem minor and readily soluble. Perhaps this "moral" is what the ending of the Dinah story is meant to teach us.

In reading this story, it is hard not to notice other "morals" that are presented. Here I am thinking specifically of the contrast in moral values the sons of Israel and the Hivvites represent. Unfortunately, the two societies do not reflect well upon each other, for Hamor and Shekhem convince the men of their city that an alliance with the Israelites, even at the painful price of circumcision, is in their best interests. What are those interests? Hamor spells them out: peace, business, trade in livestock and cattle, marriage to desirable women.

The other side of this picture is the thumbnail sketch drawn of Jacob, Shimeon, and Levi, the dominant males of Dinah's tribe. They practice deceit, vengeance, tribalism, murder, and despoilation. Their chief worries are about shame and reputation. Now, I know that this is an unfair characterization. I could equally well have argued that Shekhem practiced rape and abduction while Jacob *et al.*, practice love and loyalty to family. It need not be an either/or construction; indeed, it never really is an either/or construct. For if we choose to characterize these stories (or our own lives) as black and white, good guys versus bad guys, we misconstrue the complexities of the situation (life) and arrive at extreme characterizations or decisions that do no fair service to either understanding the narrative or acting upon it.

However, as my last sentence illustrates, either/or does serve as a heuristic device. Such an extreme set of readings, setting off characters as antinomies, does help us begin to understand the stakes involved in the dilemma we are confronting. When we take the story of Dinah's family's reaction to Shekhem, we can characterize it as a question of either passivity or naked aggression. This does help us see the distinction between Jacob's reaction, on the one hand, and Shimeon and Levi's on the other. But it is also important to realize that they have much in common. They are on a continuum in the middle of which there is a great deal of gray area. That both father and brothers are concerned about reputation and control over their women is an important point to mitigate the extreme either/or passive/aggressive distinction.

Moral dilemmas are often quite messy, just like life. Extreme distinctions in our characterization of the dilemmas are useful only to begin a discussion, not to reach a conclusion. Inasmuch as life remains messy, the extreme conclusion does not really help sort out the dilemma in the end. Once the borders have been drawn through a use of either/or, then we must go back to fill in the middle of the picture—much like a complex jigsaw puzzle. Only through a good deal of sorting, a lot of analysis and careful fitting together of all the pieces, can we complete the entire picture.

A final example may be drawn from the Dinah dilemma. When the brothers tell the Shekhemites that the only possible way they can intermarry with the Israelite tribe is through circumcision, we see the rudiments of conversion. However, even as we see that, we know that the brothers hold a differing system of values and, in fact, are lying to their enemies. If what they said about circumcision was sufficient to permit the tribes to commingle, if circumcision was conversion to Judaism (as in the modern sense), then there is an added dilemma that after circumcision, Shimeon and Levi are killing fellow Jews! Jews killing fellow Jews! Oy!

I draw this extremely, even as caricature, again to emphasize the problem. If the basis for their deception is sound, then Shimeon and Levi have truly been evil. It was bad enough to kill strangers and despoil their riches, troops, women, and children. Is it not that much worse that they should kill fellow klansmen, members of their own tribe? In a tribal system, the answer to this question is a resounding yes. In a tribal system it is worse to kill members of your own tribe than it is to kill outsiders.

But as my ironic "Oy!" above indicates, I am not much taken by this argument for our own society. We are no longer tribal in the sense that the Israelites were in the time of Jacob. So I would ask what possible difference might it make that the men of Shekhem were or were not "of the tribe"? How could it matter if they were in or out? Murder is murder. There cannot be one morality for us and another for them. There cannot be one law for Jews and another for Gentiles. There cannot be one lunch counter for whites and another for blacks. There cannot be one standard for men and another for women. A society that makes certain members invisible is doomed to have moral dilemmas explode from the shadows and rain carnage upon every member of the tribe. They will forever be doomed to justifying their violence by asking "Should our sister be made a whore?"

17

GRACE

JOSEPH ARRIVES ON THE scene not a moment too soon. The family of Israel is falling apart. Although Shimeon and Levi bellow with triumph at the rescue of their sister, the brutal violence they unleash makes Jacob realize only too clearly that the tribal morality of the clan is insufficient for survival in the promised land. With other nation-tribes ranged roundabout, each ready to join in the fray against his family, Jacob-Israel understands that the very precepts he has lived by until now are insufficient to become a nation. "Trick or be tricked" did not even work very well within his own family, truth be told. Now that he is faced with a cycle of violence and retribution, Jacob fears for his life and for his off-spring. He finally understands that narrow tribalism leads to brutality, while blithe assimilation leads to extinction. Nor can being a shrewd trickster guarantee survival. So Israel seeks to find a better way. With the greatness of vision that earns him the name Israel, yet with the short-sightedness that keeps his name also Jacob, he turns his sight to his son, Joseph. Jacob's hope is this: that through his special grace, Joseph may bring salvation to the children of Israel.

Of course, Joseph is young and foolish, much as his father, Jacob, is old and foolish. Jacob shows unchecked favoritism to his darling youngest boy, Rachel's son. And young Joseph, well, young Joseph is a dreamer, who although aware of his grace has no understanding of its power or the responsibility it demands. So Joseph boasts of his ar-rogant dreams to his jealous brothers and soon finds himself sold into slavery in Egypt. Much as Great-grandfather Abraham went to Egypt and found himself in Pharaoh's court, so would it be Joseph's fate. But the sequence of events was as different from Abraham to Joseph as it would be from Joseph to Moses, after him. And I, remembering all too well that the novelist Thomas Mann set out to write a short story about Joseph and wound up three volumes later with *Joseph and His Brothers,* think it meet at this juncture to cut short our meditation on this phenomenal character.

It is not Joseph that is the focus of our interest here, captivating though he is. For now, our interest lies more in the change he marks rather than in the person himself. At the very end of the last chapter, I judged the tribal morality displayed by Shimeon and Levi as less than adequate for our own society. Indeed, as this chapter opens, I have remarked that it was insufficient for Israel's nationhood. Since the Bible study offered in this book is intended to exemplify a method of moral development, it is worth our while to take a step back and examine the systems of morality under discussion.

I have characterized the morality of Genesis as tribal or appropriate for the clan. I have also made it clear that the type of moral development I am seeking to encourage with the study of these Genesis narratives is founded upon Lawrence Kohlberg's theories, which are based, in turn, on the philosophy of John Rawls. As I pointed out in Chapter 1 of this book, the notions of fairness, spelled out in Rawls' *A Theory of Justice,* are the very notions that I am promoting. This philosophy, recently described by a lawyer acquaintance of mine as "sixties liberalism," is a very far cry from the philosophy of Jacob or Shimeon and Levi or Isaac or Abraham or, most probably, even God in the book of Genesis.

It is essential that this difference in moral philosophy is made clear. Kohlberg's theory of moral development is based upon another philosophy than that of Genesis. As a result, one stands outside the other and runs the danger of judging its predecessor. I am not at all sure I wish to make this judgment, or, having made it, that I wish that it stand as a condemnation of biblical morality. I argued long and hard with Kohlberg about this when I was his student (and he was yet alive to respond). Genesis presents itself as a divine morality. We have seen the implications of this again and again, as metaethical assumptions are made throughout the book. Whether it is God acting as protector for trickster Abraham, or God demanding that the same Abraham slaughter his son, human ethical assumptions are tossed aside in the face of the divine imperative. What Kierkegaard referred to as "the teleological suspension of the ethical" often seems to be the normative ethic operating in Genesis.

Let me put this into English. Genesis does not share the same ethics that we "sixties liberals" seem to hold dear. When God enters the story, the balance of the story shifts radically. The reason for the shift when God arrives on the scene is because the ethics and morality that philosophers speak of are what people decide among themselves as a system for getting along. The entire system is between humans and they have to agree on the basis for it. For Kohlberg and Rawls it was fairness. For the ancient Greeks it was The Good. Various philosophies offer various bases for their systems to rest upon, be they Aristotelian, Pragmatic, Stoic, Communist, or what have you. All agree that there should be some agreement on the underlying philosophy. Once that is accomplished, working out the ethics—the rules by which that moral philosophy is achieved—is a communal task.

It is intriguing, then, that the Bible differs in two ways from this system. First of all, at least by Exodus Chapter 20, the means of working out the details are presented as commanded by God. Second, the underlying philosophy is also dictated by God—it is divine, not human. So theoretically, systems like Kohlberg's, or any others that rest on human ethics, do not do a very adequate job of judging biblical commandments or the metaethical God Who ordains them. Supernatural religion and rational philosophy go head to head here.

Genesis makes the story even more complex, for although God is a central character in the drama, the humans in it do not work under any prescribed system of divine rules. Although God commands individual characters in Genesis, God does not offer the nation Israel any prescribed system of commandments or ethics. Yes, it is true that the patriarchs and matriarchs go when God tells them, "Go." It is also true that God provides protection, promise, and blessing. However, the descendants of Abraham act, for the most part, by relying on tribal morality, something that makes them just like any other tribe.

If anything, they are craftier, more deceptive, and, when it is necessary, more brutal. The morality of Israel is such that were it all that they brought with them as a legacy into Egypt, they would not have survived the ordeal of slavery.

Joseph arrives not a moment too soon. For all that his forefathers had communion with God, it is he, Joseph, who recognizes again and again that God's grace imbues his personal and his family's history. It is he, even in the dungeon, who knows that he acts on a larger stage than that of the family, as a boy whose brothers sold him to slavery. It is he who can say, with all the assurance of having been the savior of Egypt, "It was God Who sent me as a lifesaver before you." Joseph takes the tribal ethic and insists that it become something grander, that it transform to something divine.

Were he to continue living only by the tribal ethic, how might he have responded to the offer that the Egyptian woman, the wife of Potiphar, made to him? When she said, "Sleep with me," he might have rationalized that she was a Gentile and therefore permissible to him. Further, tribal mentality might have led him to think he was doing no more than settling the score for Pharaoh's behavior to Sarah when she and Abraham fled to Egypt during the famine four generations previous. But Joseph has a broader sense of morality and ethics. He sees beyond narrow tribal borders and recognizes universal principles. Hence, when she attempts to seduce him, he responds by telling her that her husband, "my master, need not know what goes on in his household because he has given everything to my trust . . . he has not denied me anything except you. So how could I do such evil to him? Further, I would be sinning against God."

Joseph has a sure sense of loyalty to his master, Potiphar. In this he is unlike his father, Jacob, who only showed loyalty to his own nearest kin. Joseph is marked by a grander ethic as well, in his ability to recognize that immediate pleasure (for no one doubts the woman's charms) must be deferred for a greater sense of order. Finally, and most intriguing, is Joseph's sense that his morality is not merely predicated on interpersonal ethics—it is divinely ordained. To sin against his master, Potiphar, to commit adultery with his master's wife, is, in Joseph's eyes, equally well a sin against his greater Master, God.

But even God's law must stand the scrutiny of human ethics. We learned that principle when God responded to Abraham's query, "Shall the Justice of all the earth not do justice?" Or, in the book of Deuteronomy 16:20, when the Israelites are commanded, "Justice shall you do, justly." By rabbinic interpretation this requires that human means of justice be employed in pursuit of God's law. Apparently it is reasonable for the God of the Torah to be judged by human ethical and moral standards, so when we read the stories of Genesis as moral dilemmas, we apply the Bible's own canons of justice to the book itself.

Here is not the place for an extended defense of ethics in the face of divine law. I am keenly aware that there are as many readers who would argue that human ethics is the only law that matters as there are readers who argue that divine law is the only reality in this God-given universe. I seek to find a middle ground. I do so because I believe that among the gifts God gave to human beings (who were created in God's image) was critical intellect. I also believe that God can withstand our severest ethical scrutiny. If I rage against God's justice, God is not diminished by it—God remains God. If I learn by my rage, if I develop morally, then it will have been a worthwhile exercise for me. My revisionist readings of Genesis are a valuable undertaking if they help achieve ethics, morality, justice, or fairness.

I believe moral development should be practiced using the Bible as a text for study. Here I respond to the secularists. "Abraham and Sarah on the road" is at least as good a dilemma as "Should Heinz steal the drug?" What we gain by studying the Bible as a text of moral development is a connection to a classic of Western thought, a religious document that has served as the basis for much of our ethical thinking for two millennia and more. This connection to history, to community, to the broader religious world, serves to broaden the community of ethical discourse. Since Kohlberg sought to prove that his system of moral stages was universal, this expansion of his system to the Western religious world should be a natural growth of his teaching. If anything, it serves to mitigate the nasty exclusivism that secularists and religious moralists (myself included) correctly complain about as a shortcoming of biblical morality.

This is a good juncture to reply to two other common criticisms that my use of Genesis as a source for moral dilemmas often raises. The first is what I have come to think of as the "Why not Shakespeare?" question. In short, if discussion leads to moral development, why do I insist on the Bible? Why not Shakespeare? I was, I confess, winking at this question when I quoted from *Romeo and Juliet* in the last chapter. I would answer the question: Well, why *not* Shakespeare? Indeed, let us study Shakespeare and Bacon and Marlowe and all English, French, German, and other European literature as a means to moral development. And why stop at Dead White Males? African literature, Asian literature, women's literature, secular literature, all literature—if it leads to moral development, I am in favor of including recipes and laundry lists in our canon.

I am, however, aware that we do have a canon. I understand that the canon is undergoing some significant revision these days. In fact, the canon has always been undergoing revision, even the biblical canon. The canon of Jews differs from that of Catholics. The Catholic canon, in turn, differs from that of Protestants. Even among Protestant denominations there are differences of opinion as to which books are sacred and which are not. If the borders of the canon are fuzzy, nevertheless, the Bible has enjoyed a very long run on virtually every list of canon in Western civilization.

The very notion of canon carries with it a certain weight. Communities agree upon what texts serve as the very documents by which they define themselves. Sometimes the canon of a community is clearly spelled out, sometimes the notion of canon is inchoate. In any case, communities form around canons of literature they deem the essential embodiments of the communal "myth." Those texts, whatever they may be, carry within them the code of the community's moral system. Whether that system remains in actual force, it is the touchstone against which all subsequent communal myth and ethics are measured. For two thousand years and more, Genesis has been part of our Western canon. We cannot help but begin there as we seek to grow and develop.

The second issue, which I have already briefly mentioned above, bears repetition in a more explicit formulation. I addressed both religious and secular readers and their varying concerns for finding ethics in a "divine document." What lies behind this concern is a broader issue, the same one that forced my senior professor to worry about my Freudian analysis of Jacob's ladder dream. It is the issue of piety. I, for one, believe that all piety is but a means to an end. True piety is not a series of actions or even attitudes displayed in a community— those are ritual. Ritual can be carried out with deep piety or with virtually no piety at all. Piety is, rather, a means to a godly end. In this case, I believe God wishes human creatures to behave in moral and ethical ways toward one another. Doing so is an expression of piety. Teaching others to do so is also piety. If hard questions and cynicism lead to the same end, then they, too, may be construed as piety. So I think myself pious, a student of the Bible who uses the same means as my ancestors, the rabbis of the midrash, may their memories be blessed. I intend my revisionism of Genesis to force readers to reread (or in some cases read for the first time) the Bible with moral development as a primary goal. There are those who will find my method in this book impudent, even blasphemous. I say to them, "Let God be the judge. But wonder, please, how many more people will read the Bible as a result of having read this book?"

This brings me to reading the Bible. We have read through one half of the book of Genesis together. From Genesis 12 through Genesis 36 makes twenty-five chapters by my count. Since Genesis is fifty chapters total, we're only halfway done. There are yet fourteen chapters to go to the end of the book—the story of Joseph. But that is a subject for another book or, better, for you to do on your own. Form a study group, ask hard questions, listen to one another, listen to one another, listen to one another. In questions and in listening lie the keys to the formation of enduring communities and to moral development.

We have seen throughout this book how discussion of the dilemmas of Genesis lead to a broad variety of opinions. Exposure to varying opinions, debate, and discussion—these are the keys to moral development. Among the rabbis of the fourth and fifth centuries, for instance, when they read the story of Joseph, they hotly debated the scene involving the wife of Potiphar. Some rabbis suggested that Joseph, in fact, was ready to bed her, but he was impotent. Other rabbis suggest that when he went to bed with her, Joseph beheld the image of his father before him and at that sight deflated. Other rabbis suggest that it was his mother's image he beheld. Still other rabbis suggest that as an act of resistance to the allure of his seductress, Joseph dug his fingers into the ground and ejaculated through his nails! Each of these colorful opinions carries more than a wink and giggle. Each rabbi couches a moral philosophy in his earthy language. In considering Joseph, the rabbis of old were discussing the ethics of sexuality and the effect of psychology upon those ethics.

We must do no less ourselves as we read Genesis. As you turn from this book to your own study, you could choose to ignore Joseph and remember that there are eleven chapters at the very outset of Genesis that also require study. You could read about Adam and Eve and Noah and the Tower of Babel. Or you could finish with Joseph and then return to Genesis 1. It is equally good to start your journey "in the beginning" and work your way through to the end. Form a study group, ask hard questions, listen to one another. Do not worry about repeating the materials that have been covered in this book. By the time you arrive at those chapters of Genesis, they will seem like a different story entirely. Along the way, you will have changed, grown, experienced a little more of life. In doing so, the ways in which you read the Bible will have changed. The story, then, will appear different to you. As your moral development changes, the very dilemmas you perceive in the text will also shift. So we have to read, ask hard questions, and listen to one another. The study of Scripture, like moral development itself, is an unending journey.